ON THE ROAD
WITH
RABBI STEINSALTZ

Photo © Gary Eisenberg.

ON THE ROAD WITH RABBI STEINSALTZ

Twenty-Five Years of Pre-Dawn Car
Trips, Mind-Blowing Encounters,
and Inspiring Conversations
with a Man of Wisdom

ARTHUR KURZWEIL

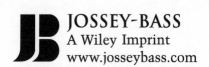

JOSSEY-BASS
A Wiley Imprint
www.josseybass.com

Published by Jossey-Bass
A Wiley Imprint
989 Market Street, San Francisco, CA 94103-1741   www.josseybass.com

Jossey-Bass books and products are available through most bookstores. To contact Jossey-Bass directly call our Customer Care Department within the U.S. at 800-956-7739, outside the U.S. at 317-572-3986, or fax 317-572-4002.

Jossey-Bass also publishes its books in a variety of electronic formats. Some content that appears in print may not be available in electronic books.

Credits are on page 291.

Library of Congress Cataloging-in-Publication Data
Kurzweil, Arthur.
On the road with Rabbi Steinsaltz: twenty-five years of
pre-dawn car trips, mind-blowing encounters, and inspiring
conversations with a man of wisdom / Arthur Kurzweil.
p. cm.
Includes bibliographical references and index.
ISBN-13: 978-0-7879-8324-6 (cloth)
ISBN-10: 0-7879-8324-1 (cloth)
1. Steinsaltz, Adin—Teachings. 2. Steinsaltz, Adin—Anecdotes.
3. Steinsaltz, Adin—Interviews. 4. Kurzweil, Arthur. 5. Spiritual life—Judaism. 6. Jewish way of life. I. Title.

BM755.S6915K87 2006
296.092—dc22   2006010546
Printed in the United States of America
FIRST EDITION
HB Printing   10 9 8 7 6 5 4 3 2 1

Contents

For Bobby

". . . build your world around her."

The Bible calls the Jews "the House of Israel" or "the House of Jacob," meaning that the Jews are essentially and principally a family. This family began as the small group of the offspring of Abraham. With natural increase, we became a clan and then a tribe and ultimately a nation. But in spite of its extraordinary proliferation, this tribe, and eventually the nation, remained what we have always been—a single family. We are not really a religion or a nation; we are a family.

—RABBI ADIN STEINSALTZ, *We Jews,* p. 48

Acknowledgments

In the twelfth century, Rabbi Yehudah HaChasid taught that the Almighty puts books into some people, and it is the obligation of these people to give birth to the books they find within themselves. I hope and pray this book is one which was meant to be born. If so, I must begin with my thanks to the Holy One for all that I have received in my life. In the words of the Psalms, *my cup runneth over.* Many individuals helped with this book's birth. I am grateful to them, as well as for the opportunity to express my thanks and gratitude. Heartfelt appreciation goes to:

Alan Rinzler. You urged me to write this book, you cheered me on as I wrote it, and you brought your abundant talents toward making it a better book than I could have ever done without you. Thank you for this, for your friendship, and for your confidence in me.

Margy-Ruth Davis. Your devotion to Rabbi Steinsaltz as well as the many years of hard work on behalf of the Jewish people inspires me and so many others. I cherish our friendship and admire you deeply.

Rebecca Allen. This book would never have happened without your editorial skills and talents. Thank you for being there, for your friendship, and for your words of Torah.

Ruth Friedman. How lucky we are to have you as national director of the Aleph Society. Your talents, your hard work, your professionalism, and your dedication to Rabbi Steinsaltz are always so uplifting to me. I am delighted to know you and eternally grateful every time you are on the other end of the phone and say, "Rabbi Steinsaltz will be coming to New York soon. Can you pick him up. . . ?"

Rabbi Simcha Prombaum. Our friendship is a gift from Above. Thank you for your help in making this book happen. Nobody helped me more than you.

Gary Eisenberg. Can a friendship be more awesome than ours? I don't think so.

Rick Blum. Lifelong friend, *chevrusa,* confidant. Thanks for sticking with me all these years.

Richard Carlow. Who would have guessed when we first met forty-five years ago that you and I would still be discussing the meaning of life? As you will see, these pages include the story of some of our early efforts to grasp the Infinite. Our friendship is a true blessing.

Marc Felix. We are soul brothers, and we knew it from the moment we met. I am deeply grateful for all that we share.

Ed Rothfarb. We began to discuss the Universe with each other during our carpools to Hebrew school and our walks to public school, and here we are, still sharing our spiritual journeys. Our friendship is so precious to me.

Rabbi Steve Shaw. You are a unique and special soul. Thank you for paving the way to my first meeting with Rabbi Steinsaltz.

Elie Wiesel. You took me under your wing thirty years ago. But you insisted I fly on my own. Thank you for all that you know to have done for me, and for so much more.

Yehuda Hanegbi, z'l. Your translations of Rabbi Steinsaltz's books have nourished me and countless others. I miss you and will always be grateful to you.

Saul and Evelyn Kurzweil. Some say that before birth we pick our parents. If so, I made the right choice. How fortunate we are to have each other.

Joanne Clapp Fullagar. Thank you for your editorial skills and talents. Fortunate is the author whose manuscript is under your care. Every encounter we have is a true pleasure for me.

Seth Schwartz. I wish you lived around the corner; I know we'd be friends. Thank you for giving your talents to every book in which you are involved.

Rea Kurzweil. Thank you for your friendship and for the children we share. You were there from the beginning of my connection with Rabbi Steinsaltz, and I'm so glad you were.

Moshe Kurzweil. Your spiritual explorations are an inspiration. Your kind heart is a model for everyone. You are the son every father hopes for.

Malya Kurzweil. You dazzle all who know you well. Your wisdom and wit are awesome. I am enhanced every moment I am with you.

Miriam Kurzweil. Your smile brings me profound joy. Your insights are deep and wise. You see into my heart and teach me about myself every time we are together.

Moshe, Malya, and Miriam Kurzweil. How blessed I am to be in this world with you. Thank you for listening to my stories about Rabbi Steinsaltz, for sharing words of Torah with me, and for filling my heart with joy.

Ken Kurzweil. I am grateful for our connection, our eagerness to share mutual interests, and our genuine care for each other. And thanks for all your computer expertise. You've gotten me out of every jam.

Ruth Rothwax. Thank you for your love and support. How fortunate I am to have you in my life. I am grateful for your advice, your wisdom, and for always being there for me.

Bobby Dor. I know what you'll say: "Thank *me*? For *what*?" Which is exactly why I must thank you. Giving is so natural for you. We put the finishing touches on this book together. Just the way I like it.

And, of course, I owe far more than a thank you to Rabbi Adin Steinsaltz. Each time I say goodbye to you I thank you, and each time you look at me like I'm crazy. So, here I am saying thank you again. I guess I'll never learn.

Blessed are You, Lord our God, Ruler of the universe, Who keeps us alive, sustains us, and has permitted us to reach this season.

Passaic, New Jersey   Arthur Kurzweil
Great Neck, New York
June 2006

Becoming the Rabbi's Driver: Stepping Down to a Higher Position (1980–1985)

Ｏne day, in 1985, I did something smart.

Unfortunately, I can't say that about all the choices and decisions in my life. But there was one time when I have no doubt my action was right.

Six years earlier, I had learned of Rabbi Adin Steinsaltz. From the first moment I read his words in a published interview in a 1978 issue of *Parabola* magazine,[1] I knew there was something special about him. I felt he was speaking to my mind, to my heart, to my soul.

In that interview, among many other things, Rabbi Steinsaltz said, "Whether a Jew is knowledgeable about his tradition or not, there comes a time when he has to re-meet and re-understand his tradition in a way that will be applicable to him and will say something to him as he is. You see, every person has to, at some time, re-create Sinai for himself."

And he said, "We believe that the Law has at least 600,000 different paths within it for individuals to enter. There is what is called the 'private gate' for each of us. And we each have to find our own gate."

And he said, "A man may search for years and find only doorways that are not his; he may go on through all his life without really finding it. That is the basis of the transmigration of the soul (reincarnation), which contrary to what so many nice people wrote is a part of Judaism."

And he said, "Among our people, violent one-minute conversions are extremely rare. So that any change seems not to be very easy, and not instantaneous. Now, that means that if there is a change, the change comes not by leaps and bounds, not in an immediately illuminating moment when everything is changed, but very gradual."

✸ **Why Me?** ✸

In 1978, when this interview was published, I knew something about that process of gradual change. I knew that although I grew up in a family with great respect for Judaism but with little Jewish education or practice, I was feeling a pull toward Jewish tradition.

When I grew up, Saturday was the best day of the week—for shopping, for traveling, for watching TV. By 1978, when I was twenty-seven years old, Saturday was becoming Shabbos, the Jewish Sabbath, with its customs, traditions, and sanctity.

When I was growing up, I loved ham-and-egg sandwiches. By 1978, I was beginning to learn about the *miztvot,* the sacred commandments of Judaism, including the commandments concerning kosher food.

When I was growing up, I prided myself on knowing every Bob Dylan lyric and every Beatles lyric. In just about any conversation, I could quote an appropriate line from Dylan or the Beatles with ease (and still can). But by 1978, I was beginning to see a shift within the free associations of my mind. I was starting to hear lines from the classic Jewish texts that I was just beginning to study. In 1978, I was like a hidden Jew, a Marrano. I would go into my apartment and put on my yarmulke. I would be reading several Jewish books at a time; I was beginning to say some blessings throughout the day as recommended by the Jewish sages.

I was also on the verge of wearing my yarmulke full time, inside my apartment and out, and I was trying to drum up the courage to do so.

During one period in the late 1970s, I knew who among my friends had already seen me wearing a yarmulke out of my house and who had not. One day, a longtime friend, a woman several years older than I whom I saw over a meal two or three times a year, called me and asked me to breakfast. We were to meet at a corner on upper Broadway in Manhattan.

I decided to wear my yarmulke.

I felt self-conscious. She knew I was interested in Judaism, but wearing a yarmulke, outside, on a weekday, in the middle of New York City, was, for me, quite odd.

Moments before I reached the corner, I quickly took off the yarmulke and stuffed it into my pocket, just in time for her not to see me. I got scared. I chickened out. Even though I felt inside I was a Jew who was being pulled toward and inspired by traditional Jewish observance and that the yarmulke was a tool I could use to help me stay conscious of my spiritual work as a Jew, I apparently wasn't ready to tell the world.

At breakfast, my friend said, "I have something to tell you, Arthur. I'm a lesbian."

I went home that day thinking she was brave enough to come out of her closet, but I was still a Marrano, a hidden Jew. From that day on, I've worn my yarmulke full time and have done so to this day.

Yet coming from the world in which I came, a secular world with little connection to traditional Jewish life, I often felt that traditional Judaism was far too rigid, that it was forcing me to fit into a mold. Yet I was realizing that I am a spiritual person with God on my mind just about all the time, and I was apparently eager to find expression for that kind of feeling, the feeling that God is truly present always.

Growing up in a world where God was regarded as superstition and the opiate of the people, as the reason for too many wars, and the topic on the minds of stupid, narrow-minded TV preachers, I had no opportunities to talk about God and no real knowledge about how to give expression to my inner life.

But there in the *Parabola* interview, among the words of Rabbi Steinsaltz, an Orthodox rabbi with a most impressive bio, were ideas that were speaking to my concerns. I didn't want to fit into an Orthodox mold, or any mold. I didn't want to take on everything in a sudden conversion.

I wanted to stand at Mount Sinai and hear the voice of God.

But not if it meant giving up my individuality, not if it meant going through the same gate as everyone else.

And there was Rabbi Steinsaltz telling me how I need to find my own gate, need to re-create Sinai for myself, and need to do this slowly. His passing remark about reincarnation, a topic I have believed in and studied for years, just added to my delight.

When I asked around and did a little research about Rabbi Steinsaltz, I quickly learned I was not alone. In fact, every person I spoke with and every article I read seemed to echo the same view: Rabbi Adin Steinsaltz of Jerusalem is a rabbi among rabbis, a profound thinker, a brilliant scholar, an extraordinary teacher, an exceptional person, a rare being.

Reading *The Thirteen Petalled Rose*

In 1980, the year of its publication, I learned of Rabbi Steinsaltz's masterpiece of Jewish theology, *The Thirteen Petalled Rose*. It has become, in its brief time in print, perhaps *the* classic statement of Jewish spiritual belief. It does not describe Jewish history or customs or laws or holidays, like so many other books on Judaism. Rather, in its brief 180 pages, *The Thirteen Petalled Rose* offers a concise description of reality as seen through the lens of Jewish mystical tradition, based on the structures of Kabbalah.

When I encountered the book, due to the reputation of its author and by its very feel, I was confident it was a book I could trust. I felt it was not just one man's opinion; it was not one more rabbi giving his personal view of things. Rather, the book felt like the pure, distilled, essence of Jewish theology itself. It was the kind of book—and author—I was looking for.

I learned, throughout the years of reading so many books on Judaism, that every author had his or her own version of Jewish belief.

For example, so many books about Judaism teach that Judaism does not speak much about death and the afterlife. They say that Judaism is a "this world" religion. While I understand that Jewish thought does pay close attention to the details of our lives, it is a gross distortion to say Judaism does not pay attention to the afterlife. In Judaism's vast literature, there is a great deal written on the afterlife and on death.

The problem, in my view, is that too often, liberal rabbis, in an effort to fit Judaism into their own modern, rational views, write off big chunks of Jewish tradition because they don't fit snugly into what they personally believe. Rather than teach about things they might not agree with, they seem to write them out of the tradition.

The Thirteen Petalled Rose was the first Jewish book that truly spoke of the essence of Jewish belief. It addressed the spiritual questions that until that time I had encountered only in books outside of Jewish culture. It addressed the questions that were on my mind and being asked by the core of my being: Who am I? Where do I come from? Where am I going? What is life all about?

While reading *The Thirteen Petalled Rose,* I learned that Rabbi Steinsaltz is a scientist, a mathematician, a skeptic, and a man of God. In combination, they result in a wholeness of vision that to this day I have never encountered elsewhere.

The book has helped me understand that not only does my body have a soul, but more accurately, my soul has a body. And my soul has five parts to it. By understanding these five parts, my soul is better able to function as it should, since awareness sheds light on things. The less we function in the dark, the better.

Becoming the Rabbi's Driver

So one day, as I said, I did something smart.

I called the office in New York City from which, I was told, Rabbi Steinsaltz's activities in the United States are coordinated. Although he was born, grew up, and resides with his family in the holy city of Jerusalem, he regularly travels throughout the world.

On the phone, I reached a woman who told me that she was responsible for the Rabbi's travels in the United States. I said I was glad to speak with her and I wished to work for Rabbi Steinsaltz.

I made it clear that I wasn't looking for a full-time job and wasn't looking for money. I simply wanted to help Rabbi Steinsaltz in his work. I knew from my reading and investigations that Rabbi Steinsaltz has ambitious goals, that a motto of his is "Let My People Know," and that he is trying to rebuild the Jewish people, a people who have, in the last few generations, been decimated by the Holocaust on the one hand and rapid assimilation on the other.

I've seen it in my own family. My grandparents came to America from Eastern Europe in the first part of the twentieth century, along with some of their siblings. Today, many of the grandchildren of those immigrants have either little interest in Jewish tradition or no longer consider themselves Jewish. Some of my cousins even deny being Jewish and make efforts to hide it from the world.

For some reason, I was one of the few exceptions. Although I did not begin the process of becoming an observant Jew until shortly before I encountered Rabbi Steinsaltz's writings in my late twenties, for some mysterious reason Judaism has called to me since childhood.

Once, when I was in the second grade, I announced to my teacher that I could not eat in the cafeteria because it wasn't kosher. I did not live in a kosher home, and I have no idea why I said that, but for some reason I wanted to declare my identity in that way. By the next day, I was eating in the cafeteria again, but it was the first of a continuing string of little moments that reflected an inner yearning.

Immediately after college, when I no was no longer kept busy reading what my professors wanted me to read, I read every Jewish novel I could get my hands on. When I traveled for several months through Europe after college in the early 1970s, I asked my father to send me an English translation of the Holy Scriptures and a few other books on Jewish history and tradition. And when I returned from Europe, I became obsessed with Jewish genealogy. For several years, I told everyone, including myself, that my interest in my family genealogy reflected my interest in Jewish history. But I was being disingenuous. I was really looking for God.

When I was speaking on the phone with the woman from Rabbi Steinsaltz's New York office, I stressed the fact that I wasn't looking for remuneration. I simply said, "Do you have any work for me? I'd like to help."

I told her that in my own far lesser way, I had chosen the same career as Rabbi Steinsaltz had. Since the age of twenty-three, from the end of 1974 to the present, all of the dozens of newspaper and magazine articles I have written; all of my public speaking and teaching at hundreds of synagogues and Jewish community centers throughout the United States, Canada, and Mexico; all of my professional work as a publisher of hundreds of books of Jewish interest; and even my frequent performing as a magician in my Jewish magic show have been directed to my one great passion, the Jewish people.

"That's a lovely offer," I was told. "But what do you have in mind?"

"I'll do *anything*," I said. "Give me *any* kind of work you have. I just want to help Rabbi Steinsaltz."

Although I have learned much about Rabbi Steinsaltz since then, I knew enough about the Rabbi at that time to know that he was doing something no one man had done in nearly a thousand years. Not since the twelfth century had any one individual written a comprehensive commentary on the Babylonian Talmud, that extraordinary spiritual document containing thousands of years of Jewish teachings. Edited about eighteen hundred years ago and continuously added to over the centuries by commentators, it now consists of dozens of huge volumes containing what can aptly be called the wisdom of the Jewish people.

Rashi, the great biblical and Talmudic commentator, who was born around the year 1000, did it centuries ago. Rashi's quickly became the standard and authoritative Talmudic commentary throughout the Jewish world.

Since then, many commentaries have been written by scholars and sages on various sections of the Talmud, but only Rashi and now Rabbi Steinsaltz have tackled the entire sixty-three-volume work single-handedly. And just as Rashi's commentary is considered a masterpiece and a work of genius, Rabbi Steinsaltz's Talmud commentary is considered a watershed event in Jewish history and is often described as the most important Talmudic publication since Rashi.

I had begun to fall in love with the Talmud a half dozen years or so before I learned about Rabbi Steinsaltz.

When I was introduced to some of the great stories and sayings from the Talmud in the mid-1970s, nothing excited me more than trying to navigate the "sea of Talmud," as it is often called—discovering its wisdom and being inspired by its tales and teachings. Texts from the Talmud offered me spiritual nourishment, dazzling ideas, and deep pride in being Jewish.

I later learned that Rabbi Steinsaltz and his editions of the Talmud have probably done more to spark interest in the

The Talmud is the repository of thousands of years of Jewish wisdom; and the oral law, which is as ancient and significant as the written law (the Torah), finds expression therein. It is a conglomerate of law, legend, and philosophy, a blend of unique logic and shrewd pragmatism, of history and science, anecdotes and humor. It is a collection of paradoxes.

—Rabbi Adin Steinsaltz, *The Essential Talmud,* p. 4

contemporary study of the Talmud than anyone or anything else in our time.

"Well, I have nothing to suggest at the moment," said the woman at the other end of the phone, who by this time was probably feeling the burden of the phone call more than my offer to help. "If you could come up with something specific, I could tell you if it will help."

"Please believe me," I insisted. "I'll do anything for him. Give me the crummiest job you have," I repeated. "If you want," I quipped, "I'll pick him up at the airport at five in the morning!"

The woman on the other end of the phone said, "You *will?*"

🍃 Behind the Wheel 🍃

And from that moment on, almost every time Rabbi Steinsaltz visits the United States, usually flying in from Israel to John F. Kennedy Airport in New York and arriving at 5:00 A.M., I pick him up and take him to some of his appointments. I have been doing this at least three times a year for twenty-five years. Sometimes I pick him up, bring him to his first appointment, and do not see him again during the remainder of that trip. Sometimes I see him almost every day for a week, getting him to his appointments and lectures. I have heard Rabbi Steinsaltz lecture at least two hundred times (and it is never a canned lecture—it is always original, fresh, and brilliant).

Traffic in New York City and vicinity is almost always bad. But of course, it all depends on one's definition of "bad." A big traffic jam is heaven for me when Rabbi Steinsaltz is sitting next to me. From my point of view, the more traffic the better, for it always results in my spending more time with him, asking more questions, and discussing more issues with an amazing, creative, brilliant, holy man. Sometimes I am with him for forty-five minutes at a stretch, and at other times it is closer to two or even three hours.

The first time I picked him up, I prepared by washing my car, vacuuming it thoroughly, and keeping the windows open to air it out. My income has never allowed me to own anything fancier than a small inexpensive sedan, so I tried my best to make it as nice as I could. Over the years, I've relaxed about it, to the point where I no longer give my car the ablutions I did at first. For the past dozen years, I've driven him in my modest-model Saturn. And while most of my private time with Rabbi Steinsaltz has been in my car, I have also had at least three extended meals each year with him since our first encounter.

In East Meadow, Long Island, the middle-class neighborhood where I grew up, we did light Hanukkah candles, had two Passover Seders each year, and went to the local synagogue on Rosh Hashanah and Yom Kippur, where I usually failed to stifle my boredom. The most meaningful Jewish experiences of my childhood occurred the year after my grandfather, my father's father, died.

Grandpa died a few weeks before my bar mitzvah. As a result, the grand catered party we had planned to celebrate the occasion was cancelled. Instead, we hosted a modest gathering after the synagogue service. No music, no celebrating. After all, my father and the rest of us were in mourning. To try to soften the experience for me, my parents told me they would buy me any gift I wanted. That is how I obtained my first electric guitar and amplifier, both of which served me well in my teens when I was part of a local, amateur, and quite dreadful rock band.

But every day for almost a year, my father went to the local synagogue twice a day to recite the mourner's Kaddish, the traditional Jewish prayer that mourners recite. It is so interesting to me that in a family where most Jewish observance was absent, my father never failed to go to the synagogue each day. I often went with him. And each time I went, I felt like I belonged there.

My responsibility during Rabbi Steinsaltz's U.S. travels covers New York City and vicinity. Over the years, most of my private time with Rabbi Steinsaltz has been with me behind the wheel and the Rabbi, almost always smoking his pipe, in the passenger seat. The sweet smell of his tobacco lingers (I say with delight) for days.

Sometimes I simply pick up Rabbi Steinsaltz at the airport, take him to his first appointment, and go on with my own day. At least twice each year, the Rabbi and I manage to have a complete conversation, sometimes for ten minutes, sometimes for an hour or two. On many occasions, at least three or four times a year, I have been in the position of having to wait for Rabbi Steinsaltz to finish a meeting or a lecture, after which I take him to his next appointment. So I have had the fantastic opportunity to sit in on a number of Rabbi Steinsaltz's classes and lectures every year for a long time.

At times we've had to stop for a meal together. In New York, there are lots of kosher options; My Most Favorite Dessert Company on West Forty-Fifth Street, a great kosher restaurant right in the middle of the theater district, has been a frequent stop for us. We've also done our share of gobbling down some kosher sushi from time to time. And when there are no kosher options, we have been able to find a hard-boiled egg and some black coffee, which is always an option for a person who observes the kosher laws but can't find kosher food. Rabbi Steinsaltz is also a chocolate fan. So a bar of good chocolate is frequently somewhere within reach.

Walking the Jewish Spiritual Path

For me, being Jewish is primarily a spiritual thing. Though I've learned and have been captivated by Jewish history, though I love Jewish culture and our Jewish artists, novelists, and playwrights, it is our theological tradition that has captivated me and transformed my life from a secular one to a religious one.

In the 1970s, I had invested a huge amount of time in doing genealogical research on my family. By the late 1970s, I was seriously exploring the religious lives of my ancestors, and since the early 1980s, I have been living a traditional Jewish lifestyle. I study holy Jewish texts every day, sometimes for five minutes, sometimes for hours. I observe the Sabbath and all of the holy days of the year. Each of my three children has been educated in Orthodox yeshivas. I try to work on my character traits, to stay involved in acts of loving kindness, to pray every day.

So what does being Jewish mean to me today? Like Rabbi Steinsaltz says, it's like being in a big diverse family. I have never thought that an Orthodox Jew is somehow "more Jewish" than non-Orthodox Jews. Perhaps, in part, this is due to the fact that having lived among Orthodox Jews now for more than two decades, I know too many who take our living tradition and freeze-dry it.

In a conversation I had with Elie Wiesel in the late 1970s when I was beginning my search to answer the question "Who is an authentic Jew?" he taught me something I have subscribed to ever since. Elie Wiesel said to me, "An Israeli soldier who is guarding Israel's border but never put on tefillin [ritual objects worn by traditional Jewish men at morning prayer] in his life— is he an 'authentic' Jew? Yes, he is an authentic Jew protecting our people. A person who follows all the laws of the Torah—is he an 'authentic Jew'? Yes, he is an authentic Jew who observes the Law."

For me, Judaism is my way of life. I have tried to immerse myself in its thinking, its words of wisdom, and its religious disciplines and traditions. After exploring many of the world's spiritual traditions, I have concluded not that Judaism is the best for everyone but that it is the best for me. The more I have learned about being Jewish, the more at home I feel.

I was thrilled, after my bar mitzvah at age thirteen, to be out of the boring Hebrew school I had been attending two or three afternoons each week. I went to public school in a town where Jews were in the minority, and my family belonged to the local Conservative synagogue. There was also a Reform synagogue. Those were our two choices.

I showed little interest in Judaism until, one day when I was in college in the late 1960s, going for my bachelor's degree, I saw a poster on a bulletin board announcing that Theodore Bikel, the folksinger, was going to be appearing that afternoon at an auditorium on campus. All I knew about Theodore Bikel was that he played the guitar, and since I also played the guitar, I wanted to hear him perform.

My dear lifelong friend Richard, who was also a student on campus, went with me. We arrived at the auditorium to discover that the event was sponsored by an organization known as Hillel.

When the door opened and Theodore Bikel walked in, he did not have a guitar with him, and he was dressed in a suit. I quickly realized that he was not on campus to sing but rather to give a lecture.

He began by saying, "I have been traveling around college campuses lately and have met a lot of Jewish Buddhists."

The year was 1969. The Beatles, with their interest in transcendental meditation, the Maharishi Mahesh Yogi, and Indian music, permeated the culture of which I was a part. At the time, I was not involved with any Jewish spiritual practice or any religious practice from any other tradition. Many young people were reading books of wisdom from Eastern religions. I was reading books on Zen Buddhism by Philip Kaplow and Alan Watts and Suzuki. I was also listening to tapes on the Bhagavad-Gita by Ram Dass.

Inspiration from Theodore Bikel

I certainly didn't consider myself a Jewish Buddhist or Hindu, nor did I ever identify in name with any Eastern religion. But I had been dabbling in Eastern religions since high school, and I understood quite well what Theodore Bikel said about Jewish Buddhists.

His lecture went on and basically made one point. He said to the students, "If you want to reject Judaism, you are free and entitled to reject it. But don't reject it until you know what it is."

Richard and I decided he was right; we had indeed rejected Judaism with very little idea of what it was about. I did have a bar mitzvah and I did go to Hebrew school, but I came out knowing very little.

Worse than that, I came away from my Hebrew school experience, like most of my friends, with hostility toward and alienation from Judaism and Jewish education.

The individual journey begins when a person tears him-self away from the state of aimlessness. This is the first step. At this point everything is still in the embryonic stage. Clearly, at this stage one does not fully understand the significance and future consequences of the sponta-neous first step into the unknown.

—Rabbi Adin Steinsaltz, *On Being Free,* p. 36

That night, I looked up the phone number of a Conservative rabbi who served in a congregation a couple of towns away, who I knew was friendly and interesting. My high school girlfriend's family attended that synagogue, and I went with them a few times and discovered that he was a great speaker. It was known that this rabbi had been in the advertising business, and I heard it said he used his advertising skills and talents to deliver a great sermon.

I reached him on the phone, introduced myself, and told him I was interested in learning more about Judaism. Could he help me?

He invited me to his office, and I brought Richard along. The Rabbi spent about ten minutes with us and handed us a half-dozen pamphlets on various aspects of Jewish tradition.

One pamphlet was on the Sabbath, one was on the kosher laws, and so on. We found all of them to be uninspired, uninteresting, and irrelevant.

But countless times over the years as I look back on my reading of those pamphlets, I have realized it was during that time that the miracle occurred.

The miracle was that after reading these boring pamphlets, I didn't say to myself, "OK, now I know about Judaism, and it doesn't interest me; I'll go back to Eastern religions." After reading those six boring, uninspired pamphlets, I said to myself, "I can't believe that my ancestors died for this, for these superficial, one-dimensional words."

I had to find out more, and the best way to do that was by reading more. We are the People of the Book. So I needed more and better books about Judaism and being Jewish. It was then that I discovered a very important number in American Jewish life. That number is 296.

296 is the number the Dewey Decimal System has assigned to the subject of Judaism. I went to my public library, located 296, and discovered that the library had dozens and dozens of books on Jewish tradition and Jewish thought.

I began reading those books systematically, one by one by one; some of them I hated, and some of them were quite informative, interesting, and inspiring.

I spent the 1970s reading just about every Jewish book, in English, I could get my hands on. And then, in 1978, I discovered Rabbi Steinsaltz. By 1980, I was beginning to feel the impact that his book *The Thirteen Petalled Rose* was having on me, leading me to knowing I had found my teacher, the man who would help me ultimately find myself.

⚜ Why This Book? ⚜

I have written this book to encourage you, my kind readers, to track down some books by Rabbi Steinsaltz, who is a prolific writer, and to discover his genius for yourself. The good news is that his seemingly endless lecture schedule continues to afford many people around the world regular opportunities to hear him

Our real problem is that our people, especially our youth, are ignorant. Their ignorance is not a matter of not being able to pass their Hebrew, biblical, or other tests. They are ignorant because they have nothing really to do with Judaism. There is a critical level of Jewish knowledge under which no effective tie with Judaism will ever be reached. Below this level all attempts to teach Judaism are quite useless. Below this level the only thing a Jewish youth learns is what I heard from a Jewish student in an American university: "The only thing I learned in my Sunday school was to hate Judaism."

—Rabbi Adin Steinsaltz, *On Being Free,* p. 47

in person. I would urge you to watch for his appearances and learn from him in person.

I have also written this book to recall some of the moments I have shared with Rabbi Steinsaltz over this past quarter century, with the hope they will nourish you as they have nourished me.

How has Rabbi Steinsaltz nourished me?

He has written a few dozen of the most profound books on Jewish belief, tradition, and theology.

He has helped me understand the purpose of religious observance and has transformed my life from thinking there were too many commandments into knowing that every commandment is really an opportunity to connect with God.

He has helped me understand how to develop a personal relationship with a God I can't conceive of.

He has been a role model for me, showing me how to deal lovingly with Jews of all backgrounds and levels of religious observance.

He has introduced me to some of the most sublime ideas of Kabbalah.

He has helped me understand why God has created a world with so much suffering.

He has helped me see how to live a religious life without having to isolate myself and how it is possible to be religious and yet live fully in the world.

He has shown me that one can be religious and still have a sense of humor.

He has taught me that one does not have to abandon one's intelligence in order to believe in God. He once told an audience, "I never saw it written that to be religious one has to have a lobotomy."

He has helped me understand how to determine what is important and what is unimportant, what is crucial and what is expendable, what is big and what is small.

He has supported my personal spiritual quest to the point where my first thoughts each day are thoughts of gratitude to God, as are my last.

And he has, through his books, his lectures, and the personal conversations we have had, helped me transform my life from that of a secular Jew with little knowledge of Judaism into that of someone who appreciates and participates in the extraordinary inheritance of the Jewish family, the way of Torah.

I invite you to come along for the ride.

CHAPTER ONE

Photo © Gary Eisenberg.

"A Series of Small Turnings" (1986)

*Since all of life is permeated with Torah,
the sages are not merely teachers. Their very lives
constitute Torah, and everything pertaining to
them is worthy of perusal.*

—Rabbi Adin Steinsaltz,
The Essential Talmud, p. 96

I first met Rabbi Steinsaltz in 1982, two years after *The Thir- teen Petalled Rose* was published. Its title is a phrase found in the opening lines of the Kabbalistic text *The Zohar,* in which the House of Israel is compared to a rose in a garden. The number 13 is significant in several ways, one being the ancient tradition of thirteen attributes of God. So the title is a reference to Kab- balah, signaling to the reader that the book is based on Kabblis- tic notions of existence.

In 1980, the year of its publication, *Newsweek* magazine devoted a full page to Rabbi Steinsaltz and his new book. "Jew- ish lore is filled with tales of formidable rabbis," *Newsweek* wrote. "Probably none alive today can compare in genius and influence to Adin Steinsaltz, whose extraordinary gifts as a scholar, teacher, scientist, writer, mystic and social critic have attracted disciples from all factions of Israeli society."[1]

When I located a copy of *The Thirteen Petalled Rose,* I couldn't put it down. Not that the writing captivated me. On the contrary, when I read the first three lines of the first chapter, I was confused and dumbfounded.

The book begins, "The physical world in which we live, the objectively observed universe around us, is only a part of an inconceivably vast system of worlds. Most of these worlds are spiritual in their essence; they are of a different order from our known world. Which does not necessarily mean that they exist somewhere else, but means rather that they exist in different dimensions of being."[2]

What did this mean? What was this about? How could I read the book when I could hardly grasp the first few lines?

I confess that sometimes I am a demanding or perhaps a lazy reader. Often unless a book speaks to me and delights me from the very first sentences, I put it aside. I often feel, however foolishly, that there is just too much to read to have to work my way through something dense and obscure.

It takes both time and considerable introspection to get beyond the elaborate mental constructions, the words and ideas, devised by everyone.

—Rabbi Adin Steinsaltz, *The Thirteen Petalled Rose,* p. 140

When I finished the book, I started it again, from the beginning, and found, of course, that I had picked up enough insight as I chiseled my way through the chapters to gain a little more understanding from my second reading.

But when I first read those confusing, almost unintelligible sentences in *The Thirteen Petalled Rose,* rather than toss the book aside, I reread the lines and reread them again, working my way, phrase by phrase, sentence by sentence, through the entire book.

Then I read the book a third time, and then a fourth, and a fifth. Today, twenty-five years later, I have read the book surely more than a hundred times; I consider it my favorite work and the most important of all the books I have ever read.

It was sometime during the year after I discovered *The Thirteen Petalled Rose* that I realized the book was having a deep and life-changing impact on me.

So I wrote Rabbi Steinsaltz what can only be characterized as a fan letter bordering on a love letter. Not a romantic love letter, of course, but a love letter written by a disciple to his Teacher. In it, I told Rabbi Steinsaltz about my upbringing and lack of much Jewish education. I told him of my attraction to Eastern religions and my alienation from Judaism. I described my unhappiness with the afternoon Hebrew school I attended before my bar mitzvah and how it was such a turnoff. But I also told him about my genealogical research and the powerful way in which I was drawn to the religion of my ancestors. I told Rabbi Steinsaltz I was reading *The Thirteen Petalled Rose,* that it was blowing my mind, and that I had some questions I wanted to ask him.

I added a line saying that if the Rabbi were ever in New York, I'd love to meet with him, and mailed it off to his address in Jerusalem.

❧ Becoming *The Thirteen Petalled Rose* ❧

Writing to famous people and expecting responses was not new to me.

One such effort was inspired by Ray Bradbury's science fiction novel *Fahrenheit 451.* I had been moved by the film version of the novel, directed by François Truffaut.

Fahrenheit 451 is about a society in the near future where books are banned. The last scene of the film shows the organized underground trying to save books. The underground does not hide books to save them from the antibook regime. Rather, people memorize books and "become" them. A person who memorized a book might say, "Hello, I'm *The Thirteen Petalled Rose*" and would be able to recite it in its entirety from memory.

I wrote to lots of famous people, including some of my favorite authors, asking them which book they would "become."

Amazingly, I did get responses, and many of them were fascinating: Bernard Malamud wrote that he would become Shakespeare's sonnets, John Fowles told me he would become the *Oxford English Dictionary,* and Allen Ginsberg said he would become *Songs of Innocence* by William Blake. In fact, the most interesting part of the project was my discovery that famous people often *do* write back.

At one time in my life, I would have become *Franny and Zooey* by J. D. Salinger.

Today, of course, I would become *The Thirteen Petalled Rose.*

So when I wrote to Rabbi Steinsaltz asking for a meeting when he came to New York, I actually expected a prompt reply. Instead, a year went by with no response.

My Teacher, Ram Dass

Allow me explain my situation when the phone call finally occurred.

For many years, I was a serious student of the teachings of Ram Dass, formerly known as college professor Richard Alpert. Ram Dass was known, among other things, for his being fired from Harvard University on the same day and for the same reason as Professor Timothy Leary. Both men were engaged in LSD research at the university.

Much of their research, as Ram Dass tells it, consisted of ingesting the psychoactive (they called it "psychedelic") drug and noticing its effects on themselves. Harvard would have none of it and threw them out.

Leary went on to lead a colorful public life. Alpert, a Jewish boy from New England, went to India, found his spiritual teacher rooted in the Hindu tradition, changed his name to Ram Dass, and then returned to the United States, developing a huge following of students and admirers. I was and still am one of them.

Ram Dass is probably best known today as the author of *Be Here Now,* an influential and classic best-seller that is still being read more than thirty-five years after publication. He's been on the cover of the *New York Times Magazine* twice. He is an amazing teacher and a gifted storyteller, writer, and public speaker.

I was not interested in psychedelics. I was interested in the spiritual ideas Ram Dass discovered in India and elsewhere and how marvelously he expressed those ideas.

I would say that Ram Dass helped me see that I am not simply my rational mind. I *have* a rational mind; it is a wonderful and useful tool. But it is not who I am. It is just one aspect of me. I also learned that we all experience various levels of consciousness and that we all have souls that are eternal.

I am one of many serious Jewish seekers who have Ram Dass to thank for what he has taught us.

One day in 1982, I attended an event held at Columbia University. It was recommended by Ram Dass. A woman named Pat Rodegast claimed to be able to "channel" a being named Emmanuel. She went into a trance, and Emmanuel spoke through her. What ensued was a very powerful discussion about death, the afterlife, and the meaning of it all. I went home, had dinner, and went to sleep.

In Judaism there is nothing extraordinary or unacceptable about extrasensory experience. It is quite natural for people to have the capacity to rise above the usual human level of functioning and to reach a higher spiritual consciousness. Judaism even recognizes different forms and levels of this capacity, such as prophecy, magic, and mystical powers.

—Rabbi Adin Steinsaltz, *The Strife of the Spirit,* p. 177

The secret of the positive *mitzvot,* the commandments to perform certain actions, lies, in a manner of speaking, in the activization of the limbs of the body, in certain movements and certain ways of doing things which are congruous with higher realities and higher relationships in other worlds. In fact, every movement, every gesture, every habitual pattern and every isolated act that man does with his body has an effect in whole systems of essences in other dimensions with and against one another. Clearly, an ordinary person does not know anything of this; at best he is conscious only to a very small degree of the things he does and of their higher significance.

—Rabbi Adin Steinsaltz, *The Thirteen Petalled Rose,*
p. 118

The next morning, I woke up and went into the living room, where I was in the habit of studying some Jewish text or other for a while at the start of each day. On the way to the living room, I collapsed, managed to crawl back into bed, and was literally unable to get out of the bed or move at all for ten days. My doctor never figured it out. And it never happened again.

It was during those ten days in bed, almost paralyzed on my back, when a woman called on the phone and said, "Rabbi Steinsaltz will be arriving in New York this week. He can talk to you just for a few minutes while he's here, so how's a week from Wednesday at ten A.M.?"

This is not to say that there is no use for these powers, or that mystical manifestations have no value. They are only worthless in themselves, when they are isolated from all else; but when they are properly understood, they can guide the soul better than any other forces in life. Here too, as with all else, it is the use and the direction of a faculty that determines its value: It may be turned one way to fantasy and empty vision or another way toward God.

—Rabbi Adin Steinsaltz, *The Strife of the Spirit,* p. 181

I quickly accepted the invitation, even though at that moment I was unable to get down the hall to the bathroom, let alone to the address in midtown Manhattan where I was asked to meet with Rabbi Steinsaltz.

And it was on the morning of that Wednesday when I successfully managed, for the first time in ten days, to get out of my bed, out of my apartment, and down the stairs.

"The Rashi of Our Times"

The phone call actually came from the offices of Rabbi Steve Shaw, who is a friend, student, and adviser to Rabbi Steinsaltz and was instrumental in helping the Rabbi launch his publishing and teaching activities in the United States. "I don't think it's exaggerating to say that Rabbi Steinsaltz may come to be known as the Rashi of our times," Rabbi Shaw has suggested.

From the time I received the phone call until the morning of the appointment, I spent my time in bed thinking about the meeting I would have with Rabbi Steinsaltz.

I tried to think about why I had originally asked to see him, but even more important, I was going to take the opportunity to ask the Rabbi the most profound questions in my life. As the days passed, I composed my list of questions.

In the end, I had eleven questions to pose to Rabbi Steinsaltz. Some were large, abstract questions; others were far more specific or personal. But all were, at that time, of great importance to me.

After all, I thought, if Rabbi Steinsaltz is who they say he is, if he is indeed one the greatest rabbis of the century, if he really is a genius and a mystic and a scientist and a profound thinker, if he is in fact a "once in a millennium scholar," as *Time* magazine described him, if he really is a unique, brilliant, and holy man, I have to seize the moment, grab the opportunity, ask the most important questions of my whole life. I'd have to go for broke.

I called a car service and traveled from my apartment in Brooklyn to an office building on Forty-Second Street, across from the world-famous New York Public Library. My back was still quite sensitive and sore, but I managed to slowly walk to the elevator and up to the office number I was given.

I was nervous. The last thing I wanted to do was to say something to Rabbi Steinsaltz that I would later regret—some foolish comment or inarticulate question. I approached the receptionist, but suddenly the Rabbi himself appeared, reached out his hand, and said, "Hello." I had the impression that he had already been meeting with other people, as he suggested we take the elevator to another floor where there was a place for us to sit and chat.

His hair and beard were red, with hints of whitish gray. His hands did not look like the hands of a scholar but rather like those of a worker, a man who uses his hands to build and repair and tinker. I am five feet seven inches tall, and Rabbi Steinsaltz was shorter than me. His eyes were bright, almost twinkly. His beard was long and wild, his hair slightly long in the back. He was wearing what looked like a blue velvet smoking jacket, and he was carrying his pipe and a pouch of tobacco.

We walked together to the elevator. He noticed that I was partly bent over, so I told him that my back had "gone out" and that this was my first time out of bed in ten days. When we reached our destination, we sat on comfortable chairs in a sitting area outside a row of offices.

I began by telling Rabbi Steinsaltz that I had been, for many years, in search of a Teacher. I remember saying, "I am looking for a Teacher with a capital T," and he smiled for the first time. Rabbi Steinsaltz has a great smile, which you can often barely see behind his mustache and beard, but it is usually accompanied by a smile around his eyes.

In those days, it was permissible to smoke in public spaces in New York City buildings, so Rabbi Steinsaltz was occupied with packing his pipe with tobacco and lighting it several times during our conversation. I had no idea how long I would have with him, but he didn't seem at all in a rush. He gave me all the time I wanted. We spoke for two and a half hours on that Wednesday morning.

&ᘔ My First Questions &ᘔ

Of the eleven questions I had brought with me, we discussed, to my absolute satisfaction, nine of them. I had written the questions in a little notebook and held it in my lap as I asked them one at a time. Although I had listed the questions in a particular order, when I was with the Rabbi I quickly switched the order around. I don't know why.

I was nervous. I didn't really want to interview him. I wanted to have a conversation.

But it didn't happen that way. There was no way at that first meeting of ours for me to chat with Rabbi Steinsaltz, to have a back-and-forth conversation.

Some of my questions were straightforward and were answered with a quick yes or no. Others were more detailed, profoundly personal, and needed some air and some light.

I began, "Since high school, I have been reading books that teach the ideas of the Eastern religions. I don't pretend to really know too much about the history, similarities, or differences among the various forms of Buddhism, Hinduism, or other strands of Eastern thought."

I went on, "But I drifted toward books about these spiritual traditions and have found myself being nourished by them."

"And then," I explained to Rabbi Steinsaltz, "I discovered your book, *The Thirteen Petalled Rose,* and I found that so many basic notions about life as you describe them in your book are similar to or the same as those in the East.

"How could it *be*?" I asked.

Rabbi Steinsaltz, lighting his pipe, took it away from his mouth and with a smile said, "One might say, 'How could it be *otherwise*?'"

I understood what he meant immediately. But not only did I understand; I also experienced something that happened often when I was with the Rabbi: I would have a question in mind that had attained immense proportion. And then Rabbi Steinsaltz would help me bring it down to the right size.

Why would I be shocked that the various spiritual traditions in the world teach some of the same basic teachings? As Rabbi Steinsaltz suggested, wouldn't it be more of a shock to think that the world's great spiritual traditions *differ* profoundly?

After all, just as one plus one equals two all over the world, there are surely spiritual principles, like "Do unto others," to use a simple example, that also find expression in the various religious traditions of the world.

Even the notion of reincarnation, which is so central to the theology of the East, has been taught by some of the greatest spiritual masters in Jewish history.

In a way, my question was the wrong question. My shock was really not that the Eastern spiritual masters taught similar ideas to those I found in *The Thirteen Petalled Rose.* My real shock, although I didn't realize it or express it during my first meeting with Rabbi Steinsaltz, was that after reading hundreds of books about Judaism, I had never encountered a Jewish book as inspiring, as profound, as *The Thirteen Petalled Rose.* There were lots of books on Eastern thought that inspired me, but nothing came close in the world of modern Jewish books.

Rabbi Steinsaltz went on to say, "History is usually taught backward. You will hear historians say, 'A long time ago there were pagans. And then came Abraham, who invented one God and introduced monotheism to the world.'"

The Rabbi spoke very softly. His pipe was well lit, and its aroma sweetened the air.

I do not mean to imply that holiness is in any way restricted to one people or that the approach to the Divine is not equally available to all of mankind. It is only that the Jews undertake a greater burden.

—Rabbi Adin Steinsaltz, *The Thirteen Petalled Rose,* p. 97

"But there are still pagans, I would say, all around us right here in New York City. One does not have to go back hundreds or thousands of years to find pagans."

I understood what Rabbi Steinsaltz was saying: a pagan is a person who does not acknowledge the existence of God. It is not that a long time ago the world was without belief in God and that Abraham introduced the idea of God to the world. Rather, the world was *created* by God, and God's creations knew Him—but came to forget Him. Then Abraham came along and reminded the world of God.

Today, we are still in great need, I believe, of reminders that this is God's world that we are in.

Rabbi Steinsaltz added, "Abraham did not introduce God to the world. Abraham was, so to say, a Renaissance man. He reminded the world of God. God created the world, and everything in it stems from the same Source. Everything grows from that Source and in some ways resembles it."

I was moved and surprised by his response. I suppose I foolishly expected him to quickly point out the differences between Judaism and the Eastern religions. Instead, he established the reasonableness of spiritual traditions' being similar.

He told me that he was once invited by the BBC to participate in a documentary about the world's religions and that he was asked to represent Judaism—and they gave him one minute.

He told me that he said, "What can I say? I can say that Jews believe in God. But *other* religions believe in God. I can say that Jews believe in revelation. But *other* religions believe in revelation. I can say all kinds of things that Jews do, but other religions do these things too. I suppose all I can really say is that we Jews do it in a *Jewish* way."

During the hours that we spoke, I was half bent over. I winced from time to time.

When he said to me, sympathetically, "You know, you didn't have to come," I disagreed and said that I certainly *did.*

Another question I asked Rabbi Steinsaltz—not one of the deeply personal ones—had to do with my relationship with family members who were not observers of Shabbos restrictions.

I was celebrating Shabbos each week on Friday night, including a beautiful Shabbos dinner, complete with candle lighting, two challahs, a cup of wine, songs and words of Torah shared at the table, and grace after meals.

My question was this: since it is not permitted to drive an automobile on Shabbos, was it OK for me to invite family members and friends to my Shabbos table who do not observe the laws of Shabbos and who would have to drive a car to visit me? After all, on the one hand, my invitation would prompt them to drive. On the other hand, wouldn't it be better for them to see our Shabbos celebration and to join in?

This might appear to be a small question, especially since I have described my questions for this first meeting with Rabbi Steinsaltz as being profoundly important ones. This question was really symbolic of a whole series of issues that arise in nonobservant Jewish families when one member, like me, decides to become observant.

We have in our time witnessed a phenomenon unprecedented in Jewish history: the return of Jews to traditional observance. The phenomenon, sometimes known as the *ba'al teshuvah* movement,[3] is that of Jews like me, who were brought up in mostly secular homes and who have decided to enter into traditional Jewish life with its values, dedication to Torah study, prayer, customs, restrictions and celebrations but may be the only ones in the family to do so.

"Well," Rabbi Steinsaltz began, "if your family or guests never go out on Friday night, even if not for religious reasons but just that this was their habit, then I would not invite them. By staying home, they are doing the right thing as far as the laws of Shabbos are concerned. However, if they would just as quickly drive to the theater on a Friday night, you might as well invite them to your Shabbos dinner."

Rabbi Steinsaltz also referred to a category that is described in discussions among the Jewish sages in the Talmud, and that is the case of Jewish infants being kidnapped by Gentiles. Clearly, such an infant is not obligated to observe the laws of Shabbos. Rabbi Steinsaltz explained that this kind of Talmudic case is similar in many ways to the *ba'al teshuvah* today.

During that first meeting, I asked some questions about Jewish practice, about reincarnation, and about several other topics, much of which was personal and pressing for me. I had no hesitation sharing some deeply private psychological stuff with him, and I reaped great benefit from doing so.

But eventually my first conversation with Rabbi Steinsaltz was over. My mind was spinning.

There was no arrogance. No smugness. No air of superiority. No overwhelming force of authority.

Instead, Rabbi Steinsaltz was like a wise, experienced fellow seeker who was farther along the trail and had the generosity to turn back and call back to me, describing the terrain that I was approaching.

The ordinary man who has been granted contact with the holy person is thereby brought into a certain contact with true holiness.

—Rabbi Adin Steinsaltz, *The Thirteen Petalled Rose,* p. 83

I left my first encounter with Rabbi Steinsaltz deeply satisfied, spiritually nourished, and greatly uplifted. In fact, I was blown away.

"Some People Have More Than Twenty-Four Hours in Each Day"

A year passed after that first conversation. It was the spring of 1985. I felt that I needed to arrange a second meeting with Rabbi Steinsaltz. But I was a little hesitant about bringing him more of my questions. I felt that I would be wasting his time. I had not yet had my brilliant idea to become Rabbi Steinsaltz's driver.

So I asked Marc Silver, who is now an editor at *U.S. News and World Report* but was then the editor in chief of the *National Jewish Monthly,* the official monthly magazine of B'nai Brith International, if he would give me an assignment to interview Rabbi Steinsaltz for the magazine. In this way, I would get to meet with Rabbi Steinsaltz under the pretense that it wasn't personal.

Marc assigned me the task of writing an article on "a day in the life of Rabbi Adin Steinsaltz"—the perfect excuse for spending more time with him. I wasn't able to arrange to follow him around for a day. But I was able to talk with him about his life.

Rabbi Steinsaltz was known for both the large quantity and the high quality of his work, so I asked him, "How do you get so much done?"

When not traveling, he explained, "I go to my office very early and leave sometime in the early afternoon. I go home for lunch. And then I go back to the office and stay there until sometime in the evening. So you might say that I have two working days each day."

He then added, "Most people think that everybody has twenty-four hours in a day, but that it might not be true. Some people, like the Rambam [the great Jewish thinker Maimonides], seemed to have more than twenty-four hours in a day.

"I wake up in the morning, and in what seems like a very short time, I discover that it is midnight or two A.M. And I wonder, What has happened to this day? Where did it go?"

I didn't stay on the subject of his day. It wasn't really of interest to me. Instead, I was eager to ask him a question that was often on my mind, a question about marijuana.

Marijuana: Who Is the Master and Who Is the Slave?

I knew people who smoked marijuana, and had one friend in particular who smoked it at least twice a day, in the morning and at night. My friend once said to me, "Why don't you ask Rabbi Steinsaltz what he thinks of marijuana?" I said I would and so I did.

Rabbi Steinsaltz said to me, "First of all, I never tried it. There are two issues with marijuana. One is small, and the other is big. The small issue is the idea in Jewish law of *dina d'malchuta dina,* 'the law of the land is the law.' Generally speaking, we're supposed to follow the law of the land where we live. So if marijuana is illegal, you have an illegal situation there. So perhaps you need to follow the law."

That was the small issue. The big issue, he said, has nothing to do with marijuana; it has to do with anything in life.

"The issue is who is the master and who is the slave. If you are the master, fine. If you are the slave, then you are in trouble no matter what you're the slave of, whether it be coffee, exercise, or Torah study.

"So you have to ask yourself, 'Who is the master and who is the slave?'"

Rabbi Steinsaltz was, as usual, smoking his pipe. He was smoking pipe tobacco. He told me that he stops smoking every year on Pesach. One of the reasons he does it is to see what his reaction might be, and he is convinced that he is not addicted to tobacco. Smoking his pipe is a habit, but he is not its slave.

More Meetings

After my second meeting with Rabbi Steinsaltz, I felt that I had found my Teacher. There was something about the way he listened to me, the way he sometimes went to the heart of the matter and also circled around a question, making sure it was well defined and explored from various angles; and the way he always spoke to the heart of the matter.

Fortunately, any further hesitation about pursuing Rabbi Steinsaltz a third time, and a fourth and then a fifth, was reduced by a conversation I had with Rabbi Jonathan Omer-Man.

Jonathan used to work with Rabbi Steinsaltz in Jerusalem. He was editor in chief of a magazine called the *Shefa Quarterly,* which came out of Rabbi Steinsaltz's offices under Jonathan's direction.[4]

During the summer of 1985, I taught a class introducing people to *The Thirteen Petalled Rose* at the wonderful annual Jew-

The Jewish approach to life considers the man who has stopped going—he who has a feeling of completion, of peace, of a great light from above that has brought him to rest—to be someone who has lost his way.

—Rabbi Adin Steinsaltz, *The Thirteen Petalled Rose,*
   p. 132

ish educator's conference sponsored by the Coalition for the Advancement of Jewish Education (CAJE). Jonathan attended the conference and joined my class.

That day, I said to him, "You know, I've been inventing reasons to get the chance to see Rabbi Steinsaltz again. But I don't want to waste his time. I'm afraid that I'm asking him for too much and taking up too much of his time."

And Jonathan said to me, "Rabbi Steinsaltz is a big boy. He can take care of himself. Believe me, if he didn't want to see you, he wouldn't be seeing you. Don't worry about it." From that point on, I stopped hanging back.

That same summer, I moved to an apartment located just a few streets away from the neighborhood known as Boro Park, in Brooklyn, New York. Boro Park was once described in the media as "the largest ultra-Orthodox neighborhood in America." It occupies dozens of city blocks. The neighborhood has a few hundred synagogues, many groups of Hasidim, and is possibly the most Jewishly religious place in the United States.

My first child, Malya, was a year old and during that time I was interested in intensifying my Jewish life. I was beginning to love Torah study more than anything else in the world. One of the attractions was the opportunity I had to spend much of my time praying and studying Torah and celebrating Jewish holy days at the world headquarters of an amazing Hasidic group called Bobov.[5]

My friend Tovia, a Bobover Hasid whom I had met a few years earlier through our mutual interest in genealogy, urged me to come to Bobov, in particular to see the Bobover Rebbe, the spiritual rabbi of rabbis in the Bobov world, and he intensified his efforts to get me to visit the community when he learned that I lived just a short walk from Bobov's world headquarters in Boro Park. Tovia invited me to sample Bobov at the

He whose search has reached a certain level feels that he is in the palace of the King. He goes from room to room, from hall to hall, seeking Him out. However, the king's palace is an endless series of worlds, and as a man proceeds in his search from room to room, he holds only the end of the string. It is, nevertheless, a continuous going, a going after God, a going to God, day after day, year after year.

—Rabbi Adin Steinsaltz, *The Thirteen Petalled Rose,*
   p. 133

Rebbe's tisch ("the Rebbe's table") on a Friday night in the fall of 1985.

I walked into the synagogue's large room, which was used as a study hall. There were hundreds of bearded Hasidic men, all in black hats or round fur hats called *streimels* and dressed in black suits. They were all gathered around their rebbe. I felt as if I had walked into a different century.

Roman Vishniak is famous for his photographs of the Hasidic world in Eastern Europe before the Second World War. What I see in Bobov today is exactly the same as what I see in those photos: the same faces, the same garb, the same traditions, the same books, the same relationships.

I must confess, however, that the first time I walked in there, I felt that I had been there before; deep inside, I felt that this was not the first time my soul had been in such an environment.

🦋 "When It Comes to Your Soul, 🦋 There Are No Gentlemen"

The evening was filled with eating, drinking, and singing. The Bobover Rebbe sat in the center of a dais, his Shabbos dinner before him. Hundreds of Hasidim, plus me, sat or stood around the table. We were all guests at the Shabbos table of the Rebbe.

At a certain point, the Bobover Rebbe spoke. He told stories from the Talmud about Rabbi Akiva. He reminded us that Rabbi Akiva, known as one of the greatest sages of all times, did not even begin to study Torah until he was forty years old. I was familiar with Rabbi Akiva and about the fact that, as the Talmud says, he didn't know an *aleph* from a *beit* until he was an adult. Every person like me who returns to Judaism as an adult loves Rabbi Akiva.

The evening, which ended around two o'clock early Saturday morning, culminated with the Hasidim going before their Rebbe and receiving a *l'chaim* (a toast "to life") with a raised cup of wine or a blessing from the Rebbe up close and personal, with touches and embraces. Often the Bobover Rebbe would put his arm around a person's shoulder and speak intimately.

All of a sudden, I found myself in the midst of a pushing and shoving and elbowing crowd of Hasidim surging toward the Rebbe with great hunger and what I felt was rude selfishness. It was horrible, a mob, with people cutting ahead and pushing others aside. I said to myself, "This is not for me. I'm not coming back here."

Nevertheless, the following week I returned. There was something so wondrous, so magnetic, so spiritually uplifting for me there that I couldn't resist a second session at the Rebbe's tisch.

Once again the evening was glorious, with eating and drinking and singing and listening to profound teachings from the Bobover Rebbe.

And once again the evening ended with the chance to get a blessing from the Rebbe, and once again I found myself in the middle of a pushing, shoving mob. I said to myself, "Didn't I learn my lesson last week? This is horrible! Everybody is so inconsiderate! I hate this. I'm not coming back."

And I left that evening once again at 2:30 in the morning, and I promised myself I would not return.

Nevertheless, the third week, there I was again, walking to Bobov looking forward to the uplifting atmosphere, the warmth of the Hasidim, the shining face of the Rebbe and his profound teachings.

The evening progressed as usual, again ending with the crush of Hasidim surging toward the Rebbe. I couldn't take it, and I said to the guy who was elbowing me to my right, "Why is everybody doing this? Pushing and shoving like animals! What is going on here?"

The Hasid looked at me in the midst of the tumult and said, "We have a rule around here. When it comes to your *neshama* (your soul), there are no gentlemen."

All of a sudden, the whole scene flipped for me: my body was being jostled, but my soul, my *neshama,* had one direction and one aim, and that was to receive a blessing from the Bobover Rebbe; like whipped cream on a cake, it was the culmination of the joyful evening at the Rebbe's Shabbos table.

Years later, I was told by Rabbi Zalman Schachter-Shalomi that a Rebbe is not someone who acts as an intermediary between the Hasid and God. The Rebbe is not the person who makes the connection between the individual and the Almighty. The Rebbe is the one who goes underneath the student and pushes him up.

And certainly the Bobover Rebbe was somebody who lifted me up.

> Most souls are not new; they are not in the world for the first time. Almost every person bears the legacy of previous existences. Therefore the destiny of a person is connected not only with those things he himself creates and does, but also with what happens to the soul in its previous incarnations.
>
> —Rabbi Adin Steinsaltz, *The Thirteen Petalled Rose,* p. 64

All of a sudden, I wasn't being pushed around. Rather, I was a salmon swimming upstream.

"When it comes to your *neshama,* there are no gentlemen." That advice has ever since meant to me that my body is temporary but my soul is eternal. And when one's focus is on one's soul, one doesn't mind a little tumult.

❧ Getting Acquainted ❧

January 1986. The phone rang.

"Rabbi Steinsaltz is arriving at JFK one morning next week." Could I pick him up and bring him to Manhattan?

I said yes immediately.

It was my first assignment. I would be Rabbi Steinsaltz's driver. I imagined what it must have felt like to be the wagon driver of Rashi, the great Talmudic commentator of a thousand years ago.

But this was the twentieth century, so I brought my car to the car wash, I vacuumed the inside several times, I cleaned out all of the accumulated junk on the floor of the back seat and the trunk, and I prepared to fulfill my obligation. The flight was scheduled to land at 5:00 A.M. I got up at 3:00, showered, dressed, and arrived at the airport about an hour early.

By the time the aircraft had landed and Rabbi Steinsaltz had cleared customs, it was another hour and a half before we met. While waiting, a flood of thoughts danced in my head: "I can't believe I have this job. What should I say to him? How can I help him? Do I take his luggage and carry everything for him? Do I make small talk and ask him how his flight was? Do I open doors for him? Do I dare ask him my own questions again? Should I ask him if he wants to listen to music when we're in the car? Does he want to sleep in the car at this hour while I get him to his first appointment? Do I wait in the car while he has his breakfast? Do I tell him when his first appointment must end to allow enough time for me to get him to his next appointment? Can I speak with him about God?"

Rabbi Steinsaltz finally came out into the hall of the International Arrivals Building. He was rolling his suitcase and carrying a small case. I said hello and asked him if I could carry his suitcase. He gave me the lighter one. It was a little awkward for me. After all, I wanted to help him, but I have also been in his position, where I am picked up at an airport for a lecture and the person wants to carry my suitcase and carry-on case.

Rabbi Steinsaltz did the same thing I do: I give the person one thing to carry and I carry the other.

I don't like small talk, and the last thing I wanted to do was make small talk with him. I wanted to avoid clichés like "How was your flight?" and "How are you?" Frankly, I wish I could have said, "Hello, can we talk theology for a few hours?"

Instead, I asked him how his flight was, and I inquired as to whether he is able to sleep on a plane. I have no recollection of what he said; I was too preoccupied with making sure everything went smoothly.

A Shared Interest in Genealogy

At the time of my first car trip on the road with Rabbi Steinsaltz in 1986, I was in the middle of my own book tour.

In some ways, that book tour has never ended because it is now twenty-five years since my first book, *From Generation to Generation: How to Trace Your Jewish Genealogy and Family History,* was published, and I am still speaking around the country on the subject of how and why to climb one's Jewish family tree.

But for the first six years of the book's life, I lectured in forty cities a year. And I was exhausted. The Jewish Lecture Bureau told me that for four years in a row, I was their most frequently booked speaker.

The book tour was grueling. Night after night, city after city; there were actually some nights that I looked out at the audience and did not know which city I was in. One night, I remember thinking, "I know I'm in Wisconsin, and I know the place starts with an *M,* but I don't know if it's Madison or Milwaukee."

When Rabbi Steinsaltz and I got to my car, I opened the trunk and put his things in. I opened the passenger door for him but let him close the door himself. I can understand opening a door for someone, but it has always felt more awkward to have someone close a car door for me, so I treated Rabbi Steinsaltz the way I want to be treated. Good principle, that Golden Rule.

When we were both in the car, he asked, "Do you mind if I smoke my pipe?" I gave him instructions on the use of the lighter and the ashtray, the electric window openers, and the car seat adjustment so that he could make himself as comfortable as possible.

He then asked me if I flew much.

I mentioned my book and the book tour, and he started discussing his own interest in genealogy and his own genealogical research and discoveries and then asked me about some of mine.

Kurzweil the Entertainer

Rabbi Steinsaltz also brought up the subject of surnames and their meanings. I knew from my genealogical research that there is a name for the study of surnames and that word is *onomastics*.

I told Rabbi Steinsaltz, "*Kurzweil* means an amusement or diversion, something you do for fun. *Kurz* means "short" in German, and *Weil* means "time," so the compound "short time" means "someone or something that entertains and makes the time seem short."

Kurzweil is thus fun, the opposite of boring. The original Kurzweil must have been quite entertaining.

"And I think the name fits me. I have been a successful lecturer and performer in synagogues and for other Jewish organizations for years. Kurzweils in our family are often great storytellers."

Rabbi Steinsaltz said, "There have been great rabbis who always began their studies or lectures with a joke, wishing to put their audience and themselves into the proper frame of mind, to prepare them for awesome truths."

I said, "Isn't there a story about the prophet Elijah?"

"Yes, there are many stories of Elijah in the world. One has Elijah in a marketplace filled with people. One of the elders in the community comes over to him and asks, 'Who, of all those here in the marketplace, belongs to Heaven?' Elijah looks around and says, 'I don't see anyone here who belongs to Heaven.' Then two strangers enter the marketplace. Elijah points to them and says, 'These two are among those that belong to Heaven.'

"The elder asks who they are.

"'They are clowns. Jesters. They earn their living by making people laugh.'"

Rabbi Steinsaltz told me that in Kabbalistic writings, there are discussions of how to transform the hard, outer "shell" of the soul into holiness through humor.

As our talk of family trees went on, I was keenly aware of two things: that the time was rolling by and that I still had many questions to ask about *The Thirteen Petalled Rose* related to issues that were stirring in my soul, and here I was, talking about genealogy, the very subject that had me on this book tour and that I wanted to get away from for a while.

Genealogy was the last topic I wanted to speak about with Rabbi Steinsaltz. Or anyone else.

But as I drove to the Rabbi's destination in Manhattan, our discussion of genealogy continued. Rabbi Steinsaltz asked me whether I had discovered anything interesting in my genealogical research.

I told him that I discovered that I have illustrious rabbinic ancestors. I assured Rabbi Steinsaltz that I don't brag about those ancestors. Instead, I am humbled by the knowledge of them.

"When I learned that my great-great-great-grandfather, Rabbi Chaim Yosef Gottlieb, who was born in 1790, was a Hasidic rebbe from a town called Stropkov in Slovakia, I wanted to find out about that town. I wanted to find out about this Hasidic rebbe. I wanted to find out who his teacher was.

"I wanted to find out as much about him as I possibly could.

"When I found out that I was a direct descendant of Rabbi Isaiah Horowitz, who was born in 1555 and was known as the Shelah HaKodesh,[6] I wanted to find out who *he* was.

"I was intrigued to learn that he was a great Kabbalist, a great Jewish mystic, and that the *Encyclopedia Judaica* says that it was Rabbi Isaiah Horowitz who brought Kabbalah to Poland. He is credited with being the primary Kabbalist in Poland, which is an amazing achievement.

"I'm a direct descendant of his. The more I learn about him, the more connected I feel to what he taught and the spiritual world in which he lived.

"When I learned that I was a direct descendant of the *Rama,* Rabbi Moses Isserles of Krakow, who was born in 1530 and who wrote a commentary on the *Shulchan Aruch*, the Code of Jewish Law, it gave me a sense of pride, but it also humbled me and stimulated me to continue my own spiritual work."

Looking back, I now understand what was going on. I know it to be true that there were many years when I was involved with my family tree research when I had no idea what I was doing.

I thought I knew. Had you asked me, I would have said that I was tracing my family tree. I was interested, I would say, in my Jewish history.

But my genealogical activities were really a spiritual search, not a historical research hobby. From the outside, it looked like I was doing Jewish genealogy, but from the inside, I was really looking for myself and for my relationship to the Absolute, to God.

Who am I? Where did I come from? Where am I going? What is this life all about? These are the questions that the genealogist asks, and these are the same questions at the heart of *The Thirteen Petalled Rose,* based on the major structures of Kabbalistic thinking about existence.

The search for roots, even in the simplest genealogical sense, is likely to be a meaningful experience on both the personal and religious levels. Lineage is not just a matter of empty self-congratulation. All lineage, and not just that of nobility, carries with it a certain responsibility.

—Rabbi Adin Steinsaltz, *Teshuvah,* p. 60

✿ Different Gates for Different People ✿

Rabbi Steinsaltz said to me, "I have recommended to many people that they trace their roots. When someone becomes a *ba'al teshuvah*"—a person, like myself, who did not grow up with Jewish observance but has "returned" to it—"he sometimes thinks that he should forsake his own historic roots. I urge people to seek them out."

I remarked to Rabbi Steinsaltz that I thought that genealogy teaches tolerance. When I traced my family tree, I discovered that my family has everybody in it. We have Hasidim, we have socialists, we have Orthodox Jews and assimilated Jews, we have Israelis and Americans and Australians and Hungarians. We have city people and country people. We have Democrats and Republicans and Communists.

I told Rabbi Steinsaltz that I discovered a second cousin who was almost exactly my age and who grew up under the Communist regime in Hungary. Her grandmother and my grandmother were sisters. My grandmother came to the United States when she was fifteen; her grandmother stayed in Hungary. Things could so easily have turned out so differently.

Rabbi Steinsaltz had written about it. In his book *Teshuvah,* the Rabbi writes, "A family search often becomes an acceptance of diversity in Jewish life." He remarked that I seem to know some of his books better than he does!

At one point in our conversation, we began to talk about the individual paths that each of us finds ourselves on. He began to tell me about the mystic vision of Ezekiel.

"It is said that there are different gates to the Temple for each of the twelve tribes," Rabbi Steinsaltz explained to me. "These are different gates for different people."

The Rabbi quoted from the Torah in Hebrew and then translated: "Each of the Israelites must remain bound to the ancestral portion of his father's tribe" (Numbers 36:7). He said, "It is not a statement about the inability to unite. Rather, we have to recognize human diversity. Elijah's role, when the final redemption comes, is to restore the Israelites to their tribes and to their families."

I once wrote in my notebook that Rabbi Steinsaltz said, "Israel will be united, but only when each can relate to the others on the basis of, confidence in, and open expression of its own distinctiveness."

When I told Rabbi Steinsaltz about my illustrious ancestors and my mixture of pride and humility at my discovery of them, he said, "Of course, it's not a matter of self-congratulation. Lineage carries with it responsibility. We don't brag; we learn from them.

"There are many individuals among the Jewish people who claim that they descend from an illustrious lineage. They must understand, of course, that they ultimately stem from Abraham and, before him, from his father, Terah, which is not exactly a proud lineage."

The car ride to Manhattan didn't take long—at least, it wasn't long enough for me. But I had to admit that it was mean-

A further reason that man was created one is related to genealogy: families should not fight over questions of superiority. Even after knowing that man was created one, families still argue over who is of more venerable descent. . . . What would have happened if there had been several pristine men?

—Rabbi Adin Steinsaltz, *On Being Free*, p. 74

ingful to talk with Rabbi Steinsaltz about genealogy, a subject that had been an obsession of mine for decades.

I dropped Rabbi Steinsaltz off at the building where he was to have his first appointment; I got his suitcase and carrying case onto the curb for him as he assured me that I didn't need to park and that he could manage with his suitcase by himself. It didn't feel right to drop off Rabbi Steinsaltz at the curb, but that's what he wanted.

"I Read Marx Before I Read the Bible"

Rabbi Steinsaltz doesn't usually like to talk about himself, but the next day, when I once again was asked to drive him to a synagogue in a New Jersey suburb for a lecture he was scheduled to give, I asked him directly about parts of his life and I was able to glean a number of pieces of his biography.

"I read Marx and Lenin before I read the Bible," he remarked. Thus he shared with me one of the most wonderful pieces of information about his youth: that this supremely outstanding rabbi and Talmud scholar didn't begin studying until his midteens. An only child, he was introduced to Jewish studies by a private tutor his father had hired.

On this second-day drive, Rabbi Steinsaltz told me that his father, a secular man and a leftist, proclaimed at the time, "I don't care if my child is an *apikores* [heretic], but no child of mine is going to be an ignoramus!"

He told me that he grew up in a nonobservant household, "and I disliked those Orthodox Jews. I used to throw rocks at them.

"Like Kafka's story, 'Metamorphosis,'" Rabbi Steinsaltz said. "One day, you look in the mirror, and you see that you've become a cockroach.

"My mother and father were skeptics," Rabbi Steinsaltz said. "They brought me up to be a skeptic. In fact, I became such a skeptic that I became skeptical of skepticism."

He said that he had no religious epiphany and that Jews generally don't have them.

The starting point of repentance is precisely this fulcrum point, away from the pursuit of what he craves, and confronts his desire to approach God; this is the moment of conversion, the crucial moment of repentance. It is rare for repentance to take the form of a sudden, dramatic conversion, and it generally takes the forms of a series of small turnings.

—Rabbi Adin Steinsaltz, *The Thirteen Petalled Rose,*
    p. 129

NOTES FROM THE ROAD:
A Heretic Among Heretics

I asked Rabbi Steinsaltz about his own spiritual quest. He said, "It was many years ago. I didn't want to annoy people, but I began asking questions, many questions, about things that were accepted in Israel, where I was born, and in other places. I was perhaps a better nonbeliever than the rest of my countrymen. They were such great nonbelievers that they didn't believe in Judaism; I was such a nonbeliever that I didn't even believe in heresy. So this was the turning point, a very important one. I discovered that one has to believe in many heresies in order to be a heretic. But to accept heresy, one has to be a believer. And if you have to be a believer, it becomes a matter of choice in what to believe in."

I mentioned that in *The Thirteen Petalled Rose,* he speaks about the process of becoming religious as "a series of small turnings." The Rabbi smiled, perhaps realizing for the first time that I was able to quote from *The Thirteen Petalled Rose* even better than he could. I suspect that like most authors, after he finished writing it, he never looked at it again. I, on the other hand, had read it scores of times.

"To become more religious doesn't just mean believing or affirming but rather entering a whole culture," he said. "It was a very lonely time for me. I had to fight my way into Judaism step by step."

I told Rabbi Steinsaltz that I had heard that at age fifteen, he left his secular school for a year to attend a yeshiva. This he confirmed and also confirmed that he had studied physics and mathematics at the university level. "I was a slight boy with red hair, blondish red curls," he said. A few moments later he said, "I came to the point that this world was not enough."

❦ "I Was Born in Jerusalem— ❦ Nothing Else Is Interesting"

At one point Rabbi Steinsaltz said to me, "My biography is simple. I was born in Jerusalem, and I still live there. Nothing else is very interesting."

("I *love* Jerusalem," he has said many times with passion. "I love the light in Jerusalem. And I'm not speaking mystically.")

"My life has been very undramatic and even boring. I didn't climb any tall mountains," he said, "and I didn't kill any lions."

"My Only Official Position Was That I Was on the Board of the Jerusalem Zoo"

His parents had come to Palestine in the 1930s, and he was born in 1937. He has memories that go back to when he was about a year old. He told me that he grew up in a household of socialists; his father was "one of the few Palestinian Jews who fought in the Spanish Civil War." Just as people in the United States formed the Abraham Lincoln Brigade, which went to Spain to fight the Fascists in the 1936–1939 conflict, Rabbi Steinsaltz's father did the same as a Jew living in pre-statehood Israel.

Rabbi Steinsaltz told me that he himself had gone to Spain a number of years earlier to visit some of the places that his father had told him about.

He described himself as a "nonbelieving teenager." But by the time he was in his early twenties, he was the youngest principal of a high school in Israel. And he was also teaching adults, including people like the first president of Israel, Zalman Shazar, who was an old man when he was a student in the young man's class. Rabbi Steinsaltz told me that the way he was able to teach classes to students who were sixty years his senior was to imagine that he himself was three thousand years old and the students were eight-year-old babies.

"I have no official position and am not the rabbi of a synagogue. The only official position that I've held is a seat on the board of directors of the Jerusalem Zoo."

Rabbi Steinsaltz likes zoos. He told me that as a young man, whenever he was feeling blue, he would go to the zoo. Something about the animal world settled his mood. He told me that he loves animals.

Rabbi Steinsaltz is married. His wife, who is from a Lubavitch family, the Asimovs, is related to the famous American scientist and author Isaac Asimov. My understanding is that the Asimovs are a religious family and that Isaac was the exception. Rabbi Steinsaltz has three children. His daughter is the director of a battered women's shelter in Jerusalem dedicated to helping Orthodox women in need. Rabbi Steinsaltz said to me, "Unfortunately, she's busy there." Rabbi Steinsaltz also has two sons, both of whom have been ordained as rabbis.

"Nobody Seemed to Want to Operate on Me"

I told Rabbi Steinsaltz that when I mention his name to people, they often ask if I know how he is feeling, and I wondered why.

He told me that there was a time in his life when he was very ill. In fact, he was gravely ill, and he spent a prolonged amount of time in the United States seeking medical attention for his illness.

He was born with a genetic disease that tends to run in Jewish families: Gaucher's disease (pronounced "go-SHAYZ").

"I am suffering from one of those Jewish maladies," he said, "Gaucher's disease. You possibly know about it. Friends showed me a medical textbook that incorporated all the pertinent new material about this malady that appeared in the past twenty years. And it contained a recommendation that if there is the chance that a child will suffer from Gaucher's disease, the parents are advised to abort the child.

"So in my case, either my parents didn't know or their doctors didn't know, and so I escaped the best medical advice of the time!"

Rabbi Steinsaltz told me that when he was very ill, he went to a physician, who said to him, "Rabbi, you are gravely ill; you must be operated on immediately. I will recommend a surgeon." He went to the recommended surgeon, and the surgeon said, "Rabbi, you are very, very ill; you need to be operated on immediately. I'm going to recommend a surgeon."

Then he went to the third doctor, and the man said to him, "Rabbi, you are gravely ill. You need to be operated on immediately. I'm going to recommend a surgeon"—at which point Rabbi Steinsaltz realized that he needed the surgery but nobody wanted to perform the potentially dangerous operation. So he said to the doctor he was with at the time, "I would like you to do the surgery. Let's schedule it."

Well, the surgery was scheduled, and it was a success. It also happens that in the past several years, major progress has been made regarding the treatment of people who have Gaucher's disease, and Rabbi Steinsaltz is participating regularly in that treatment. It is, as I understand it, extremely successful.

"On the eve of the operation, I worked late and slept well," he told me. "I was either still needed here, or my job was done." He then said, "In any case, with the operation behind me, I was able to plan ahead realistically. With God's help, I was able to go on."

He then added, "I had the advantage of being a very obstinate person. One must keep one's aims clearly in mind. Life is a constant compromise. If you don't keep your aims clearly before you, you come to a situation where means and ends become confused."

It so happens that when Rabbi Steinsaltz's older son was in his teens, he was diagnosed with a certain kind of leukemia. The Lubavitcher Rebbe was told about it, and the Rebbe advised the Steinsaltzes to change their last name. (It is more usual for a Rebbe to suggest that people visited by misfortune change their first name.)

The name *Steinsaltz* means "stone of salt." But that is not the name on Rabbi Steinsaltz's passport. The name that appears is the name that the Rebbe advised the Steinsaltz family to change it to, *Even Yisroel,* "Stone of Israel." Rabbi Steinsaltz's son wrote an article about the experience and told the story of the name change. Shortly after the name was changed, the leukemia went into remission and has not returned.

"I Belong to Hasidus"

I decided to ask Rabbi Steinsaltz about his relationship to Hasidism.

He replied, "I belong to Hasidus. My background is that of Hasidus. It is how Judaism has always appeared to me in any significant way. Looking at Judaism in the recent era without Hasidus would be like looking at the Talmud today and ignoring the *Acharonim,* the Talmudic commentators from the 1600s to the present."

He added, "Hasidism was halted. Hasidism didn't spread all over the world mainly because of the destruction of the Jews in Europe—the pogroms in Russia and the Holocaust. But if you 'count heads,' you'll find that a majority of Jews are connected, in some way, to Hasidic tradition."

Many times, people have asked me if Rabbi Steinsaltz is a Lubavitcher Hasid. I too have wondered from time to time if he would consider himself a follower of the Lubavitcher Rebbe, but for some reason that day, I didn't feel comfortable asking him.

What business was it of mine what label he might or might not give himself? And in fact, for years, it really wasn't *my* question.

Other People's Questions

When I was in my early twenties, I spent some time with Elie Wiesel. He is perhaps known best as a recipient of the Nobel Peace Prize and as a witness of the Holocaust, but during the years that I have had opportunities to spend time with him, I have never asked him about the Holocaust. My questions for Elie Wiesel have always been of a different nature, a religious nature.

But during one of our conversations, I did ask a question about the Holocaust. I asked, "What did you learn from your Holocaust experience?"

Two things, he replied. The first thing he learned is not to delay when fighting evil. "Fight evil immediately," he said. "Don't wait. Don't try to convince yourself that it's going to get better."

And the second thing he learned was this: "Don't let other people tell you what your questions should be. Don't let other people's questions become your questions."

I asked him to explain, and he said, "For example, if somebody says to you, 'Why do you wear that beard?' don't feel that you have an obligation to answer that question. It may not be

What is Hasidism? What is its innovation? Hasidism strives for consciousness of one's inner essence and simplicity—in relation to Torah, man, and divinity—and for this, there are no adequate words or direct definitions. Because it deals with man's inner essence, Hasidism defies easy definition or description.

—Rabbi Adin Steinsaltz, *Opening the Tanya,* p. xi

your question. It's somebody else's question. You don't have to justify yourself to others. Don't let other people's questions become your questions. Don't let others force their questions on you."

So the question of whether Rabbi Steinsaltz was a Lubavitcher was for a long time not my question.

I confess that I did once ask a close colleague of the Rabbi's if he knew whether Rabbi Steinsaltz considered himself a Lubavitcher. And the response was, "If Rabbi Steinsaltz is a follower of any rebbe, I think he is a Hasid of the first Lubavitcher Rebbe, the Baal HaTanya, Rabbi Schneur Zalman of Lyadi."[7]

Although it was not a pressing question for me, so many people ask me about this that I ultimately did speak with him about it. "People have asked me many times if you are a Lubavitcher Hasid. What should I tell them?" I asked.

With a familiar twinkle in his eye, he first said, "It depends, of course, on who asks."

I understood what he meant. I knew that Rabbi Steinsaltz has tried, as far as he possibly can, to stay independent of any specific groups throughout his life. He is for the unity of the Jewish people and he is working tirelessly to achieve that goal. So for example, I wouldn't say to a person who *is* a Lubavitcher that Rabbi Steinsaltz isn't a Lubavitcher. After all, his wife was born into a Lubavitcher family, his sons both prepared to become rabbis in Lubavitch schools, he prays at an old and well-known Lubavitch shul in the Old City of Jerusalem, and he visits the Rebbe's grave almost every time he visits New York (which is about three to five times a year).

On the other hand, if a secular Jew asks me, I am more inclined to say that Rabbi Steinsaltz dislikes labels, is really for Jewish unity, and considers every Jew to be just as Jewish as any other Jew.

I know from my reading about Rabbi Steinsaltz, as well as from my countless discussions with people far and wide who know him and have known him for years, that the Rabbi has made an effort not to affiliate with any one particular movement or group. He considers himself a Jew and a teacher within the Jewish family, but he transcends all movements.

One can ask rabbis of every denomination—Reform, Conservative, Reconstructionist, Renewal, Orthodox—and one will find so many rabbis in all of those movements who will agree that Rabbi Steinsaltz is one of the most extraordinary Jewish teachers and that his teachings transcend individual movements.

But when I pressed him on the subject, suggesting to Rabbi Steinsaltz that I might not always know what to say to whom, he said to me, "The Rebbe always considered me to be one of his." He then remarked, "What do people say? If it looks like a duck and walks like a duck . . ."

"Being a Rabbi Is My Hobby"

When we arrived at the synagogue, there was no place to park. The synagogue parking lot, as well as every street in the vicinity, seemed to be overflowing with automobiles. The synagogue was filled to capacity. The one available spot was right next to the synagogue, reserved for the synagogue rabbi. I took a chance and parked there. I later learned that the synagogue was between rabbis, so I hadn't actually usurped anyone's spot.

Rabbi Steinsaltz used the rabbi-less synagogue to make some observations about synagogue life in America. He began the lecture by saying, "My training is in science; being a rabbi is my hobby.

"I do not want to deliver a sermon that was written somewhere in heaven. Or in the words of the Kotsker Rebbe, 'Other rabbis want to speak so that their words can reach the sky; I want to speak so that my words will reach the stomach.' I do not want to offer sparkling words about Torah and *halakhah* [Jewish law] or mysticism or about what can and has been done but rather to instill in all of you the feeling that time is so short and the work is so great, how can anyone be idle, how can anyone say, 'I am not trying to do something'?"

Rabbi Steinsaltz told the audience he's never taken an official job as a rabbi and joked that being a rabbi is an unappealing job. He also said that if he could do one thing for the American synagogue, he would ban sermons.

He then said, "In too many places, the rabbi doesn't teach and the congregation doesn't learn. It's a kind of colossal trick. The community knows it has to have a rabbi. But it doesn't feel it needs a rabbi in the sense that a man needs a doctor when he is ill or a drink when he is thirsty."

He went on, "When I come to America, I see these big American synagogues and sometimes I wonder whether Americans build these big synagogues thinking that if you go to a synagogue big enough, you can keep God *in* it. Unfortunately, God won't stay in the synagogue. He is also in the bedroom and also in the kitchen and also in the marketplace."

Rabbi Steinsaltz then reminded the audience that "a Jew can be born, can be circumcised, can be named, can be a bar mitzvah, can be married, can be buried without ever meeting or needing a rabbi."

The Rabbi went on to encourage the congregation to take advantage of the fact that there wasn't an official rabbi and increase the learning and praying that goes on there.

"Gentle by Definition"

At six o'clock the following evening, I brought Rabbi Steinsaltz to a modern Orthodox synagogue in New Jersey. We crossed the George Washington Bridge in my car, with little conversation, as I needed to focus on the unfamiliar driving directions and making sure that the Rabbi would get to his destination on time.

The place was packed. There were people out the door. I was sitting way in the back. But I was able to see and hear everything well.

Rabbi Steinsaltz came in and walked to the front of the sanctuary with the rabbi of the synagogue. Everyone stood up in complete silence. A journalist reporting on another lecture Rabbi Steinsaltz once delivered wrote, "His own life's work has sparked not only excitement but reverence, evidenced by the hush that fell over the packed hall as he entered, when the mixed crowd of Orthodox and non-Orthodox people rose to their feet."[8]

The rabbi of the synagogue then introduced Rabbi Steinsaltz.

Rabbi Steinsaltz began his talk by saying, "Ladies and gentlemen, I am extremely uncomfortable at the moment."

You could hear a pin drop. The place was jammed to capacity, people had come from far and near to hear Rabbi Steinsaltz, and the rabbi began with a reprimand. "I am *very* uncomfortable with the way you have situated me here this evening. I am uncomfortable with my position."

Now, I have seen Rabbi Steinsaltz many times over the years, and sometimes he's harsh and sometimes he's gentle. When he is harsh, he can be very harsh. He is not vulgar, never vulgar. But giving individuals, organizations, or audiences a kick in the pants is something that he is very capable of doing.

He has joked that his first name, Adin, means "gentle" and that since his first name is Adin, he's "gentle by definition."

The audience in this particular Jewish community, as I said, was completely silent, wondering what it was that prompted Rabbi Steinsaltz to feel so uncomfortable that he made a public statement about it. Where did we go wrong? they wondered.

The Rabbi then clarified. "I am very uncomfortable speaking in the synagogue with my back to the Aron HaKodesh," the Holy Ark, which contains the Torah scrolls.

"Help Me Become a Torah"

The next moment, he turned and almost whispered to the rapt audience. In a soft, loving, voice, he said to them, "But there is *one* way that I can continue. There is *one* way I can have my back to the Aron HaKodesh and speak to you here this evening. And that is if I become a Sefer Torah, a Torah itself. If I can become a Sefer Torah, then I can proceed. So I am asking you all here this evening for your help, to make me a Sefer Torah tonight. So then we can speak with one another."

As Rabbi Steinsaltz said this, I recalled a line from the Talmud: "Oh the fools who stand up for a Torah but not for a living Torah." A great teacher can embody the wisdom of the Torah, but he also needs the help of eager students. Together, the transmission can occur, with the congregation elevating the teacher and the teacher seeking to rise as high as possible in order to earn the right to teach.

He then, of course, delivered, as he always does in my view, an extraordinary lecture.

Advice on Raising Children

As we left the lecture, I had a pressing question based on my relatively new status as a father. I asked the Rabbi if he had any advice on raising children.

Not seeming the least bit tired after his busy days of lectures, appointments, and more, Rabbi Steinsaltz gave me two pieces of advice, which in some way are two sides of the same coin and were words of advice and wisdom that I have made sure to follow over the years with my children.

His first piece of advice was this: "Don't only teach your children things that they can understand. Just because they can't understand something is no reason to avoid teaching it."

The example Rabbi Steinsaltz gave me was that of the recital of the *Modeh Ani* each morning. The sages of Jewish tradition urge us, in our spiritual work and our spiritual practice, to wake up each morning with feelings and thoughts of gratitude on our mind for the new day that God has given us. Our first thoughts of waking consciousness each morning should not be "What's for breakfast?" or "I better get to my appointment" but *Modeh Ani,* "I am grateful," an expression of gratitude to God for my soul's presence in the world.

"Your grandmother can teach you, when you are a tiny child, to recite the one-line prayer *Modeh Ani,* the daily prayer of gratitude, recited as the first words on your lips each morning when you wake. And you can have no idea what it is about, what it really means at that young age. But when you grow up a little and learn what it means, you already have it in you."

The second piece of advice was this: "Teach your children the most abstract theological notions. Don't dumb it down."

His words called to mind a Bob Dylan line: "Don't wanna learn from nobody what I gotta unlearn."[9]

Rabbi Steinsaltz said to me, "Don't teach your children things that ultimately they're going to have to overcome. If you teach your children that God is an old man with a long beard who lives in the sky, then when that child gets older, it will be even more difficult to come close to God because before any progress can be made, first an old image has to be discarded. Always aim for the highest expression of the truth with your children."

Rabbi Steinsaltz went on to tell me that if you were to say to a group of adults that God is everywhere, they would almost surely have all kinds of difficulties and all kinds of theological problems with that statement. But if you say to a child that God is everywhere, usually that child finds no obstacles at all to a clear grasp of what that might mean.

I brought those two pieces of advice home that day. And it became a guiding force in my life as a parent. My children and I have been speaking about God, about faith, about the most abstract theological ideas in life for many years now.

It has been an extraordinary trip.

CHAPTER TWO

Photo © Flash Rosenberg.

"Let My People Know" (1989)

When a man purifies himself of all the illusions and distortions of his self-centered desires, when he opens up to the divine plenty, he can be like an instrument in the hands of the Supreme Will and so the way he does anything will be Torah.

—Rabbi Adin Steinsaltz,
The Thirteen Petalled Rose, p. 90

It is 5:00 A.M., winter of 1989.

I am standing at JFK Airport in New York, at the International Arrivals Building, waiting for Rabbi Steinsaltz. He's coming this time because Random House is beginning to publish the English translations of the first two volumes of his commentaries on the Talmud.

Only a few people are scattered around, waiting for the same flight. Although Rabbi Steinsaltz's flight gets in at five o'clock, passengers usually do not come out of the International Arrivals area for up to an hour after the jet lands due to delays at customs. But I am here early, as usual. More people will be here soon.

What a privilege I have received, to pick up Rabbi Steinsaltz and take him to his appointments.

I have a copy of the Rabbi's itinerary for this trip and can see that it will keep him very busy. He has interviews with print journalists, TV stations, and radio stations, plus some lectures and a class or two.

The first two volumes of the English translation of his commentary on the Talmud have just been published. It feels like a historic occasion! People who know far more about these things than I do tell me that Rabbi Steinsaltz is the greatest Talmudic scholar of our generation. Many even say that he is the greatest Talmudic scholar of the past thousand years. Experts are saying that his commentary on the Talmud will live forever and will become part of the standard canon of Jewish studies.

He has done something that no one has accomplished for a millennium: to write a comprehensive commentary on all sixty-three volumes of the Talmud. He is almost finished; he began it in 1965. His commentary is widely acknowledged as a work of genius.

But it was written in Hebrew, yet at last we have it in English. At least two volumes, that is.

For the first time, English speakers like me can study the Talmud. The Talmud is the most important literary work in all of Jewish culture, but it has been closed to countless Jews for generations. Rabbi Steinsaltz's commentary is opening up the Talmud in Hebrew. And now, with this English translation, he is opening it up for us.

There he is. . . .

❧ A Visit to the Lubavitcher Rebbe ❧

Rabbi Steinsaltz had not yet seen copies of his groundbreaking publication. Random House sent me copies so that I could give them to Rabbi Steinsaltz when he arrived from Jerusalem.

As always, Rabbi Steinsaltz wandered out into the hall of the International Arrivals Building, and within moments our eyes met. He always gives me a warm and welcoming smile and the handshake of a friend. And as usual, he was wearing a black suit, with a blue shirt and no tie.

By this time, I knew exactly how best to help him, by taking one piece of his luggage and escorting him to my car in the parking lot. I showed him the two volumes of the Talmud, and we agreed that it would be best to look at them in the car. After loading the trunk and getting him settled in the front seat, I handed the books to their author.

He looked at them, flipped through them quickly for a few seconds, and handed them back to me. I saw little emotion or reaction of any kind until Rabbi Steinsaltz said, "I hope they do some good."

I have heard Rabbi Steinsaltz say several times that he has a motto: "Let my people know." His efforts with his commentary on the Talmud and his translation of that commentary are to help fulfill that motto. He has said, "I don't want people to read *about* the Talmud. I want our people to be able to encounter the Talmud itself."

His first appointment was not until noon. On other occasions when Rabbi Steinsaltz and I had found ourselves with extra time, we had done a variety of things. Sometimes we would go to a Jewish bookstore together. Each time, a crowd would gather and word would quickly spread throughout the store and into adjacent stores that Rabbi Steinsaltz was there. Sometime I'd feel like the chauffeur to a rock star.

On a few occasions, we went to a synagogue where we prayed *Shacharit,* the morning service, together. On this occasion, when I asked what he might like to do, he replied, "Let's go to 770."

770 Eastern Parkway is the street address for the world headquarters of the Lubavitch movement, and it has come, over the years, to be referred to as simply 770. So when Rabbi Steinsaltz said, "Let's go to 770," I knew we were on our way to Crown Heights in Brooklyn.

It was a Sunday morning, one of those days during the life of Rabbi Menachem Mendel Schneerson, the seventh Lubavitcher Rebbe, who died in 1994, when hundreds or even thousands of people lined up, usually out the door, down the street, and around the corner, to greet the Rebbe as that great man offered a blessing and handed each person a dollar bill.

The custom of the Lubavitcher Rebbe handing dollar bills to people as he greeted them was based on the tradition of asking someone to be a *shaliach mitzvah,* a messenger in the performance of a mitzvah (religious commandment). Basically, the Lubavitcher Rebbe was saying to each of the visitors, "Here is a dollar. Be my messenger and help me perform the mitzvah of giving *tzedakah* [charity]." His custom to do this with thousands of people became legendary.

NOTES FROM THE ROAD:
The Lubavitcher Rebbe

"The most remarkable thing about the Rebbe—and this is something you could see in everything he did, you could hear this in snippets of his discussions with people, in virtually every sentence he spoke or wrote—was his enormous drive. To always supersede oneself, to always do more."

—Rabbi Adin Steinsaltz

We parked a few blocks from Eastern Parkway and walked to the headquarters of Lubavitch, the most influential Hasidic group in the world.

When Rabbi Steinsaltz and I arrived at 770 Eastern Parkway that morning, the line extended out from the main building and was wrapped around the block. The Rebbe was standing in the lobby of the building as the line passed by. It was impossible to get near the Rebbe unless you waited patiently for your turn, but as Rabbi Steinsaltz and I walked up to the building, someone in a position of authority apparently recognized Rabbi Steinsaltz and ushered us directly to the front of the line.

The Lubavitcher Rebbe and Rabbi Steinsaltz exchanged a few words. Rabbi Steinsaltz handed the two volumes on the Talmud to the Rebbe, who congratulated him on the publication and whispered some private words into Rabbi Steinsaltz's ear. There wasn't time for more; after all perhaps more than a thousand people were waiting on line for their moment with the Lubavitcher Rebbe.

It seemed obvious that the Lubavitcher Rebbe and Rabbi Steinsaltz were on the same mission: they were both reaching out to Jews and helping them become more connected to the Jewish people and Jewish life. They greeted each other warmly, and for a moment I had an odd sensation. The way that Rabbi Steinsaltz related to the Rebbe reminded me of the way that I related to Rabbi Steinsaltz. There was reverence, affection, and profound respect.

A moment before we left, Rabbi Steinsaltz encouraged me to come closer to where the two of them were standing. He encouraged me to stand in a spot where the Lubavitcher Rebbe looked at me, offered me a blessing, and whispered something into my ear as well: "Be his driver, but be your own driver. Add more mitzvahs."

Years ago, I wrote a letter to the Rebbe. I tried to describe what I was doing, tried to explain that one project I'm involved with is enough work to occupy me all day, every day.

There was also a second project, which was also enough work to fill my entire day.

And then there was a third undertaking, which was a full day's work.

I told the Rebbe that I find it hard to carry on with them all and that every day is more difficult than the one before because there is just so much. So what should my priorities be? What should I cut out? This is the letter I wrote.

So he responded—this is practically the last letter I received from the Rebbe—the Rebbe's answer was, "Continue all these things that you are doing and add more to all of them."

He demanded these things. How can I explain? You know the famous story about the farmer who comes to the rabbi complaining about his small house so full of children. It's unbearable. So the rabbi tells him to take a goat into his house, a noisy, smelly, dirty goat. Very soon the farmer comes back to the rabbi. "Every problem I had is worse!" he cries. The rabbi tells him to take the goat out. So he takes the goat out of his house and soon he's back to tell the rabbi what a big wonderful house he now has.

A very old story, but what the Rebbe did was similar and yet quite different. When people complained about how hard their work was, he would give them more to do. When they complained how terrible that was, he would give them even more.

He told them to add the goat, and then he'd give them the camel too to put in their house! That was the way he worked all the time. Whenever people complained about their inability to cope or the hard times they endured, he would suggest, "Take on something more."

Obviously, this is against the laws of nature. You have a certain amount of space; you are confined by the limits of the human condition. What did the Rebbe do? How could he overburden people like this?

I will give an answer from the realm of physics. Once, when I was a nice, honest young man, I was interested in that field. There is something in physics—you have a

(continued)

certain amount of pressure on something, and there is a point at which it can take no more. When you put ten times, one hundred times that pressure on it, something happens. The molecules collapse, and the very nature of the object changes.

In astronomy, you have what is called "white dwarves." These are small stars, the size of the earth, sometimes even smaller. The mass they contain is many times that of the sun. Each cubic centimeter weighs many tons. Why? Because the matter collapsed and became something else; the laws themselves changed.

In a way, this was what the Rebbe wanted to do. He wanted to change the very nature of human matter, human behavior, the very way the human being operates. With all whom he encountered, he tried to change their nature into something completely different. They weren't people anymore; they were something else.

The first person that the Rebbe tried this experiment on was himself.

—Rabbi Adin Steinsaltz, speech marking the tenth anniversary of the death of the Lubavitcher Rebbe, delivered at the John F. Kennedy Library, Boston, June 17, 2004

The Rebbe did not leave a legacy. The Rebbe left marching orders. This is an entirely different concept. The Rebbe did not just leave a collection of books, videos, and speeches. He left a task to be completed, and the books and other resources provide the understanding that will enable people to carry it out.

—Rabbi Adin Steinsaltz, speech delivered at the Library of Congress, Washington, D.C., March 11, 2002

🌾 A Visit to the 🌾 Senate Dining Room

During this same period, a luncheon was held in one of the dining rooms of the United States Senate in honor of Rabbi Steinsaltz and the publication of his first two English-language volumes of Talmud commentary. My understanding is that Senator Joseph Lieberman of Connecticut and Senator Patrick Moynihan of New York sponsored the lunch.

We flew to Washington, D.C. I was grateful to be asked to accompany Rabbi Steinsaltz and to help facilitate two of the events that were planned. At the Senate luncheon, Rabbi Steinsaltz was asked to teach from a passage of his choice taken from the new English translation of the Talmud. It was my responsibility to make sure there were enough copies and then to make sure that the copies were distributed to everyone in attendance.

I was like a grade school monitor, and I was pleased to be cast in that role.

We arrived at one of the Senate buildings and went through security. The halls were long and narrow. We entered a dining room where dignitaries and invited guests were assembling. I spotted Senators Lieberman and Moynihan immediately. My understanding is that several members of one of the Christian prayer groups in the Senate also attended, but I didn't recognize any of them.

Senators Moynihan and Lieberman

The order of business for that lunch at the Senate dining room was first a little mingling; then Rabbi Steinsaltz was introduced, along with appropriate words on the historic nature of the day; and finally, Rabbi Steinsaltz expounded for ten minutes on a page from the English-language Talmud commentary that had been copied and distributed. Then we had lunch.

First, Senator Moynihan got up to speak. He was such an impressive man, with a unique look and a wonderful delivery. He spoke with great admiration for Rabbi Steinsaltz and also expressed his gratitude for their friendship.

Then Senator Lieberman spoke, talking about his relationship with Rabbi Steinsaltz and how honored the senator was to have the Rabbi visit his home and synagogue in Connecticut. Though both senators towered over Rabbi Steinsaltz in height, it was interesting to see how humble these two senators appeared before their friend and teacher, Rabbi Steinsaltz.

My big responsibility ended up being almost irrelevant, for even though I did have enough copies of the page of Talmud that had been selected and I did manage to get everyone a copy, Rabbi Steinsaltz did not refer to a single word on the page. Instead, the Rabbi spoke about the Talmud itself, its history, its significance for the Jewish people, and its virtual disappearance from the lives of the average Jew, which is something the English translation was intended to change. And the Rabbi spoke specifically about his

NOTES FROM THE ROAD:
Surgeon General's Warning

The Talmud should have the surgeon general's warning on it: "Caution. This book might have an impact. It may be dangerous."

—Rabbi Adin Steinsaltz

goal. His goal in translating these volumes of Talmud into English, he said, was simply "to change the meaning of the word *Talmud*. This, I would say, is an important goal. Just to make the word *Talmud* no longer a 'dirty word.'"

At the Senate luncheon, I found myself seated at a table next to a Conservative rabbi, who served as the leader of one of those megacongregations with something like eighteen hundred member families. After Rabbi Steinsaltz's ten-minute Talmud lesson, we started to chat.

One of the questions I asked him was whether he had a Talmud class going in his large congregation. He replied in the negative.

"Why not?" I asked.

"It would take me about twenty hours to prepare what Rabbi Steinsaltz just did there in ten minutes."

Later that night, sitting next to Rabbi Steinsaltz on the plane back to New York, I mentioned that snippet of my conversation with the Conservative rabbi.

From the strictly historical point of view, the Talmud was never completed, never officially declared finished, without need for additional material. The final edition of the Talmud may be compared to the stages of maturity of a living organism; like a tree, it has reached a certain form that is not likely to change substantially, although it continues to live, grow, and proliferate. Although the organism has taken on this final form, it still produces new shoots that draw sustenance from the roots and continue to grow. The principle that the Talmud is unfinished holds out a constant challenge to continue the work of creation. It is incumbent on every scholar to add to the Talmud and to contribute to the work, although it can never be finally completed.

—Rabbi Adin Steinsaltz, *The Essential Talmud,*
   pp. 272–273

Rabbi Steinsaltz looked at me and said, "You see, this is one of the problems. Somebody convinced that guy that he was too stupid to do it. So he doesn't do it, and his congregation doesn't do it."

I told Rabbi Steinsaltz that one of the advantages that I'd had in my life and in my relationship with the Talmud is that nobody ever told me that I was too stupid to do it. Unfortunately, I have learned that some professors in the rabbinical seminaries had been guilty of intimidating their students and convincing them that they were incapable of studying Talmud.

NOTES FROM THE ROAD:
The Difference Between Talmud and Sex

The study of the Talmud is not passive. In Talmud study, if you are passive, you can't get any enjoyment from it. It's much worse than being passive at sex.

—Rabbi Steinsaltz

📚 A Conversation with Ted Koppel 📚

Before we went back to New York, however, there was one more stop in Washington. That evening, a public dialogue was being sponsored by the Washington, D.C., Jewish Community Center between Rabbi Steinsaltz and Ted Koppel, the host of ABC's renowned news show *Nightline*. It was being held at the Carnegie Institute.

The large auditorium was buzzing. Every advance ticket was sold, and there was excitement in the air.

I took a few notes that night.

Ted Koppel began by saying to the audience, "Let me just tell you, by way of a very brief introduction, about my relationship with Rabbi Steinsaltz. It is only a few hours old. But the Rabbi was kind enough to come to my office this afternoon so that he and I could chat. I want to say that Rabbi Steinsaltz is one of the very few wise men that I've ever met."

Koppel then said, "Rabbi, you have devoted much of your life—and apparently you're prepared to devote much of the rest of your life—to the translation and interpretation of the Talmud.

"I'm going to ask you what may sound like a discourteous question, though I don't mean it to be—"

Rabbi Steinsaltz interrupted and said, "You can ask. I can defend myself."

"I certainly have faith in *that*," Koppel said confidently.

Rabbi Steinsaltz was already pleased by the exchange. He said, "OK, we are beginning now in the right way."

Koppel returned to his question. "Do you have any expectations that your life's work is going to do any good in the practical world? You are almost like a medieval scholar, something out of the fifteenth or fourteenth century. There you are, doing your translation. What good is it going to do?"

"What good does it do?" Rabbi Steinsaltz repeated. "To define it, I would say that I am talking to my people, to the Jews. I am talking to the Jewish people, who are in the strange situation of a people that has somehow lost a part of its soul. Most of our people, who belong in one way or another, don't really understand what it means to be Jewish.

"For many Jews, being Jewish is something like a hereditary malady. They just have it. Some are slightly embarrassed about it, and some are actually ashamed. For others, it is a perplexing experience. There are very few for whom being Jewish is a source of pride, very few.

"There are so many people who are hurt not only religiously and theologically, but even deeply psychologically, because they do not feel that they belong anywhere. People have a certain set of notions, of ideas, that belong to them. Without those ideas, they are like a machine in which some of the parts have been taken out.

"You can take certain parts out of a car and it will still drive. Perhaps the brakes are not there, but it still goes on. It happens also in more complex machines, like in computers. Sometimes there is a mistake, but the machine goes on, not in the right way, but it still goes on.

"Just imagine, somebody wakes up and he has just found that he lost his heart on the way to his bedroom or he doesn't even know he lost it, yet miraculously, he is walking around without it. The basic problem of the majority of our people is that some parts are missing. It is not that the people know what is missing, but there is a deep feeling of unrest, which is traumatic.

"I am devoting a fair amount of time and attempting to replace, to put back, things that I suppose our people need. But possibly I am *not* doing important work—"

Koppel interrupted and said, "Well, you know you are. I mean, you're being a little bit cute when you say 'I don't know how important it is'—you *know* how important it is—"

Rabbi Steinsaltz bounced back. "I'm not cute. I'm not trying to be, so to say, coy. You can't tell, with a work that doesn't have any kind of immediate results, where some of the results may happen after years, ten years, twenty years."

Rabbi Steinsaltz continued. "By being a Jew and a part of a very ancient history, it is as though we are in a clock that ticks once in ten years. I have devoted something like three seconds, three ticks, three beats of that clock. It's a very large part of my life, but it's a very small time within the history of the Jewish people. Will it continue to be valuable? I just don't know, but it doesn't mean that I don't have to go on."

The evening concluded with a few unmemorable questions from the floor. And then we went to the airport. A few other people who knew Rabbi Steinsaltz and who help him with his work were on the same flight. I took my seat and got back home quite late that night.

As I said my prayers before bed and reviewed my day as I always do, looking for moments to be especially grateful for, I felt thrilled to be the driver or the guy who passed out handouts for Rabbi Steinsaltz. He is recognized by world leaders, politicians, and well-known personalities in so many nations and fields. But even more important, he is creating the first tool that a Jew speaking only English can use to enter into the eternal conversation that the Jewish people have been having with God for the last few thousand years.

𝕰 First Encounter with the Talmud 𝕰

But why should *I* care about the Talmud? Why should I be interested in a written collection of oral laws from nearly two thousand years ago? And why would I be interested in a commentary on those laws?

My own introduction to the Talmud occurred almost thirty years ago, well before I had met Rabbi Steinsaltz. I had just begun to lecture on Jewish genealogy. My book, *From Generation to Generation,* had not yet appeared, but thanks to some magazine and newspaper articles I had written on discoveries I was making in the field of Jewish genealogical research, I was invited to give lectures and classes in various places, including synagogues, Jewish community centers, and other Jewish gatherings. At one particular gathering, I was one of a number of teachers giving different classes at different times throughout a weekend, so that not only did I teach a class but I was also able to take other people's classes.

And it happened that one of the students in my class on Jewish genealogy was a teacher who would be leading a work-

The Jewish notion of "a kingdom of priests and a holy nation" rests to no small degree on the fact that Jewish knowledge is not restricted to a separate learned caste but incumbent upon all. One need not become a *talmid hakham* (i.e., achieve the pinnacle of scholarship), but one must not remain an *am-ha-aretz* (ignoramus) either.

—Rabbi Adin Steinsaltz, *The Essential Talmud,* p. 88

shop on the Talmud later that day. His name was Danny Siegel, a moving poet and a gifted teacher. Danny attended my Jewish genealogy session, and I attended his session on the Talmud. It was my first real exposure to Talmud texts, and it changed my life forever.

After that day of teaching and learning, Danny and I stayed in touch with each other. When Danny, who had been living in the Boston area, moved to New York, he contacted me, told me that he was looking for private students, and asked if I knew anybody who might be interested in studying with him. I told him that I knew of nobody but myself. The result was a weekly get-together for the better part of a year, for the purpose of studying the Talmud together.

Danny introduced me to some of the leading personalities who lived during the first two centuries of the Common Era and whose words of wisdom can be found in the Talmud, including Hillel and Shammai, Rabbi Akiva, Rabbi Meir and his wife Beruria, Rabbi Yosi, Rabbi Eliezer, and Rabbi Yochanan ben Zakkai. Each of these extraordinary people, and many others, were dazzling and uplifting and life-altering for me.

> The Talmud is not merely important on an intellectual and literary plane; it also has far-reaching socio-historical implications. It is reasonably certain that no Jewish community could survive for long without the ability to study Talmud.
>
> —Rabbi Adin Steinsaltz, *The Essential Talmud,* p. 267

Who Is Rich?

Since the Steinsaltz Talmud was not and would not be available in English until many years after Danny and I studied together, we jumped around from volume to volume of the traditional Aramaic and Hebrew text, with Danny translating short passages and introducing me to this personality and that story and this idea and that conflict and this drama and that poetic image from the great Jewish sages.

For example, Danny introduced me to a Talmudic personality whose name is Ben Zoma. Ben Zoma offers four definitions that appear in the Mishnah, which is a collection of halakhic traditions incorporated into the Talmud: Who is wise? Who is strong? Who is honored? And who is rich?

Who is wise? The person who learns from everyone.

Who is strong? The person who has control over his passions.

Who is honored? The person who honors others.

And who is rich? The person who is satisfied with what he has.

Simple and profound. Imagine a world or even a life where riches are measured not by wealth but rather by satisfaction and gratitude.

Danny showed me that the sixty-three volumes of the Talmud were an immense pool of Jewish creativity. He showed me that the Talmud was perhaps unlike any sacred document in the world. For example, it is probably the only sacred document that objects to itself. Within the Talmud, you will read passages that object to the very point of view it had just expressed a moment before.

The Talmud is timeless. A question asked in the 1800s can be answered three centuries before, in the 1500s, in the commentaries included on the pages of the Talmud.

Not only do generations talk to each other in the pages of the Talmud, but people living on various continents speak to each other in pages of the Talmud.

I will forever be indebted to Danny Siegel for introducing me to that world.

When I purchased my own set of the Soncino Talmud, a literal English translation with no commentary, which was for years the only tool that those of us who could only study in English had, I threw a party in celebration of my purchase, which Danny of course attended.

The set of books cost $300, which was a lot of money for me. With Danny's encouragement, I bought refreshments, asked some close friends to join us, and we inaugurated the set of Talmud by having me teach a passage or two to the group. I couldn't believe it. I was teaching Talmud!

But what does that mean? Surely not that I was a master of the Talmud but rather that I was able to do what is asked of me by Jewish tradition: to get involved with our sacred texts and to share their wisdom with others.

I taught two brief passages from the Talmud that night, which means that I opened one of the volumes to a favorite passage, read the passage aloud, and then explained it.

The first was the story of a rabbi whose name was Eliezer ben Dordia who visited as many prostitutes as he could find. The text can be found on page 17, on the "a" side of a volume of the Talmud called *Avodah Zara,* Strange Gods (every edition of the Talmud is paginated the same way: each leaf has a number, and each side is either "a" or "b").

Rabbi Eliezer ben Dordia once heard of a certain prostitute whom he decided to hire. She was very expensive, but he gave her the fee. When he was with her, she did something and said something. What did she do, and what did she say?

The text says, "She blew forth breath and said, 'As that blown breath will not return to its place, you, Eliezer, will never be able to repent.'" So one question, of course, is, what does the text mean when it says, "She blew forth breath"?

I looked up at my teacher, Danny Siegel, and said before my friends, "Danny, can you tell us what it means?

And Danny said, "Kurzweil, I learned that some say it means she flatulated."

So I added, "And so what she meant when she said, 'As that blown breath will not return to its place, you, Eliezer, will never be able to repent' is that just as gas ejected from the body will never go back in from whence it came—a wild metaphor to say the least, but quite effective and memorable—Eliezer, the so-called rabbi, is never going to mend his foolish ways."

In other words, the prostitute was telling Eliezer that he had sunk so low that he would never be able to get out of the hole he had dug for himself. But the Talmud text goes on to say that the prostitute was wrong. At first, after realizing his bad ways, Eliezer prayed to the hills and mountains, the sun and moon, and the stars and constellations. Then he saw that what he really had to do is to change by himself and within himself, that *teshuvah* is inner work, and when wholehearted change was sincere, it would be accepted by Heaven. When he died, in Heaven he was even addressed as "Rabbi."

In Jewish tradition, an important idea is that change is always possible for the soul. No matter how low a person sinks, he or she is able, through the Divine free will we have been given, to choose freely and to get on the right path. A few years later, I would encounter this same idea in *The Thirteen Petalled Rose,* in which Rabbi Steinsaltz points out that according to traditional wisdom, every descent is for the sake of ascension; when we fall, what we get is the opportunity to pick ourselves up and perhaps be even stronger than we would have been had we not fallen.

This was the first Talmud passage I ever taught. The story of a rabbi and a prostitute may seem frivolous, perhaps, but a profound notion is embedded in the story, and students of the Talmud need to break open the text and find the eternal idea within.

The second passage I chose to teach that evening allowed me to introduce my favorite Talmudic personality to my friends. Of the many hundreds of rabbis who appear throughout the sixty-three volumes of the Talmud, my favorite is Rabbi Nachum, the man of Gamzu. The Talmud teaches that Rabbi Nachum of Gamzu was Rabbi Akiva's teacher for twenty-two years. Yet whereas Rabbi Akiva appears in the Talmud many hundreds of times, his longtime teacher Nachum appears only seven times. But if we look carefully at what the texts are about, this becomes more understandable. It is recorded that Nachum taught Rabbi Akiva two things. The first is that every letter of the Torah has meaning.

And the second is the profound lesson represented by the word *Gamzu.* What does it mean that Nachum was a man of

Gamzu? Some say that he comes from the town of Gimzo. But it is generally agreed that his name, Nachum of Gamzu, refers to his favorite saying, his philosophy of life, *"Gam zu l'tova,"* the Aramaic way of saying, "Everything is for the best." Rabbi Nachum taught that we must understand that in some inexplicable way, everything is for the best, nothing happens without God allowing it to happen, and the Almighty knows what he's doing.

I had learned the same notion from Ram Dass, who often said, "Everything is perfect."

But how, in light of all the suffering in the world, can one possibly say this? Years later, I would explore the question in depth with the help of Rabbi Steinsaltz.

Oral Tradition Preserved in Writing

Around two thousand years ago, a proposal was made among the great Jewish sages of the time to write down the Oral Tradition. The Oral Tradition is not supposed to be written down. Ancient Jewish tradition makes it quite clear that it is in fact forbidden to write down the Oral Tradition. This stems from the notion that when Moses encountered the Almighty on Mount Sinai, he received, in a sense, two Torahs from the Holy One, a written Torah and an oral Torah. The written Torah was obviously written down, while the oral Torah, the teachings that were transmitted not in writing but orally from God to Moses, were to remain so.

The leader of the Jewish people at that time was a man named Yehuda. He was called Yehuda the Prince and referred to in the Talmud simply as Rebbe ("Teacher"). The title of Prince (*Nasi*) is used when referring to the head of the Great Sanhedrin, the "supreme court" of the Jewish people at that time.

Yehuda the Prince was the compiler of the written form of the Oral Tradition. The leaders of the Jewish people at that time ultimately decided that the Oral Tradition was in great danger. Persecution and murder of Jews had been rampant, and there loomed the possibility of losing the entire Oral Tradition. A radical step had to be taken, in a way a transgression of the traditional prohibition on writing down the Oral Tradition, and so Yehuda the Prince wrote it down.

That work, which is a relatively small book, written in Hebrew in a kind of shorthand, is the Mishnah. The Mishnah has six sections. A popular song that is sung on Passover, at the end of the Passover Seder, is "Who Knows One?" The sixth verse says, "Who knows six? I know six? Six are the sections of the Mishnah."

The sages understood the great danger of writing down the Oral Tradition. Once the Oral Tradition is written down, readers can mistakenly think that the fixed form "is what it is." And it is, of course, *not* what it is; it is only a written reflection of something far more fluid and far more alive. But our history tells us that for practical reasons, the radical decision was made, and the Oral Tradition was written down and organized by Yehuda the Prince.

Subsequent generations needed to continue a discussion of the meaning of the ideas in the Mishnah, to discuss, debate, and interpret new meaning and obtain new answers to their questions and concerns, and many of those discussions and commentaries were also written down. The combination of the Mishnah and the discussions, known as the Gemara, constitute the Talmud. It is these two sections, Mishnah and Gemara, that comprise the basic text of Talmudic study. Everything else is commentary.

When I picked up Rabbi Steinsaltz at the airport for his whirlwind Talmud publicity tour, he said, "I hope I'm kept busy." But despite all of the various television, newspaper, and magazine people who wanted to interview him, we had one

All of life is of interest to the scholars and constitutes fit subject matter for the Talmud, to be discussed in brief or at length. Habits, customs, occupational hints, medical advice, examinations of human nature, linguistic questions, ethical problems—all these are Torah and as such are touched upon in the Talmud.

—Rabbi Adin Steinsaltz, *The Essential Talmud,* pp. 95–96

afternoon that was free, and I asked Rabbi Steinsaltz what he wanted to do.

He thought it would be a nice idea to take a group of schoolchildren to the Central Park Zoo, so we contacted a school in Manhattan and invited a bunch of children to wander around the Central Park Zoo with us on a beautiful sunny spring afternoon. The children didn't know just how illustrious a zoo tour guide they had that afternoon, but they all appreciated Rabbi Steinsaltz's endless enthusiasm as we observed the behavior of the animals.

After the few hours at the zoo, I had to take Rabbi Steinsaltz to a law firm in the Wall Street area for a Talmud study session with a small group of attorneys who offered a generous donation to Rabbi Steinsaltz's projects in exchange for the honor of the Rabbi's leading them in a half-hour of study before they went home for the day.

We arrived at the skyscraper and zoomed up the high-speed elevator to some floor high above Manhattan. The view from the conference room was spectacular. The carpets were plush, and the wooden conference table was long and polished and quite handsome. The artwork was ultramodern, the atmosphere most professional.

Seven attorneys, dressed almost exactly the same, gathered around the table as Rabbi Steinsaltz perused a Talmud text that discusses the sins of the city of Sodom. After reading a few lines of the text, Rabbi Steinsaltz said, "The city of Sodom, as the Talmud explains it, would be a wonderful idea for a play or a novel. It is the forerunner, to a certain extent, of a modern city. It's clearly a futuristic city, a very modern place, too modern for my taste. It is sometimes frightening to read about what I call the laws of Sodom as described in the Talmud.

"Now, the main point is that people coming to Sodom are measured. Any body smaller or taller has to be cut to measure or stretched to measure. The city of Sodom tries to make everybody equal, and if somebody is not equal, he is put to death because they hate asymmetry. Everybody has to be equal, and if somebody is a little bit poorer than the rest, he is just dirtying the community." Rabbi Steinsaltz went on to explain that Sodom was a very modern city, and this detail refers in part to the temptation of conformity. The people of Sodom were intolerant of differences.

Several years ago, in my office at Jason Aronson, where I was publishing books of Jewish interest and running the Jewish Book Club, I offered a Talmud class to the staff. There were twenty-two people on the staff, and six of them had requested that I teach a Talmud class.

The subject that we were discussing was the following case: Somebody owned a piece of land, and he rented that land to somebody else. One day, a third person came walking down the road with his cow, and the cow dropped a pile of dung on the land.

The Talmud asks the question (knowing full well that dung, at the time, was a valuable commodity for fertilizer and for fuel, among other things), "Who's dung is it? Who owns that dung?"

Is the dung the first person's? After all, it is his land on which the dung fell.

Does the dung belong to the man who rented that land from the owner? After all, he is renting that land now.

Or is the dung the property of the man whose cow produced the dung? After all, it was his cow.

At a certain point in the Talmudic discussion, the Talmud introduces the idea and question, "What would happen if a contraption was built that the cow would wear so that when the dung dropped, it wouldn't hit the ground; it would be caught in the contraption?" My students and I studied this case in the Talmud, and I confess that there were moments when we wondered what we were doing getting up an hour early to discuss the ownership rights of dung.

But the class was a revelation to all of us because we realized on close inspection that every fundamental issue that we deal with today in connection with environmental law is discussed in that section of the Talmud, which includes, by the way, the question of whether you are living upwind or downwind from the pile of dung. It's an important factor, for sure. Even though the dung was a commodity that had great value, you didn't want to live downwind from the pile of dung. Most of us don't live downwind from a pile of dung. But all of the issues that we deal with today regarding environmental law can be found embedded in the text of the Babylonian Talmud.

Everything Is in It

It is extraordinary to watch Rabbi Steinsaltz with both well-versed Talmud students and beginners and everyone in between as he breaks open the centuries-old text and finds the eternal. An ancient dispute about an ox becomes a modern incident about a car. A discussion about the procedure twenty centuries ago for the wedding of a first-time bride becomes an exploration of the permissibility of telling a white lie.

A close look at the laws concerning our responsibility when we find a lost object becomes a detailed discussion about how to take care of old books.

The laws of verbal abuse turn into a theological discussion about the permissibility to argue and to disagree with God himself.

A passage about a prostitute who flatulates when in bed with a rabbi turns into a profound discussion about inner spiritual work and the nature of change itself.

One of the sections of the Talmud that Rabbi Steinsaltz published in English is called *Ketubot*. Interestingly, *ketubot* is the plural of *ketubah*, the marriage document that Jewish couples sign when getting married. But *Ketubot* is not really about marriage, nor is it about signing marriage contracts (although there is much discussion about both weddings and marriage in *Ketubot*), but rather about contracts and agreements between and among people.

The reason why it is called *Ketubot* is because it does deal, quite extensively, with marriage documents. This is because marriage documents are a common kind of contract. An individual or a family in Talmudic times who never in their entire lives had any need or exposure to signing contracts would probably have some personal experience with the marriage contract. So the Talmud uses the marriage contract as an example of contracts in general.

My responsibility for the day ended when the gathering with the attorneys ended. Rabbi Steinsaltz had a dinner appointment that I was not a part of, but the next morning, I was up bright and early to take the Rabbi to the next day's events and meetings.

✿❧ Talmud with the Hadassah Ladies ✿❧

To publicize the new English-language edition of the Talmud and to spread the word on how to use it, I helped organize a special event with Hadassah, the Women's Zionist Organization of America.

Hadassah, which is the largest Jewish women's organization in the world, invited Rabbi Steinsaltz for a day of Talmud learning. Each Hadassah chapter has a Jewish education chairperson. Hadassah invited all the chairs in the United States and Canada to come to New York to spend a day with Rabbi Steinsaltz, so there were a few hundred women present that day in the Manhattan offices of Hadassah.

It was suggested that I be part of the program.

The day was to be divided into two parts. Rabbi Steinsaltz and I were to be on stage together during the morning, where he and I would study and discuss the Talmud together as the women watched. Then we would have lunch, after which I would step aside, and for the rest of the afternoon, Rabbi Steinsaltz would deal directly with the women on a particular passage of the Talmud that we were studying that day. He would also answer some questions.

Hadassah ladies are known as powerhouses—always bright and almost always tough. The leadership of Hadassah, and the women who rise in the chapters to become chairpeople, are articulate, assertive Jewish women. The auditorium was buzzing loudly as Rabbi Steinsaltz and I arrived on stage.

A hush came over the room. These were the women from each Hadassah chapter who were responsible for Jewish education in hundreds of Jewish communities throughout North America. They would all be apt to know exactly who Rabbi Steinsaltz was and what he had achieved, understand the respect due him, and be grateful for this unique opportunity to spend time in his presence.

In the morning session, I began by asking Rabbi Steinsaltz a few of my own questions. I was sitting on a stage facing the Rabbi, with a little desk between us and a volume of the Talmud on the table in front of us.

"Rabbi Steinsaltz, when I skim through the sixty-three volumes of the Talmud, I see that there are many times when it says that if you transgress, if you do some things that are not permitted, you will not have a share in the World to Come.

"Now, without getting into what is really meant by the 'World to Come,' let me just ask this: The Talmud speaks about the kinds of activities that when done have me lose my share in the World to Come. But I realize that I've already done lots of those things. The Talmud is telling me that I already do not have a share in the World to Come. So if that is the case, why should I even try? If the Talmud is telling me that on so many different occasions, I, Arthur Kurzweil, have done things that disqualify me from the World to Come, then what's the use of it?"

Rabbi Steinsaltz looked at me and then looked out at the audience of women and said, "Well, it seems clear that you are going to have to study a little more of the Talmud. First, perhaps, to understand what *Olam Haba,* the World to Come, means. And then, you will also see and come to learn of all the things you've already done that *guarantee* you a share in the World to Come."

I had, of course, seen references to the fact that I also already qualify for a guarantee of a share in the World to Come. But I was pleased that Rabbi Steinsaltz put the two together and indicated to me and to the audience that when you study Talmud, it is not possible to quote something out of context with any reliability. If I just read one or the other, I will draw an incomplete conclusion. The World to Come is a level of consciousness, a state of delight that the sages say we glimpse on Shabbos. I am able to elevate my soul and taste the World to Come, and I can, with my misdeeds, lower my soul and loose my share.

The second question that I asked Rabbi Steinsaltz before the Hadassah women was similar. "I don't remember exactly where I read this, but I once read a book about the Talmud, where somebody was quoted as saying that when you study Talmud, if you read 'ox,' the animal 'ox,' and you think about an ox, then you're doing something wrong." I said, "Did you ever hear of this quote, and if so, how am I to understand it?"

Rabbi Steinsaltz smiled. He knew precisely to whom the quote was attributed and told me the name of the scholar who reportedly said it.

But then he said to me, "You have the quote a little bit wrong. He didn't say if you read 'ox' and you think of 'ox' that you're wrong. What he said was, 'When you learn Talmud, if you read 'ox,' and you think 'ox,' *you are probably an ox.*"

I then asked Rabbi Steinsaltz a few questions about the Talmud itself, its history, and his hopes for his new English edition. We broke for lunch, and in the afternoon, Rabbi Steinsaltz led a Talmud study class. I wasn't there. As much as I wanted to stay, I needed some time off to take care of the details of my life.

I believe that one of the reasons there is a disproportionate number of Jews involved in religious cults, as well as non-Jewish avenues of spirituality, is that the rabbis in the Talmud did not speak in abstractions. When you go to a New Age bookstore or a bookstore with religion and spirituality sections and look for inspirational reading, you notice very quickly that just about every spiritual tradition in the world has beautiful, lofty books about any number of subjects in human life: love, charity, friendship. Classical Judaism does not, by and large, have such books.

When one opens up a volume of the Talmud, the major spiritual text of the Jewish people for centuries, one sees immediately, at the beginning of one book, for example, the question that arises: If Reuven is holding a *talis* (prayer shawl) and Shimon is holding the same *talis* and each thinks and claims that the *talis* is his, whose *talis* is it?

Certainly, seekers who are looking for meaning, who are looking for God, will much more quickly relate to inspiring poetry about matters of the heart than to a Talmudic debate over whose *talis* it is if two people grab it at the same time.

But as many of us have discovered, the Talmud communicates its ideas in a strange but highly effective way—once you know its method. Rather than communicate ideas abstractly, the Talmud looks at specific cases and analyzes those cases and then examines the theoretical underpinnings of specific cases.

If one gets stuck with the case itself, if one fails to crack open the case and find the eternal idea that's embedded within it, one has not connected with the potential of the deep and profound and beautiful Babylonian Talmud.

🦋 Talmud Study with 🦋 Famous Jewish Writers

The next day, in a Random House conference room, we sat at a large table, with Rabbi Steinsaltz in the middle of one side and a rather colorful cast of New York literary characters all around.

NOTES FROM THE ROAD:
Holy Books

We've been on a whirlwind of a media tour this week. Reporters, radio, TV, magazine interviews.

One of the recurring questions from journalists is whether Rabbi Steinsaltz feels that people who buy these Talmud volumes would really use them.

Rabbi Steinsaltz answers, one way or another, by saying, "Just having a beautiful Jewish book on the table or on the shelf in one's home enhances a Jewish home."

Although that might sound like a sales pitch, I've come to learn that it is true: that a holy book, even before it is opened, has an impact on the room in which it sits.

The group included theater producer Joseph Papp, literary critic Alfred Kazin, publisher Mort Zuckerman, writer Betty Friedan, writer and publisher Leonard Fein, publisher Peter Osnos, writer Lore Segal, writer Hugh Nissenson, and writer Anne Roiphe.

The gathering was the brainchild of Selma Shapiro, a terrific book publicist who was helping the effort to publicize the new Talmud edition. The gathering served a number of purposes. First, it was an opportunity for Rabbi Steinsaltz to share some Talmud with creative Jews in the literary world. This in itself made it worthwhile.

Second, it was a way to pump up enthusiasm at the publishing house. It always helps a book when the staff of the publishing house feels enthusiasm for the project. The presence of all these literary heavyweights in one room surely created a buzz in the Random House hallways.

Third, it was potentially a great opportunity for an exciting Talmud class. Each of us had a photocopy of a passage from the Talmud before us, and Rabbi Steinsaltz began eagerly, seeming impatient and intent on using the time wisely.

Random House put *kippot* (yarmulkes) in a basket on the table, but I don't think anyone used them. It was lovely to watch the theater giant Joseph Papp taking copious notes as Rabbi Steinsaltz spoke. I also noticed that Mort Zuckerman, Alfred Kazin, and Betty Freidan listened very intently to the Rabbi.

And Lore Segal, a gifted writer for adults and children who comes often to gatherings in New York when Rabbi Steinsaltz speaks, did what she often does as she listens with her deep intelligence and sensitive mind: she sketched in her notebook the people who were sitting around the table.

Leonard Fein, founder of *Moment Magazine,* engaged Rabbi Steinsaltz with questions several times, including one time when he asked Rabbi Steinsaltz what a Jew's relationship should be to the laws of the country in which he finds himself.

As long as the local laws do not force you to break Jewish law, the principle of *dina d'malchuta dina* (the law of the land is the law) usually applies. During the hour, an interesting and sometimes impassioned discussion began. The two most active students that day were the gifted novelist, short-story writer, and passionate artist Hugh Nissenson and the outspoken literary critic Alfred Kazin.

In the middle of it all, Anne Roiphe said, "It is my understanding that it is not possible for a woman to be a witness. What can you say about divine justice in light of that?"

Rabbi Steinsaltz, wearing a facial expression that seemed to imply that her question had absolutely nothing to do with the topic and that in any case this was a huge topic that he could not do justice to in a few moments, pointed out that it is God's justice, not his. The Rabbi then said that he could certainly sit and study that topic too, but it would take some time.

Rabbi Steinsaltz spoke almost the entire first half of the class, but nobody else said a word. I suppose that with so many strong literary voices in the room, each person was hesitant to begin speaking first. It was also quite possible, even probable, that these literary personalities by and large knew very little about the Talmud and didn't want to reveal their ignorance. I don't mean to say anything disparaging about anyone in the group. I admire them all. And some of them might be more educated Jewishly than others.

But in general, the class was not very exciting, perhaps also because it had to end too soon. A good Talmud class, especially with bright students, should be able to go on for hours. Of course, as Rabbi Steinsaltz often points out, one never knows what impact something will have. Sometimes one small thing is the cause of something far greater.

At a certain moment, Peter Onsos, the publisher at Random House, announced that time was up. Rabbi Steinsaltz and I left without time for small talk, off to his next appointment.

To Whom Does Life Belong?

I needed to get Rabbi Steinsaltz to a gathering of about one hundred scientists at Columbia University. We grabbed a taxi and drove uptown.

You could hear a pin drop in the hall. Rabbi Steinsaltz's talk was wonderful. It was not part of his Talmud tour but rather an invitation like many he receives all of the time, this time by a group of physicians and biologists and others in the natural sciences.

The topic was "to whom does life belong?"

By the time the lecture was over, my hand was burning from fatigue. I managed to take quite a few notes.

Rabbi Steinsaltz said, "Everywhere in the world, there is an assumption of the equality of men. This is a very common assumption that is found everywhere; everybody accepts it or says that he accepts it. Even people who make certain exceptions, you know—blacks, women, Jews, whoever they may like to include—but still, there is still an assumption of equality.

"Now, as everybody knows, and I'm sure that the audience here should know it, in reality, there is a huge inequality of man. I mean, people are not equal, by any means, physical or spiritual, or in any other way. People are not equal.

"You have something that is called 'normal' and 'average,' but people are not equal. The ability to find two equal people is an impossibility, even when you have identical twins.

"You just don't find equal people.

"The basic notion of equality doesn't come from observations. It really comes from a point of belief. Equality of man is a principle of belief. Whether a person describes himself as an atheist or a believer, the notion that people are equal is a point of belief. It is irrational, meaning it has no scientific proof whatsoever.

"Now, I don't want to doubt or dispute it but simply, as I said, to point out that equality is a point of belief.

"But from where does it stem? Clearly, it stems from the same notion as in the biblical creation of man. And the notion is that people have a soul.

"Now, I know that the medical people here who do surgery have never found the soul there. But still, the belief in the soul, the belief that there is a soul, is really the essence of the notion of the equality of man. Because when I deal with souls, I cannot then make any kind of a separation. As long as I am dealing with the body, there is a basic inequality. When I speak about souls, then and only then can I speak about the equality of man.

"So the great scholar and the simple man, the beautiful woman and the ugly hag, the philosopher and the idiot, the malformed child, the one that has barely any life in him, all possess a soul.

"About the question 'to whom does life belong?' within the Jewish view, life does not belong to the man that has this life. Life is not the possession of anybody, including the person whose life it is.

"I'll put it even more strongly. In a way, the Jewish view is that my body doesn't belong to me in the same way that my money belongs to me. I can do with my money whatever I want. There are some restrictions.

"Just in brackets, we are possibly, as Jews, the only religion that sets limits on charity—an upper limit. A person shouldn't give more charity than a certain percentage. And I would suppose that some people would say that it shows how niggardly and how money-loving we are. I do think that the fact that we had to have such a law shows something entirely different, just the opposite. You see, in the Torah itself, in the book of Exodus, there is the only law in the world that says you shouldn't favor the poor man. Many laws say that you shouldn't favor the rich and the powerful. We are the only ones who found it necessary to say that for true justice we also shouldn't favor the poor man.

"Money belongs to me. Possessions belong to me. My life, even my body, doesn't belong to me, meaning that not only am I not allowed to take somebody else's life, but I'm not allowed to take my own life, because it doesn't belong to me.

NOTES FROM THE ROAD:
Crazy Love

This evening, Rabbi Steinsaltz was introduced to his audience at an Orthodox synagogue in Queens, New York. The first thing he said when he got up to speak was, "Jews are among the most infuriating people in the world."

Rabbi Steinsaltz then said, "In my work, I mostly deal with Jews. I don't know why," he said. "It's a kind of crazy love, like a crazy love for a woman. You say she's ugly, and I think she's beautiful. You say she's got a terrible personality. I find her very interesting. You say she won't even be faithful. I say I don't care. It's a crazy love that I have for the Jewish people."

Rabbi Steinsaltz then said, "It's the same with the Almighty. We're infuriating; we're not faithful. But the Almighty loves us anyway."

"In fact, the word *suicide* [literally] means 'self-murder.' That is exactly the meaning of the word. But you see, the Jewish notion of murder contains everybody, including myself. I am not allowed to murder my neighbor. I am not allowed to murder my neighbor's children. And I am not allowed to murder my own self because it doesn't belong to me. I can tell somebody, 'Take some of my money.' But I'm not allowed to say to him, 'Beat me,' because I am not the master of my own body."

🐾 Changing the Meaning 🐾 of the Word *Talmud*

I believe that Rabbi Steinsaltz has been successful in his goal of transforming the very word *Talmud* in our vocabulary from a pejorative into a word that represents a profound exploration of human activity. More Talmudic study is going on in the American Jewish world than ever before. Rabbi Steinsaltz's work clearly inspired the creation of another English translation of the Talmud known as the Schottenstein Talmud, which is an English translation and commentary on the Talmud published by Artscroll/Mesorah. I have heard positive references to the Talmud on televisions sitcoms, and I saw an entire episode of the award-winning animated series *The Simpsons* about the Talmud!

During the promotional tour for the first two volumes of the Steinsaltz Talmud commentary, I took Rabbi Steinsaltz to many interesting places, many of them already mentioned. I took him to see the Lubavitcher Rebbe, I took him to *People* magazine, I took him to *Good Morning America,* and I brought him to the studios of National Public Radio.

NOTES FROM THE ROAD:
What's the Big Deal?

I've been in the audience of a great many lectures that Rabbi Steinsaltz has given over the past twenty years. And I remember that particularly at the beginning, whenever I went with him to a lecture and found myself in the audience, I would sit there and hope that everybody in the audience would love him as much as I do. Of course, that set me up for disappointment when I saw that it wasn't always the case.

In fact, I had to get used to the experience that sometimes when I take him to a lecture and he does his presentation, I see that some of the people in the audience are absolutely blown away by him and the others walk out thinking, "Huh? What did he say? That's the great Rabbi Steinsaltz? That's all?"

There was a time when he spoke at the Ninety-Second Street Y in New York City, and it was standing room only. It was shortly after the first volumes of the Talmud in English had come out, and he had gotten a lot of publicity. And it was a well-publicized event. The Ninety-Second Street Y is a superb institution for bringing world-class people of all kinds to New York City, and the place was mobbed.

And that particular night was the perfect example of audience reaction: half of the attendees were blown away, and the other half shrugged their shoulders and said, "Is that all there is to it?" I remember what he spoke about that night, a subject to which he devotes a chapter in his book *We Jews:* Who are we as Jews? Are we a nation? Are we a religion? Are we a race? Are we an ethnic group? We don't seem to be a religion because there are lots of Jews who don't believe in anything having to do with any religious ideas, and they're just as Jewish as any other Jews in the world. We don't seem to be a nation, since we're all

(continued)

over the world and have been for centuries. Even though there is now a Jewish state, most Jews in the world do not live there. And we're not a race. All one needs to do is to go to Israel and see all the different kinds of Jews and you'll see that we don't seem to be a race.

And after a very interesting and eloquent and funny and wonderful lecture on why we were not all these other things, why we're not a nation or a religion or a race or an ethnic group, he said, "Who are we? We're a family." Basically, the Jewish people are a family. That was his message that night at the Ninety-Second Street Y.

Now, many of us who went to that lecture walked out thinking, "What an extraordinary idea. We're not a nation, we're not a religion, there is all kinds of evidence to support the notion that we are not any of those things. What we seem to really be is a family." And just knowing that seemed to click. Just knowing that seemed to make sense of lots of things.

The other half of the audience walked out thinking, "All he said is that we are a family. That's the great Rabbi Steinsaltz? I had to go out to the Ninety-Second Street Y with a whole crowd of people and listen to him tell me that we're a family? What's the big deal?"

❧ "Your Name Is Father" ❧

Shortly before the Rabbi's visit, my wife and I had split up. Irreconcilable differences. I was not living with my children. I was very upset about it, and there were many times when I wondered if I could possibly be a good parent under those circumstances. How could I not live with my children? It was painful.

I was at the time editor in chief of Jason Aronson publishers and also ran the Jewish Book Club. At Jason Aronson, I published over 650 books of Jewish interest. For a while, I was publishing and selling more Jewish books in the United States than any other single publisher.

And one of the authors we published at Jason Aronson, indeed, our most illustrious author, was Rabbi Steinsaltz. We did not publish all of his books, but we did publish several.

I had collected and was editing a volume of essays by Rabbi Steinsaltz that would ultimately be called *The Strife of the Spirit*, after one of the essays in the collection. In the essay "The Strife of the Spirit," Rabbi Steinsaltz begins by lamenting those of us who waste our time seeking peace of mind. The spirit is at war, as its natural state, he states, and life's goal is not to achieve peace of mind. "Man's question should not be how to escape the perpetual struggle but what form to give it, at what level to wage it."

As work on publication of the book was being completed, Rabbi Steinsaltz asked if I would write an introduction.

"Why would you ask me to do that?" I replied. "What do *you* need with an introduction from *me*?"

"I think you should write an introduction, and I think you should put your name on the title page: 'Edited and with an Introduction by Arthur Kurzweil.'"

"Why?" I asked again, embarrassed.

Rabbi Steinsaltz smiled. "If the critics like the book, I'll say it's mine. If they don't, I'll say, 'Well, it was Kurzweil who put it together.'"

Of course, his request was really a gift from him to me. I was blown away to have my name on the same page as his.

During the production of that book, I needed to be in touch with Rabbi Steinsaltz on some publishing matter, so I wrote him a letter and for the first time in my life signed it with my Hebrew name.

I don't know my motive for doing so. But my Hebrew name is Avraham Abush. My great-grandfather, my father's father's father, was Avraham Abush, and I am named after him. He was a beloved member of the family.

I grew up hearing wonderful stories about him. For years, my father has claimed that his grandfather, Avraham Abush, still visits him and gives him advice, advice that my father himself often disagrees with.

Rabbi Steinsaltz wrote back to me, "Dear Avraham Abba, I am pleased to see that you have signed your name in Hebrew." He then went on with his letter.

But my name isn't Avraham *Abba;* it's Avraham *Abush. I'm* glad that *he's* glad that I'm writing my name in Hebrew, I thought, but *he got my name wrong!*

I had reason to write him back, and I chose not to point out to him that he had gotten my name wrong. Rather, I once again signed my name in Hebrew: Avraham Abush.

Once again, Rabbi Steinsaltz wrote back to me, "Dear Avraham Abba."

I decided, in my next letter, to point out his error:

"Dear Rabbi Steinsaltz, I am so pleased that you are so pleased that I'm signing my name in Hebrew. But I need to point out that my name is Avraham *Abush,* not Avraham Abba."

Rabbi Steinsaltz subsequently wrote back to me, "Dear Avraham Abba, your name is not Avraham Abush, your name is Avraham Abba. Even if your great-grandfather, after whom you were named, was called Avraham Abush all his life, his name was not Avraham Abush. His name was Avraham Abba.

"*Abush* is a diminutive, a sweet form of *Abba*. There were Hasidic masters who were known by the name Avraham Abush, but the Hebrew name is Avraham Abba. *Abush* is not Hebrew. Your name is Avraham Abba."

I knew that to be given a new name, or in my case a slightly corrected name by one's rebbe, is an important event, and it came at just the perfect time. My situation as a single parent was giving me terrible doubts as to whether I would be a good father, a good *abba,* after my divorce.

Now I knew: my *name* is Abba.

Tradition teaches, as Rabbi Steinsaltz points out in his book *The Long Shorter Way,* that when parents name their children, they're not doing it themselves; a holy spirit enters them, and so they select a name with divine assistance. In fact, it is said that if a parent resists that divine inspiration and gives the child the wrong name, then one of the major tasks in the child's life is to find the right name.

🎋 "If You Can't Fix It, Get Out" 🎋

I had been, at the beginning of the divorce process, somewhat uncomfortable and reluctant to tell Rabbi Steinsaltz about my separation from my wife, but eventually he learned about it through a mutual friend. The next time I saw him, he said to me, "I understand that you and your wife are separated."

"Yes."

"Would you like to talk about it?"

I'd already decided that I was not going to talk to him about it, that I really didn't have any great need to discuss it with him.

"I'm quite clear about it," I told him. "I know this divorce is necessary. I believe that it's a healthy move. But if I *did* ask you for advice, what would you say to me?"

And Rabbi Steinsaltz said, "Basically, I would say one thing." He said, "I would say to you, 'If you can fix it, fix it. If you can't, then get out.'"

This was Rabbi Steinsaltz's advice to *me,* in my particular circumstances, not to anyone else. And in my case, he was absolutely right. It was time to make that decision.

I didn't think we could fix it, and ultimately we were divorced. But there was a brief period of time after the divorce that I had thoughts that perhaps we should try to get back together. It didn't work out that way; it was a very short-lived fantasy.

But it was during the midst of that short-lived fantasy that I was once again with Rabbi Steinsaltz in 1994. During a car trip to Manhattan from JFK Airport, I asked him about the notion of remarrying somebody whom one had married once and divorced.

He said, "Oh, yes, it is one of the rare *mitzvot.*"

"What are the rare *mitzvot*?" I asked.

"There is a list of *mitzvot* that are considered rare *mitzvot,* meaning *mitzvot* that people only very infrequently have the opportunity to perform. There is the *mitzvah* of remarrying your divorced wife. It is actually and indeed a *mitzvah* and it is considered to be one of the rare *mitzvot.*"

"What is the meaning of it? Why would it be a *mitzvah* to remarry your divorced wife?"

"I would say that remarrying your divorced wife is like the relationship between Hashem [God] and the Jewish people. He kicked us out, but we believe that one day we're going to get back together again."

⚜ A Press Conference on the Talmud ⚜

By the end of the week, I felt that we had met with every journalist in New York City. But we hadn't.

As it happened, Rabbi Steinsaltz and the Talmud was, as it is said, an easy sell. The media recognized the historic significance of the Talmud's being available for the first time in English. There were more requests for interviews than there was time.

In order to accommodate all of the reporters and writers who wanted time with the Rabbi that week, one last interview session, actually more of a press conference, was held, with four writers in the same room with Rabbi Steinsaltz. They were from various Jewish newspapers in the New York area. I sat in on the session and took my own notes. We were in a plush conference room made available by Random House. I recorded the session.

QUESTION: Isn't the Talmud a set of books that only the most intellectually inclined can study?

RABBI STEINSALTZ: One of the most frequently misunderstood points about Torah study is the fact that intellectual achievement is not the purpose. It does not matter how much or on what level one studies, whether it is mastery of all of the Talmud or reading a single psalm. What matters is the purity of the relationship to the text and not the degree of intellectual comprehension, that is, the capacity to become a vessel of Torah. After all, irrespective of how much one may claim to comprehend God's wisdom, there is always far more that is beyond one's comprehension. The best that one can do—besides endeavoring to understand—is to be in resonance with this wisdom. To let the Torah provide the answers.

QUESTION: If you could describe the Talmud in one phrase or sentence, what would it be?

RABBI STEINSALTZ: I would say, "The Talmud is a photograph of a fountain." Or I would say, "The Talmud is a mirror of the Jewish people—we look in there and find ourselves."

QUESTION: The Talmud has been studied and commented on for many centuries. Is there anything more to say?

RABBI STEINSALTZ: The finest minds of the Jewish people have dedicated their lives to Talmudic scholarship. Sometimes students feel that they cannot add to it, since every topic and every sentence has been pored over by great scholars and sages from every possible viewpoint. But the Talmud has not yet been completed. Every day, every hour, scholars find new subjects of study and new points of view. Not every student is capable of constructing his own systems, but the individual, from his own peculiar and personal point of view, is still capable of seeing some detail, however small, in a new light.

QUESTION: What relevance does a document that is over fifteen hundred years old have for people today?

RABBI STEINSALTZ: In different circumstances, the basic notions and basic sources can be applied. It is like the multiplication table. How can it be applied in the year 300 B.C.E. and in the year 21 C.E.? It is because the rules are basically the same. The application is the same, whether I'm counting camels or computers.

Whether it's 1999 or 200, it is not very different from the year 12 or the year 13 or 112. The real work in studying Talmud is not just to understand the written material but to be able to apply it in different circumstances.

The Talmudic system thinks in terms of models. In some ways, it's very close to modern physics.

QUESTION: Which is more important to the Jewish people, the Bible or the Talmud?

RABBI STEINSALTZ: If the Bible is the cornerstone of Judaism, then the Talmud is the central pillar.

QUESTION: I understand that there are many volumes of the Talmud and that you have just published the first volume. Why did you begin with the volume you began with?

RABBI STEINSALTZ: *Bava Metzia* is generally about the marketplace. About interactions between and among people, often in the marketplace. I wanted to make a statement that God is not only in the kitchen, he's also in the bedroom, he's also in the marketplace. Of course, the Talmud never stays on its subject. The Talmud is always free-associating and bringing in other subjects to the topic at hand.

QUESTION: Rabbi Steinsaltz, what is faith?

RABBI STEINSALTZ: Well, I don't know if we have the time, but I can say in a concise way that there is a theorem in mathematics, in projective geometry, called Desargue's theorem. It is an easy theorem to understand. Any schoolchild can understand it. But it is impossible to prove it—until one introduces a point located at the infinite. Once you imagine a point in the infinite, the theorem can be proved. It is the same with our world. To begin to understand it, we must imagine the infinite.

QUESTION: Why are there so many different opinions recorded in the Talmud?

RABBI STEINSALTZ: The Torah not only has, as it is written, seventy facets, but in fact the Torah has six hundred thousand facets, because each of our people has his own point, his own direction of getting into the Torah, which is his and nobody else's.

That is the meaning of what we pray several times. "And give us our share in your Torah," that we'll have the merit and the good luck to understand what is our specific, private point of entering the Torah.

In a way, one may say that the Torah has so many locks. It has so many keys. And there is a key that is mine alone. And there is a door that is mine alone. And that is the door made for me.

And if a person has great luck, he quickly finds the way he has to enter, the special door, the special keys that he has to use.

Sometimes people are just wandering about because they don't know what is the specific key that they have to use.

Because they don't know it, they may make mistakes in getting entangled with somebody else's Torah, with somebody else's pathway because it is not theirs.

The Talmud is at once a holy book and a search for the truth—it is holy intellectualism. Although holy in each detail, one may question what is written in it, one may disagree with it, one may argue.

We kiss the Talmud before studying it and when we finish, but while we are studying from it, we pound it!

QUESTION: Rabbi Steinsaltz, are you an optimist or a pessimist?

RABBI STEINSALTZ: There is an old dispute about which Voltaire parodied Leibniz. The problem is "What kind of world are we living in?" And there are two opposite answers. The first is that we're living in the best of all possible worlds. And the other is that we're living in the worst possible world.

I've been pondering for a very long time what the Jewish

position about it is. I think that I can say with some justi-
fication that the Jewish position is something like this: We
are living in the worst possible world—in which there is
still hope.

I'm speaking as a Jewish optimist. Every Jew has to be
an optimist; otherwise we would have died a thousand
years ago. But a Jewish optimist is not a person who sees a
rosy vision before him. That is not something that a Jew
can do. He sees life, and should see life, as bitter, as harmful, as problematic, and still hopes that it can be changed.

More than that, he's doing something about changing
it. I won't say that that is the only major Jewish value that
has to be transmitted, but it's a very important one. The
ability to see black and to hope for the light is a very deeply
ingrained element of not just our tradition, our religion,
but more than that. It's a great part of our very essence as
human beings: the ability to cope with problems and to
deal with what we are facing around us.

QUESTION: What is Torah study all about? Can you make any
general statement of what you mean by Torah study?

RABBI STEINSALTZ: In many religions there is the notion of a
book or doctrine that comes from heaven. We Jews, however, believe that the Torah itself is heaven. When one is
studying the Torah, one is in direct communion with God.
One is not just reading or studying or even seeking inspiration.

When we study Torah, God and man are talking
together. We can come into direct communion with God
through his Torah. When we study Scripture, God studies
with us, the Talmud says.

When we perform actions according to the Torah, we
are not separate from Him.

When a person is engaged in Torah study without an ulterior motive, he may be said to be united with the Divine Will. He is thinking God's thoughts concerning God's world. There is no basic difference between the one who studies with the highest esoteric comprehension and the one who simply reads the written words.

QUESTION: Rabbi, what was going on in your life at age twenty-seven, when, of all things, you decided to begin to translate and create a modern Talmud?

RABBI STEINSALTZ: What was on my mind? Well. It is a good question. First of all, it is a book that I love. You see, I got entangled with it. I did not intend earlier to do anything like this. It was not that a person plans his life to do one specific thing. It was my hobby, a very big hobby. So I got entangled with a hobby.

But in one way, there was a feeling that there is something that has to be done. It is like I am walking a long way and find somebody wounded and I'm the only person that can do something about it. Now I know that I am not qualified, I am not the best person to do it, I am not the right person to do it, but I'm here.

QUESTION: (*from an obviously Orthodox man who was a reporter for an Orthodox Jewish newspaper*) Rabbi Steinsaltz, how do you do what you do? You're teaching Gemara all over the place, you're teaching Gemara to men and women sitting together. The men are bareheaded. How is it that you go around and do this?

RABBI STEINSALTZ: My teachers taught me to relate to a person's essence and not to his or her shell. As long as I do that, I'm safe.

QUESTION: (*from a somewhat arrogant reporter whose body language was showing some kind of chip on his shoulder*) Who do you think you are, writing a commentary on the Baby-

NOTES FROM THE ROAD:
The Beauty of the Talmud

The beauty and the lesson of the Talmud is that it teaches us to always see the other side, to believe and to question at the same time.

The Talmud has kept us sane by showing us that there are contradictions in the world and that we cannot solve them. We must learn to live with them.

—Rabbi Adin Steinsaltz

lonian Talmud? The Babylonian Talmud has a commentary by the great scholar Rashi. Who needs another commentary?

RABBI STEINSALTZ: (*with a big smile on his face*) What do you mean, who do I think I am? Every schoolchild is supposed to write his own commentary on the Talmud. We're all supposed to write our own commentary on the Talmud. This is what the Talmud is asking of us, to bring ourselves to the Talmud, to write our own commentary.

My chutzpah is not writing my own commentary on the Talmud; we're all supposed to write our own commentaries on the Talmud.

My chutzpah was publishing it.

CHAPTER THREE

Photo © Gary Eisenberg.

"Kabbalah Is the Official Theology of the Jewish People" (1998)

A real secret can be open and apparent to everyone. All can see the matter clearly and examine it from all sides. Nevertheless, the more it is looked at and examined, the more of a secret it becomes, profound and insoluable.

—Rabbi Adin Steinsaltz,
In the Beginning, p. xiii

It's 5:30 A.M. on a rainy spring day in 1998. I'm in the International Arrivals Building at JFK Airport.

Rabbi Steinsaltz's flight has just landed. I have been here so many times over the years at this hour. While Rabbi Steinsaltz sometimes gets lucky and goes through customs in a few minutes, usually the line is long and it takes about an hour. I'm happy to wait.

How many times over the years have I set my alarm for 3:30 A.M. and driven in the dark to meet his flight?

I always enjoy being at the airport at this early hour. The arrivals building slowly fills with people, and the passengers trickle out. I enjoy watching parents and children, boyfriends and girlfriends, children and grandchildren as they greet each other so emotionally. This morning, a group of about twenty rather enthusiastic Hasidim are here to greet someone who is returning from the Holy Land.

Rabbi Steinsaltz has been teaching classes on Kabbalah in the basement of a Jerusalem synagogue for many years. And the gifted translator, Yehuda Hanegbi, has taped, transcribed, and edited those lectures and has produced four manuscripts, in exquisite English, that have been published in the United States. One is called *The Long Shorter Way*. The next is *The Sustaining Utterance*. The third is *In the Beginning*.

The fourth, *The Candle of God,* has just appeared. It contains a fourteen-chapter section called "The Trials of Life." In these chapters, Rabbi Steinsaltz explores an eternal question, one that has been on my mind almost all my life: Why did God make a world with so much suffering in it?

It is not only my own personal pains and suffering that have sent me in the direction of exploring this question and reading countless mostly unsatisfying books on the topic. When I look at the world around me, I just have to wonder what life's pains are all about. If God is infinite, all-knowing, all-wise, perfect, why would such a God have created a world that allows so much heartache and pain, so much hunger, poverty, sickness, and injustice?

Over the years, Rabbi Steinsaltz has invited me into the world of the Talmud, a Jewish universe, with assumptions about life that have an impact on everything we do. For example, in a part of the Talmud called "Ethics of the Fathers," which is a gathering of wise axioms from the sages, Rabbi Akiva, perhaps the greatest of the Talmudic sages, is said to have taught, "All is foreseen, and free will is given."

The question is, which is it? Is everything foreseen? Is everything known by God in advance? Or do we have free will?

Yet Rabbi Akiva teaches that both are true at the same time.

And Rabbi Steinsaltz teaches that the Talmud is a collection of paradoxes. By entering into these paradoxes, we enter into the paradox of existence, and, as the Kabbalists say, we seem to be able to glimpse a truer reality, and we can even begin to grasp the answer to the question of suffering.

I need to explore these questions.

And Rabbi Steinsaltz seems to understand that.

He has written *The Thirteen Petalled Rose* and other books based on the teaching of Kabbalah for students like me, who want to understand the meaning of our lives.

There is a hunger among Jews for an understanding of the ways our greatest sages confronted the mysteries of life.

There is a need to reveal the secrets of Kabbalah, to help us understand why God allows so much suffering.

Thanks to Rabbi Steinsaltz, these past few years—reading his books and speaking with him about these things—I was beginning to grasp a little.

Here comes Rabbi Steinsaltz now. . . .

✇ Rescuing Kabbalah from Obscurity ✇

Traffic was terrible and the rain was pouring as Rabbi Steinsaltz and I drove from the airport that morning. I dropped him at his hotel and he went inside to freshen up after his trip. The flight from Israel is long.

Rabbi Steinsaltz was scheduled to deliver an important talk at one o'clock that day. He was giving the keynote address to a gathering of the New York Board of Rabbis, to be held in the auditorium of a large synagogue in New York City. Members of this rabbinic organization are from all branches of American Judaism—Orthodox, Reform, Reconstructionist, and Conservative.

The hall in New York City was packed to capacity. It seemed like every rabbi from far and wide had come! There must have been three hundred rabbis in the room. There were Orthodox rabbis with long beards, and there were women from the liberal movements who also serve in the rabbinate. There were old rabbis and young rabbis, congregational rabbis and scholars. It was quite a scene.

There was rapt attention in the hall as Rabbi Steinsaltz began his talk by saying, "Kabbalah is the official theology of the Jewish people."

He repeated, "Kabbalah is the official theology of the Jewish people." And then he continued, "In a way, if you're not learning it, if you're not teaching it, I suppose one could question whether or not you are doing your job."

There was a little nervous laughter in the room. But enough of the rabbis in attendance understood precisely why Rabbi Steinsaltz was being so blunt and so clear. They know that Rabbi Steinsaltz is involved in a huge effort to rescue Kabbalah from the obscurity to which it had been relegated by recent generations and to put it back in its rightful place as positively central to Jewish life and thought.

❧ Why Kabbalah Went Underground ❧

Rabbi Steinsaltz proceeded to give a ninety-minute lecture on Kabbalah. He explained why Kabbalah went underground. He explained why Kabbalah is, in his opinion, the accepted and official theology of the Jews. And he made the point that there is so much misinformation about Kabbalah that there was no longer an issue of whether it is acceptable to teach these matters in public. For the sake of accuracy alone, for the sake of helping get reliable source material to sincere and qualified students, there was now an imperative to teach these matters clearly and effectively.

At the end of his talk, Rabbi Steinsaltz received an enthusiastic standing ovation.

Later that day, I had to drive the Rabbi to give a lecture at a synagogue in the New York suburbs. He rarely knew what the announced topic was and had no "canned speeches," as he calls them. Whatever the topic was, I wasn't able to attend the lecture, and someone else was being given the opportunity to drive the Rabbi back to his hotel that night. I just needed to drop him off at the synagogue where he was speaking.

While driving to the suburbs that day, I raised the subject of his talk of that afternoon. I asked for clarification and quoted something he had said earlier to the rabbis.

Rabbi Steinsaltz had said, "Since the time of the expulsion from Spain, the theology of our people is the theology of the Kabbalah. Kabbalah permeates every aspect of Judaism. Esoteric wisdom is a basic ingredient of Scripture, of our ritual, and of prayer. The history is not always known accurately. Kabbalah is accepted not only in the Hasidic world but also by people who opposed the Hasidim. The Vilna Gaon[1] was possibly more deeply involved with the Kabbalah than many of the Hasidic masters put together." I understood Rabbi Steinsaltz's reference to the Vilna Gaon. A master Talmudist and the great leader of Lithuanian Jewry, he lived at the time when Hasidism and its popularization of Kabbalah was flowering—and he was a great opponent of the Hasidic movement. Many an uninformed student has thought that the Vilna Gaon would therefore not be a student of Kabbalah. But that's simply untrue. The Vilna Gaon in fact wrote a commentary on one of the classic Kabbalistic texts, *Sefer Yetzirah.*

"Wasn't Rabbi Joseph Caro also a Kabbalist?" I asked.

The question entered my mind for the same reason. Rabbi Joseph Caro, author of the authoritative *Code of Jewish Law,* the document that still stands after centuries as the prime legal authority for rabbinic rulings, was also a mystic, a Kabbalist, although this is unknown to many. I daresay that most people who have even heard of Rabbi Joseph Caro think of him as a dry legalist, not as a mystical Kabbalist. But a Kabbalist he was.

Rabbi Steinsaltz, of course, confirmed this. "Yes," he said, "his legal text was only one of a number of his books. In addition to his knowledge of law, he was known for his mystical insight. He also wrote a manuscript—it was called *Maggid M'esharim,* clearly a Kabbalistic work. It records his mystical experiences and his visions. People have said that it was the voice of the Mishnah speaking from his mouth.

"By the way, the famous Shabbat song *"L'Cha Dodi,"* which we sing every week, is clearly a Kabbalistic poem, written by Rabbi Shlomo HaLevi Alkabetz, who is said to have witnessed Rabbi Joseph Caro when the Maggid, an angelic messenger, appeared to him."

There is also another side to the Torah, that of being the Law, of compelling men to behave in certain ways. For the Torah is, to a large extent, a plan of human action and relationship, providing guidance for what is the proper way to behave, think, dream, and desire in order that the Torah's design for the world be realized. In this respect, the Torah is a way of life, showing both how to relate inwardly and how to conduct oneself outwardly, practically. And that perhaps is why the word *Torah* is of the same root as the word *hora'ah* ("instruction" or "teaching"), providing as it does a guide to the path of God.

Theoretically, the perfect man can reach this identification with Torah from within himself.

—Rabbi Adin Steinsaltz, *The Thirteen Petalled Rose,*
  pp. 89–90

Rabbi Steinsaltz then said, "In Judaism, the greatest of the legal authorities were immersed in the world of Kabbalah."

Over the years, I've thought so often about the vast numbers of Jews who, despite their terrible Jewish education, are aware of the large volume of laws within Judaism but completely unaware that those same teachers who compiled guidebooks of Jewish law were masters and experts of Jewish mysticism. One of Rabbi Steinsaltz's many goals is to change that situation. He is a revolutionary.

I asked Rabbi Steinsaltz if I remembered correctly that he once said at a lecture that "if there is a normative Jewish theology, it is the integration of the two approaches—the Kabbalah of the Ari and the *Shulchan Aruch* of Rabbi Joseph Caro."[2]

He agreed and said, "You see, unlike most mystical schools in the world, which usually seem to stress freedom from the constraints of formal religion, Kabbalah does the opposite. It stresses the significance of the smallest details of the law and of the ritual."

🙊 "Kabbalah Is Just 🙊 Beginning to Emerge"

"How did Kabbalah become hidden?" I asked as we were driving through the Queens-Midtown Tunnel, which connects Manhattan with Queens under the East River.

"First, as I said, the tragic event of the false Messiah, Shabbetai Tzvi, caused, in great part, a frowning on the study of Kabbalah."

I knew some of the details of that history. Shabbetai Tzvi, who lived in the mid-1600s, was extremely popular and inspired countless followers, including some of the great rabbis of the generation. He ultimately claimed to be the Messiah. When the Turkish sultan told him that he must convert to Islam or be killed, he converted, and enormous numbers of his disillusioned followers were stunned by his decision. Because he was a teacher of Kabbalah, the reaction against him by the Jewish establishment included a trend to discourage the teaching of Kabbalah. The Jewish world is still reverberating from the huge scandal.

Rabbi Steinsaltz continued, "But there is also another problem of the esoteric and the occult. People were advised to keep away from subjects they did not know enough about. A little knowledge is dangerous in any field. Since the Torah is a live wire

In the literature of the Kabbalah and Chasidism, it is assumed that every human being has some capacity for making contact with a world above the concrete world, and that the way to the supernatural is available to everyone at a particular level.

—Rabbi Adin Steinsaltz, *The Strife of the Spirit*, p. 179

connecting us with God, any who get involved with it without taking precautionary measures run the risk of being electrocuted.

"At a certain point, I would say in the seventeenth century, the religious authorities believed that there was a significant danger. Important books of Kabbalah gathered dust. In Europe, only mature students were permitted to study Kabbalah. In the nineteenth century, authors of the most important books of Jewish history were fiercely antagonistic to Kabbalah, sometimes even denying its existence. It is only in our own time that Kabbalah is beginning to emerge from the obscurity into which it was thrust by enlightened rationalism."

A Conversation About Spirituality

The next day, I was asked to make sure that Rabbi Steinsaltz ate dinner before his evening lecture. I know, as a person who frequently lectures out of town, that it is easy to become the center of attention with no opportunity to eat a good meal.

Early that evening, about an hour and a half before the Rabbi was scheduled to speak in Manhattan at a private gathering of donors who are consistent and generous contributors to Rabbi Steinsaltz's many projects, we went out to dinner and had a long conversation.

We went to that favorite kosher spot of ours, My Most Favorite Dessert Company on Forty-Fifth Street near Sixth Avenue (Avenue of the Americas). As soon as we walked in, people were recognizing Rabbi Steinsaltz and approaching him to shake his hand or greet him warmly. We asked for a table in some quiet corner, and the Rabbi strategically sat with his back to the room. Even so, from time to time during the meal, diners would recognize him and would approach our table to say hello, shake his hand, or touch his shoulder. Traveling with Rabbi Steinsaltz in certain neighborhoods, such as the midtown Manhattan diamond district where we were having dinner that night, is what I imagine it must be like to be hanging out with a famous star like Bob Dylan or Mick Jagger.

I began our dinner conversation by asking Rabbi Steinsaltz if it would be all right if I brought up some questions about spirituality that were either my own or were ones I was frequently asked. Rabbi Steinsaltz told me that he would be happy to speak about anything I wanted.

So I began.

"In my conversations with lots of Reform, Conservative, and Orthodox rabbis over the years, it is clear that many of them have an aversion to spirituality, even sometimes claiming that Judaism is not spiritual! What in the world is going on when rabbis represent spirituality as some fringe element in Judaism?"

Rabbi Steinsaltz said, "What is the problem? It is really a double or triple problem. One of the big problems is historical. Most of these people you encounter are relics. The oldest relics are what I call the Reform dinosaurs. But you have as well very well-dried Conservative and Orthodox rabbis. They live in the past, when anything about spiritual matters was something of a taboo.

"You have to remember that in a strange way, we are still living in nineteenth-century Judaism. Nineteenth-century Judaism was a completely rationalistic age in which the highest spiritual move was perhaps some kind of a charitable feeling to others, and you didn't even overdo that!

"So because of the historical burden, people are, in a certain way, afraid of anything that had to do with spirituality. If you look at the work of a great historian like Heinrich Graetz, when he deals with anything spiritual, he's more than suspicious—he outright despises it.

"When Jews came to America, they unfortunately wanted to be modern. But they even didn't catch what modernity is. Modernity changed on them, and they didn't notice it. It is as true about Orthodoxy as it is about Reform. They live in a culture that is over a hundred years old and is no longer of any meaning to anybody, except for these rabbis and possibly, here and there, some university professors.

"So this is one reason."

Between the Psychedelic and the Psychotic

Rabbi Steinsaltz paused as the waiter arrived, handed us menus, and asked us if we wanted anything to drink. Water was fine.

Rabbi Steinsaltz put down the menu without looking at it and continued talking.

"Another reason is that spirituality in America has had a tendency to be very crazy. Often, for example, American spirituality is, well, somewhere between the psychedelic and the psychotic. And you have it in so many hundreds of forms. Some of them are quite bizarre. Some of them are obnoxious. Some of them, like Charles Manson's type of spirituality, are outright harmful.

"So you have all these kinds of rather odd spiritual groups sprouting up all the time. Spirituality in America is in the hands of so many quacks, shams, and cheats that you cannot take it anymore. So honest people just shy away from it. They don't want to touch it.

"So that is the reason why a seeker, a searcher, or a person who wants something, when he somehow finds his way to any kind of a Jewish prayer place, usually finds it dry, boring, and unappealing, especially if he has any kind of a spiritual tendency.

"Now, the fact is that there is a very old—I mean as ancient as anything else—a very rich Jewish spirituality that is not only a matter of esoteric corners of Judaism but very clear-cut and I would say very public forms that were always a part of Jewish life for as long as we know about Jewish life. But again, there is an attempt by so many people to take out the spiritual part and to leave sometimes the practical message and sometimes no message whatsoever in order to make it fit some preconceived notion of what Judaism is."

I was eager to discuss these things with Rabbi Steinsaltz. Most of my life, when visiting synagogues and speaking with rabbis, I have been unimpressed. I think that one of the big unspoken scandals of American Jewish life is *recruitment at the rabbinical seminaries*. Who are they accepting into their rabbinic program, and who are they rejecting?

I have met many wonderful people who are devoted to Torah and love Jews and are always working on deepening their faith but who were rejected by rabbinical seminaries. And the flipside is that the hundreds of rabbis they have ordained over the years often seem to be more interested in academics than in spirituality. I've published too many rabbis who have told me that they would prefer to be called "doctor" rather than "rabbi" on their book jackets.

The waiter returned to take our order. Rabbi Steinsaltz and I both ordered fish.

Finding a Spiritual Guide

I asked Rabbi Steinsaltz, "What advice would you give to the spiritual seeker who is searching for an authentic and reliable teacher? In the end, do we have anything to help us other than our intuition about someone?"

He replied, "Intuition is a great thing. Intuition is also a great misleader. That is, there is always a two-sided element in any kind of intuitive thinking. It is not clearly checkable one way or the other way. And unluckily, there are often people who think that they have some kind of a deep attachment to something or somebody when it was just a matter of being attracted to a show. So intuition is not a solution, not a general solution.

"I would say that there are two answers. One of them is too difficult. One of them seems to be too easy.

"The difficult one is this: if your teacher is like an angel, then go and receive Torah from him. Of course, we are handicapped in this case because, among other things, we don't know what angels look like, so if I am searching for an angel-like teacher, I may sometimes bump into something which is a very strange image that I have of angels and which is perhaps wrong.

"Of the very few things that I know about angels, one that I'm sure of is that they don't look like blond girls with big feathered wings. But again, for some people, these are the only angels they know about. Sometimes it comes as a very strong feeling. But it is, again, not readily checkable. So while it's good advice to seek out a teacher who is an angel, it is not always practical advice."

Suddenly we were interrupted by an elderly couple who wanted to shake Rabbi Steinsaltz's hand. Both of them smiled broadly and were obviously thrilled to be in his presence. The Rabbi smiled back graciously and, when they had left, continued without missing a beat.

"On the other hand, I would put it this way: the person who claims that he knows everything is most possibly a liar. The people who are undertaking to solve all the questions that you have are perhaps confidence men. Those that will undertake to heal you of all your maladies in two sessions or in six sessions are perhaps taking your money under false pretenses. Or they take your attention or your love under false pretenses.

"So in a strange way, I would say that if you are searching for a teacher, try to search for somebody who doesn't make such claims. Often people who have divine spirit are in many ways not able to express it. Even prophets were handicapped in this way. They could only claim very partial knowledge. And they did not claim more than that.

"When people claim that they know very little, there is a chance that they know something. The main point is that what people can get from one another is not the vast unknown but rather the little bit that can be transmitted. This little bit can be so very precious."

The food arrived. As we made room on the table for the plates and as the busboy hovered over us, refilling our water, Rabbi Steinsaltz continued talking, taking my questions seriously and answering as thoroughly as time allowed.

Little Nuggets of Wisdom

"I tell my pupils that when you listen to a lecture of one hour or two hours, if you get one minute's worth of something that was really important to hear, you are getting far more than the average.

"You see, people don't really find nuggets of gold everywhere on the street. In American history, you learn that people go to the creeks and to the rivers and try to find some little pieces of gold in the rubble. You don't find tons of it. But you find little pieces, and that is important enough.

"Another point is that whenever I see something very showy, very flamboyant, colorful, and impressive, I always try to find out, to search out, what is really beneath it. And in so many cases, we find out that beneath those showy garments sometimes we have nothing.

"I have had my own experience with zoology," Rabbi Steinsaltz said as he took his first bite of the zoology in front of us, a delicious piece of broiled fish as served at My Most Favorite Dessert Company, "and I remember once seeing something that made a big impression on me.

"It was a plucked peacock. When you see a plucked peacock, which looks like an ugly, emaciated hen, you are so very disappointed because when you see the peacock in all its glory, it's clearly a glorious bird. But if you want to eat it or have more contact with it, you find out what it is in truth. So when I see peacock feathers, which are wonderful to look at, I always think about the hen beneath those feathers.

"In the same way, when someone comes and makes a big show, a very impressive show, this is the time to wonder whether you are not being taken in by external effects."

Rabbi Steinsaltz then raised a subject relating to something about my life with which we were familiar. I perform as a magician. At that point, I had not gone into any detail with him about this interest other than to tell him that I have been interested in magic since I was in the third grade and that I performed from time to time.

Rabbi Steinsaltz said to me, "Arthur, you know about this because you are doing these things when you perform as a magician. The secret of magic tricks is that you make people look at the wrong things. So many of these people who are selling spirituality are really doing all kinds of tricks to take your mind off of what is really important."

Rabbi Steinsaltz continued, "I would suggest trying to look carefully at these people who are claiming or are serving as teachers. Many great teachers are very reluctant teachers. You have to push them, and you have to pull them, and you have to force them to say something. Not everybody gets the message, 'Go and spread my word.' Many people, many worthy people, don't hear it. Sometimes they are shy. Sometimes they are introverted people and you have to dig it out of them.

"It is extremely important when you find someone who seems to have knowledge. But let me add another quality. Honesty is extremely important. When people are honest, it's a high quality and not so very common. You have to search for people who are honest. Honest people may be the right teachers because whatever they say in the end will be things they honestly believe. This is someone who should be a teacher."

Suddenly the waiter comes over and asks Rabbi Steinsaltz for an autograph. Another diner was too shy to approach him but would love to have his signature. Rabbi Steinsaltz gladly signed his name on the scrap of paper the waiter handed him.

Why Aren't Jewish Books Spiritual?
I then asked Rabbi Steinsaltz, "When a spiritual seeker enters a well-stocked bookstore in America, there seems to be so many inspiring books from dozens of religious traditions. On close examination, these volumes often consist of translations of texts now available in English. There are many beautiful, uplifting

books on the spiritual life that represent most of these religious traditions. But then, when one looks at Jewish texts that have been translated into English, so many seem to be occupied with rules and regulations and cases of law. What do you make of this? Can you help me understand it?"

Rabbi Steinsaltz said, "Usually, when you translate spiritual literature, you translate the part of the literature that is obviously spiritual. In many cultures, you have details that are legal details, historical details, nonsensical details, and all these things appear in their original languages, but they usually are not translated.

"Take, for example, a collection of writings from Sufi Islam. You have lots of collections; some of them are wonderful books to read. But you see, these books are not depicting Islam, with all its vast literature, of every side and every form. You will find very few books that deal with all the legal aspects of the Muslim canon law.

"The same thing would be true about Christianity or about Hinduism. See, you may read about Hinduism in many books, but you don't have any good description, and surely not any fair, honest description, about the caste system and about what each of these castes is allowed to eat or not allowed to eat, what they are allowed to touch or not allowed to touch. It is not because people want to cheat others, but the translator doesn't think it of any importance, so it is not translated.

"Now, when it comes to Jewish literature, the tendency was different. Some of the translations, perhaps too many of them, deal with details, different kinds of details. These tend to be the books that have been selected for translation. It is a pity."

I suggested to Rabbi Steinsaltz that many of his books fill that terrible gap in English-language Jewish books. Books like *The Thirteen Petalled Rose, The Long Shorter Way, The Sustaining*

Utterance, and *The Candle of God* are not translations of all the rules and regulations but discourses on the spiritual ideas that many of us crave.

As the waiter cleared our table, Rabbi Steinsaltz said, "You see, you have books that tell you what to do under almost any circumstances. Very small, practical books or big, impractical books that deal with all these things, but most of them tell you exactly what you have to do, under any circumstances. But thinking is not a part of these books.

"But there is also another part to it that in a way goes to a far deeper level. Our language, the Hebrew language, has a tendency to avoid abstractions. Most of the abstractions in our language are modern abstractions, modern words. In the old literature, if you read a whole book, like the Torah, or even the whole Bible, you find, if you try to search for it, how few abstractions you have there. Everything is put in a different way, not always in a practical way, but it is put in a different way, because it is an entirely different style, that is unlike, say, Buddhist or Hindu literature, which tends to be abstract.

"And sometimes you are searching and you read such translations from one of these religions and you try to find one concrete word. It is filled with language like 'the sanctity of solitude' and so on. But you don't have many real words that deal with real objects.

"And incidentally, these abstract words, if you take them in a large amount, have some kind of intoxicating quality. You read them and basically you don't understand anything. But they are far more powerful than any smoke of grass. They make your mind think that you somehow got into something powerful and wonderful. You don't really know what you are talking about, but you can repeat it easily.

"And you can read them page after page and enjoy yourself immensely by being in a world made almost completely of thin air. It has an influence and is truly intoxicating. You read a few pages of it, and if you are asked to tell anybody, say a little child, what you have read, you cannot just repeat the words you find. You do not have the faintest notion what is written there. And I'm speaking about pages and pages of these things. And after you look at all of these pages, what did they really say?

"Now, Jewish literature tried not to develop abstractions and tried to deal with abstractions in a nonabstract format.

"There are Jewish books that deal with spirituality. Quite a number of them, in fact, from ancient times to modern times. Many of them are not translated, and many of them, if they were translated, would be perhaps difficult for a reader because they don't have the same quality as other kinds of spirituality. And sometimes they speak, or at least try to speak, about the highest things in the most level-headed way and with the simplest words possible. So it doesn't sound the same. As with anything of any importance, there is a demand on people—not an easy one—to bend down sometimes and look at things."

I am always struck by the patience that Rabbi Steinsaltz has to delve into any serious subject. Although the conversation was long and intense, I was delighted.

Details, Not Abstractions

Rabbi Steinsaltz continued, "I used to have lots of free time, and I'm wonderfully good at loafing. So I watched all kinds of plants. Some of these plants have tiny flowers—too tiny to be seen.

"Now, if you look at some of these tiny flowers that you can find in any field, they are beautiful, as beautiful as the most gorgeous orchids. But they are small and sometimes they don't have the same colors and they are in clusters so you don't see them. What you have to do is to bend to them and watch these things that are not so big and flashy but are as beautiful as any others. You have to watch them.

"This demand on people, to be participants, is so important for things Jewish. But in many cultures—especially in America—things are geared to make everything easy. In Judaism, things are not made to be difficult on purpose but surely not made to be easy, which means you have to participate, you have to work at it. Who now wants to work? If you can get predigested material, why should you chew anything?"

I had heard Rabbi Steinsaltz use this metaphor on a few occasions. He once said, "It is a big step for a child to go from liquid food to solid foods. They often don't want it. 'Why are you doing this? It was so easy with liquids. Now you are making me work so hard, to chew this food.' Of course, once you learn to chew, a whole new world opens up."

I asked Rabbi Steinsaltz for some clarification.

"Is part of our work," I inquired, "to see the concrete and to try to grasp the abstraction that it represents?"

Rabbi Steinsaltz replied, "In some way it is. But let's say you try to look at something in the real world, say, a bird. Look at a sparrow. Sparrows are very humble creatures.

"Look at a sparrow. And then look at the sparrow without trying to think about its being a sparrow. Look at the sparrow as it is, and try looking at it not just as something that you have to poison tomorrow if you don't want your garden destroyed. If you look at the sparrow and just look at it, you admire it, you think about it, I won't say that the sparrow will grow to the size of an angel, but the sparrow will become something different.

"That is what is called, what they used to call, 'the eye of a poet.' In a different way, it is the eye of the scientist. And in a different way, it is the eye of the lover. This is an eye that is not searching for abstractions. If I look at somebody that I love, it doesn't mean that instead of seeing a nose I see something completely different. But somehow I see the nose and it appears to be a very different and very unique nose, not like anything else.

So when looking at these things, there is a quality of being able to become transcendental without going to the abstract.

"You go to it in a different way. It's a different path, basically. It's a path that seems to be so very commonplace. There are people who will always ride on the wings of angels. But there are also people who go up on the same high mountains, just trudging, moving one foot after the other and sometimes feeling sorry for themselves because it's such a hard way.

"And after some time, without noticing, they see that they are in a much higher place than before. But you go on, you still go on and you climb on and use the same stick and go on. It's a different way. It doesn't lead to a different heaven, perhaps. But it is a different walk to spirituality.

"Now, this is a very different way, a different walk, and in some ways it's a harder walk. See, because our spirituality was basically meant for our people. And our people were meant to be, and were in a way trained to be, I would say, tough people.

"See, as Jews, we have all kinds of qualities—some good qualities and some qualities that can be used in different kinds of directions. And one of them is that there is an enormous amount of toughness in our psyche, which is one of the things that enabled us to survive. But this toughness is not only about the outside world but also about the inside world; it's a kind of ability to do hard work and somehow enjoy hard work. In some way that is a part of it.

"There's also another part, which is the ability to be obstinate. Tenacious. In the spiritual Jewish life, you don't have any charmed gateways. But you are given some kind of a path, and you have to work your way up. And again, the day after and the day after, without any promise or any kind of harps that will sing to you. And if you do hear them singing, then perhaps something is wrong with you."

The waiter came with the check. As always, I paid. And although I am always asked to turn in my receipts for reimbursement, I never do. Taking Rabbi Steinsaltz out is always my privilege.

It was almost time to get going. Rabbi Steinsaltz had to get to his next talk.

A Better Person Through Spirituality?

As we were driving to his next appointment that evening, I said to him, "With the Jewish way being such hard work, one can understand the temptation to seek a different and easier path."

Rabbi Steinsaltz responded, "Well, there are lots of easier ways. The question is, where do they lead? This is one question that has to be asked. And it's sometimes a tough question to ask. I mean, you, Ms. So-and-So or Mr. So-and-So, have been deal-

NOTES FROM THE ROAD:
On Rabbi Steinsaltz's Lecturing

I once vowed never to give talks in public because I don't do them well. So here I am on a lecture tour.

And no one thought I would be a good teacher because I have no patience; I don't tolerate fools. So here I am a teacher.

I'd like to be an engineer or an inventor or to work with my hands as a stonecutter.

—Rabbi Adin Steinsaltz

ing with spirituality for the last twenty years. Did you become a better person after twenty years of spirituality?

"You became more mushy. That is a possibility. You became less realistic. That is a possibility. But in many ways, you didn't become any better.

"I tell some of my pupils, after a year of study, 'I don't know, really, if you advanced this year. It's really hard for me to be a judge of it. And you surely cannot judge yourself. So go home. You have wives. Ask your wives if you've become any better.' Now, if your wife says, 'You definitely became better,' then it means you went in the right way. If she says she doesn't notice any difference, perhaps it was the wrong thing to do at the beginning, so stop it. Some of them have even taken my advice."

As Rabbi Steinsaltz was talking with me and doing all the things that pipe smokers do with their pipes, I was both listening to him and, from time to time, watching myself listen to him—and realizing my good fortune to have the opportunity to speak about these things with him.

He continued, "Of course, people can add all kinds of wings to their personality—from eagle's wings to bat's wings. And the question is not whether I soar into heaven. The question is, where do I land at the end? And sometimes I don't land anywhere. I'm going, really, in cloudy cuckoo-land, which is where so many of the spiritual people are, in a way, landing in the end. Is *that* the great search?

"I know that spiritual people usually don't like to be asked any questions. They are too spiritual for that. But I want to ask the question, 'What do you want? What are you searching for?' I'm asking this as a real question, not as something to taunt people with. Does spirituality have something to do with the spirit? If it has, then the spirit has to do something. It has to grow."

Our conversation had to end abruptly, as usual. We had arrived at his next appointment.

NOTES FROM THE ROAD:
Creating Leaders

One evening, I brought Rabbi Steinsaltz to a synagogue where he spoke about his book *Simple Words*. The rabbi of the congregation asked me a question privately that I had been asked several times before: "Rabbi Steinsaltz is often described as one of the most influential rabbis of our generation. And he is this amazing Jewish leader who is spoken of in superlative terms by everyone who knows him well. Where are Rabbi Steinsaltz's Hasidim? Where is his army? Where is his organization to join? Where is his magazine to subscribe to?

In addition to the great influence he has exerted through the extraordinary books he has published over the years, the answer is that Rabbi Steinsaltz is a different kind of a leader.

He's not a leader who is looking for followers. He's a leader who is creating other leaders.

That evening, Rabbi Steinsaltz spoke in the apartment of extremely wealthy philanthropists. His topic was "Hollywood," and an edited transcript of that evening's lecture became the basis of a chapter in his book *Simple Words*.

Over the years, as people have learned that I have the privilege of taking Rabbi Steinsaltz to his appointments, I've been asked questions about what he is like. As a teacher and a scholar, he is a role model. As the well-known Hasidic story relates, when Leib Saras returned from a visit to his rebbe and his students and family asked him what words of Torah the rebbe taught him, Leib Saras said, "I did not go to my teacher to hear his words of Torah; I went to see how he ties his shoelaces."

NOTES FROM THE ROAD:
Empathy

This afternoon, Rabbi Steinsaltz told his audience, "There is a story about Rabbi Levi Yitzchak of Berdichev, who was a great lover of Israel. One morning, while looking out his window, he saw a poor Jew driving his horses and wagon through the mud. The Rabbi saw that the man had his tefillin on his arm and forehead and was reciting the morning prayers.

"Rabbi Levi Yitzchak spoke to God and said, 'Lord of the Universe, do you see how devout your people are? Even while going through the mud with their wagons, they pray to you!'"

Rabbi Steinsaltz then said, "To someone else, this praying would seem irreverent. Rabbi Levi Yitzchak himself would never have considered reciting his prayers while doing other things and certainly not while pulling horses.

"But he was able to put himself in the other man's place, transferring his point of view to that of another person and his way of life."

I have been watching Rabbi Steinsaltz "tie his shoelaces" for years. He is always attentive to his questioners. He never makes anyone feel that a question is foolish. Although his answers are sometimes lengthy and even sometimes seem to work their way around and around the question, he always gets to the heart of the matter. Sometimes he doesn't accept the terms of the question, and he patiently explains why, reframing the question and then giving a brilliant answer.

He is almost always polite, though occasionally sharp or blunt. He is far tougher on Orthodox Jews than on non-Orthodox Jews and Gentiles. ("I don't like how smug Orthodox Jews often are," he once told me.)

⧉ Teaching the Rabbi's Wisdom ⧉

As soon as the English volumes of Rabbi Steinsaltz's Talmud began to appear, I eagerly started to study them. I had discovered long before that the best way to learn something is to teach it, so I began looking for opportunities to teach, using Rabbi Steinsaltz's edition.

Teaching and lecturing about the Talmud was not new to me. Years earlier, in the late 1970s, shortly after I began exploring the Talmud, I wrote up some research that I had done, using secondary sources, on the question of what Jewish tradition says about giving money to street people who ask for change. I called the study "I Can't Read Much Hebrew, I Can't Read Much Aramaic, I Never Went to Yeshiva, but I Study Talmud Every Chance I Get."

The subtitle was "Brother, Can You Spare a Dime? The Treatment of Beggars According to Jewish Tradition: A Case in Point."

The title was a long way of saying that I wanted to show how I did my research, and the subject that I chose was giving money to beggars.

Jewish traditional literature happens to be filled with teachings on the subject, with great lessons and stories about every question you can imagine. What if you suspect that the beggar is a fake? Be thankful for the beggar, say the Talmudic sages. They keep us in the habit of giving.

How much should you give to a beggar? Maimonides says a small coin to everyone. What if you think they are going to buy something other than food with your donation? It's not your business, say the sages.

The study was published in *Moment* magazine.[3] As a result, and because I already had a reputation as a speaker about Jewish genealogy on the Jewish lecture circuit, I began to get invitations from synagogues and other Jewish organizations to speak about the Talmud.

Speak about the Talmud? Me?

I knew very little about the Talmud in those days. In fact, my entire study about giving money to street beggars was done using quotation dictionaries, indexes to reference books, and even sources that quoted from other sources. The point of publishing my research was to show that if someone like me was hungry enough to dig out Jewish sources on questions of immediate interest and relevance, it was possible, using only English-language secondary sources, to discover quite a bit of wonderful material.

But I Don't Know Anything About the Talmud

One of my questions during my very first meeting with Rabbi Steinsaltz was about these invitations to lecture on the Talmud.

I said to him, "I wrote an article in *Moment* magazine on what I found in secondary sources on the subject of what Jewish sages say about giving money to beggars. And as a result of the published article, synagogues are asking me to speak to their congregations about the Talmud. I don't know anything about the Talmud. What should I do?"

Rabbi Steinsaltz said to me, "Be careful."

"That's all?" I said, somewhat puzzled.

"Be as careful as you can. Try to be careful when you check your sources," he said.

I expected Rabbi Steinsaltz to suggest that I might want to recommend that someone else be the speaker or that I start immediately to improve my knowledge. But he didn't. Instead, he clarified, "If you are in a room with all blind people and all you have is one eye, and that one eye is not even so good, you are still the sight. My advice is to work hard and do your best."

From the outside, this might not seem like such a monumental question. But I count it among the hugely important first eleven questions that I brought to my very first meeting with Rabbi Steinsaltz, because it reflected a much larger issue.

I wasn't always comfortable teaching Torah. Who am *I*? What makes *me* qualified? Who gave *me* permission to teach Torah?

But I have come to learn that there is a difference between Jewish culture and American culture in a rather revealing way. In American culture, there is no requirement to learn the law. The average American citizen does not study law. And yet ignorance of the law is no excuse. In Jewish culture, it is just the opposite. We are required to study the law all of our lives. And yet in Jewish law, ignorance of the law is often surely an excuse.

So as a Jew, I am required to study our texts and our wisdom—luckily, I love doing it. And so if there is some wisdom or knowledge or understanding I can pass on to others, why not do so?

Many times over the years, I have been asked why I never became a rabbi. (Given the way I look, with my *kippah* and beard, people all too often call me "rabbi.") And my answer is always the same: one does not need to be a rabbi to study Torah or to teach Torah.

But when I first met Rabbi Steinsaltz, I needed a little push from him. I needed permission to know that I didn't need permission—to learn Torah and to teach Torah.

The number of requests that I come to synagogues to teach people what I knew about the Talmud kept increasing. And when the Random House edition began to appear, I was asked to teach how to use Rabbi Steinsaltz's Talmud.

NOTES FROM THE ROAD:
Pregnant Times

This afternoon, at a lecture, Rabbi Steinsaltz said, "In geology, there are breaking lines between huge blocks of earth. In the same way, today we are at the juncture between great blocks of time.

This is a time of great storms—and of becoming. Today, a small act can have far-reaching consequences. This is precisely the meaning of "pregnant times": anything can be born. This is exactly the time when one must not sleep.

At a certain point, the Aleph Society, which coordinates Rabbi Steinsaltz's activities in the United States and raises funds for his many projects, agreed that it would call me the "coordinator of the Talmud Circle Project." The Talmud Circle Project, since then and still now, is the name for my efforts, and the efforts of the Aleph Society, to get people to study Talmud.

The term *Talmud circle* was Rabbi Steinsaltz's idea. When I asked him to define a Talmud circle, he said, "A Talmud circle is any two or more people who get together to learn Talmud." I am pleased to say that many Talmud circles have sprung up around the country as a result of these efforts.

✌ Teaching the *Rose* Book ✌

Rabbi Steinsaltz refers to *The Thirteen Petalled Rose* as "the *Rose* book." It wasn't surprising that I started to get invitations to teach about that book as well. I have given several ten-week courses at synagogues in the New York area over the years on *The Thirteen Petalled Rose*.

The highlight for me came when I was invited by a rabbi of a synagogue in upstate New York to offer a unique seminar on the book.

The rabbi had taken a class of mine on *The Thirteen Petalled Rose* at a weeklong retreat. He then invited me to speak about the book to his congregation, as a launch for a study of this book of Kabbalah by Rabbi Steinsaltz.

After several months of study on the part of many of the congregants, the rabbi invited me back for a weekend scholar-in-residence event, where I would once again teach *The Thirteen Petalled Rose* to the members of the congregation. The final event of the weekend, scheduled for two hours on Sunday morning, had me sitting before the congregation answering questions about the book.

The first questioner asked, "How would you recommend a person begin to study this book?"

I once heard Rabbi Steinsaltz give a talk on the observation that Jewish books don't begin at the beginning. It is said that even the Torah does not begin at the beginning but rather begins with the second letter, the *bet,* and speaks of God *creating* "the beginning," implying a time, in a sense, "before the beginning."

Rabbi Steinsaltz points out, I said, that there is perhaps only one book in Jewish history that actually does begin at the beginning, and logically and orderly goes on to the end, and that is the *Mishneh Torah* of Maimonides, who was known as the Rambam.

As Rabbi Steinsaltz once said to me, "The greatest critic of the Rambam, the Raavad, had to concede points when it came to the Rambam's structure of the *Mishneh Torah. He began at the beginning.*"

I told the congregation that Rabbi Steinsaltz said to me, "I think the *Mishneh Torah* of the Rambam is really the only Jewish book that is well organized. All other books have the tendency—which I rather like—of beginning somewhere in the middle. As you go on, you may find that the beginning is somewhere near the end. In the Rambam's book, one thing is very clear: the Rambam is well organized. The order of the book is in itself a marvelous thing.

"But generally speaking, Jewish books don't begin at the beginning."

I said to the congregation that over the years, I've recommended to people that when reading *The Thirteen Petalled Rose,* do not start at the beginning. The first chapter assumes some knowledge and some information that you don't get until you read some of the other chapters.

A woman in the audience spoke up and said, "It sounds like the Talmud. Just begin anywhere."

"That's exactly right, " I said. "*The Thirteen Petalled Rose,* like other great Jewish books and like the Talmud, is a work that you have to just jump into, and then you swim around and around.

"The Talmud is called 'a sea.' Seas don't have beginnings; you just jump in. Sooner or later you go around and around and around and you get back to where you began, having picked up, along the way, sufficient insight to now be able to navigate more smoothly and to understand things that you never even noticed the first time around, let alone the second or third or tenth time around."

I pointed out to the congregation that this is a crucial piece of information for the serious student of Jewish tradition. Jewish books do not begin at the beginning. And a corollary to that statement is the notion that Kabbalah needs to be chewed on, worked at, and invested in. The abstract, spiritual, lofty ideas of Kabbalah need to be entangled with the concrete details of the *mitzvot,* the holy acts and prohibitions.

Not History, Not Laws, Just Abstract Ideas

I was impressed by this Reform congregation and its commitment to studying Rabbi Steinsaltz's books. At least sixty people had been seriously studying *The Thirteen Petalled Rose* for the better part of a year. They were not Orthodox Jews, not Hasidim, but rather Reform Jews from the suburbs who fell in love with Torah study in general and Rabbi Steinsaltz's work in particular.

An elderly man stood up and asked, "How did the book come about?"

I replied that I have been told by the editor of *The Thirteen Petalled Rose,* Jonathan Omer-Man, and by the translator of the original Hebrew manuscript, the amazingly talented Yehuda Hanegbi, since deceased, that *The Thirteen Petalled Rose* was

Rabbi Steinsaltz's response to a series of questions and that all of the questions that Rabbi Steinsaltz was given could be summed up in one question, which is "What are the basic, fundamental theological ideas that hold up the entire edifice that is Judaism?"

I also explained that in my opinion, we have a great many books that give us the rich, long history of the Jewish people in its glorious and tragic detail; we have lots of books about Jewish customs and practices in all of their variety and volume. Rabbi Steinsaltz was asked to write a book of essences. What are the essential ideas that constitute the underpinning of the whole edifice, the foundation of the whole of Jewish thought and belief?

A woman raised her hand and ask me whether there had been any criticism of *The Thirteen Petalled Rose*. "We love the book," she said. "But are there any other viewpoints?"

I pointed out that *The Thirteen Petalled Rose,* like the *Mishneh Torah* of the Rambam centuries ago, has no footnotes. And both works have been criticized for this. Rabbi Steinsaltz gives us 180 pages on the subject of the essence of Jewish thought and makes no reference to any other books. I then held up the brand-new Hebrew edition of the book that had just been published and pointed out that it includes footnotes for every idea contained in the book.

A teenager who was in the congregation asked the next question. "Is it true that *The Thirteen Petalled Rose* is a book of Kabbalah?"

It was my chance to give a lesson in the subject area of my postgraduate degree, library science. I pointed out that like most books published in the United States, *The Thirteen Petalled Rose* has, on the copyright page, something known as the CIP, the U.S. Library of Congress's cataloging-in-publishing data. Most publishers use the Library of Congress to catalog its books for library use. The CIP data in *The Thirteen Petalled Rose* indicate that the subject heading the Library of Congress librarian

One never really extricates oneself from the context of the issue, Who am I? And from its corollaries: Where do I come from? Where am I going? What for? Why?

—Rabbi Adin Steinsaltz, *The Thirteen Petalled Rose,*
   p. 139

assigned to the book is "Cabala"—an unusual but not unknown alternate spelling of Kabbalah.

Not that the Library of Congress is the final authority, but it is interesting to see that the librarians at the Library of Congress recognize a book of Kabbalah without the word *Kabbalah* even being mentioned in it!

I told the congregation that as I grew up, the only references I ever saw in the many secondary sources that I read about Kabbalah implied that Kabbalah was some obscure branch of Jewish thought and that I heard you had to be forty years old, married, and steeped in Torah to even begin to glance at it. By writing and publishing a book like *The Thirteen Petalled Rose,* which as Rabbi Steinsaltz describes is based on the structures and assumptions of Kabbalah and deals largely with the theological system as described in Kabbalistic writings, the Rabbi is telling me not only that it is permissible to study Kabbalah but perhaps that it is essential.

The Thirteen Petalled Rose is not a book *about* Kabbalah. It is not a research paper on the history of Kabbalah, nor is it a secondary source that quotes some other secondary source that quotes still another secondary source on Kabbalah. Rather, *The*

Thirteen Petalled Rose is a book *of* Kabbalah, a book that itself has become a source, not due to any arrogance on the part of the author but rather due to a great desire on the author's part to share the wisdom of the ages and the sages with his people.

"A Little Book for the Soul"

An attorney stood up and said, "In *The Thirteen Petalled Rose,* Rabbi Steinsaltz teaches that the human form, down to its most minute detail, is divine revelation. In other words, by contemplating the detail of the human body, its structure, and the relations between and among its parts, one's understanding, one's comprehension of the divine comes more clearly into focus." The attorney paused and then said, "Am I understanding that correctly?"

I pointed out that Rabbi Steinsaltz writes, "The structure of man is a paradigm of the structure of the worlds. Man may be viewed as a symbol or model of the divine essence, his entire outer and inner structure manifesting relationships and different aspects existing in that supreme essence."[4]

This question also gave me the opportunity to mention one of my favorite ideas from the Talmud. "One of the details of the human body is known as the philtrum," I said, "the indentation on our upper lip, just below our nose. The Talmud offers a teaching about the philtrum, and so does Rabbi Steinsaltz in his introduction to *The Thirteen Petalled Rose.*

"The Talmud teaches that before we are born, while still in our mother's womb, a lamp, held by an angel, shines over the baby's head and in whose light we learn the entire Torah and can see 'from one end of the universe to the other.' Before we are born and sent into this world, the angel taps the baby on its mouth, creating the philtrum and also causing the baby to forget what it had learned."

Life is not a process of learning something new but rather of remembering what one already knows (Niddah 30b).

In his Introduction to *The Thirteen Petalled Rose,* Rabbi Steinsaltz writes, "This little book is a book for the soul. It begins, quite deliberately (and perhaps to the dismay of some readers), with a view of another reality. It does not proceed from this world, or from the familiar ways of man in our society. Instead, it seeks to go from the genuine center of all being to the world and to human life. There is no attempt here to speak of Judaism, to prove its worth or to justify it; rather, to let the message communicate itself. And if a person permits his soul to listen, the soul will soon learn that all it needs to do is remember. Because in some dim and enigmatic way, it already knows all this."[5]

The rabbi of the congregation spoke up and asked me if I would share how I had been studying *The Thirteen Petalled Rose* with Rabbi Steinsaltz over the years.

I explained that many times over the years, when I was driving Rabbi Steinsaltz to his appointments, a copy of *The Thir-*

NOTES FROM THE ROAD:
Comment by an Anonymous Blogger

I have just completed reading *The Thirteen Petalled Rose* by Adin Steinsaltz. Though I have devoted more thought per page to this book than I have to any other in recent memory, I am at a loss to describe this remarkable book's description of existence. I welcome thoughts from others who have read this remarkable but unknown gem of Jewish literature.

teen Petalled Rose sat between us in the car. There were times, at the beginning, when I chipped away at a word, a phrase, a sentence, a paragraph at a time. And there were other times that I was able to pick up speed. I'd gone around and around and around the book countless times. From time to time, I'd ask him about a phrase or a sentence or an idea or a concept or a chapter.

We never actually sat and looked at the text together. I'd quote a phrase or an idea or make a certain reference to something and he'd know immediately what I was referring to and we'd chat about it.

A young man who said he was seventeen asked me if there was anything in *The Thirteen Petalled Rose* that is similar to Eastern religions. I smiled and told him that during my very first meeting with Rabbi Steinsaltz, he and I spoke about that very subject. I asked the young man what it was about Eastern religions he liked, and he replied, "The yin-yang symbol. It is a symbol of balance. Does Jewish tradition have the idea of balance?"

With a big smile on my face, I explained that in *The Thirteen Petalled Rose,* Rabbi Steinsaltz writes, "Jewish thought pays little attention to inner tranquility and peace of mind. The feeling of 'behold, I've arrived' could well undermine the capacity to continue, suggesting as it does that the Infinite can be reached in a finite number of steps. In fact, the very concept of the Divine as infinite implies an activity that is endless, of which one must never grow weary."[6]

I went on to say that I was delighted to learn, when I encountered *The Thirteen Petalled Rose* and looked through the ten chapters, that one of them was about the Jewish view on balance. The chapter is called "The Way of Choice." Rabbi Steinsaltz writes about proper balance but not as just the middle way, an artificial middle way. Balance is being aware, as aware as you can be, of every situation and then adding your own particular contribution to create the correct harmony or balance for that moment.

So what you give to a situation is sometimes more and sometimes less, based on what you perceive as the need of that specific and unique situation.

God Created Good *and* Evil

I quoted from the book. "Rabbi Steinsaltz writes, 'As a general rule, there are no attributes of the soul that are good or bad. As the sages have said, there is no attribute that lacks its injurious aspect, its negation and failure, just as there is no attribute—even if connected with doubt and heresy—that has not, under some circumstances, its holy aspect.'"[7]

In other words, I explained, one of the basic ideas as set forth in *The Thirteen Petalled Rose* is that unlike other religious traditions that put love on a higher plane than hate, and unlike those who think that emotions and feelings have a hierarchy with some being "better" than others, Jewish theology has a different approach.

Once again I quoted from the book. "Rabbi Steinsaltz continues, 'From this point of view, the good and bad qualities are not set opposite one another, with love always on the side of the good and the other qualities always on the side of the bad. Rather all the attributes, all the emotions, and all the potentialities of the heart and personality are set on the same level and considered good or bad, not according to some judgment of their intrinsic worth, but according to the way they are used.'"[8]

Once Rabbi Steinsaltz said to me, "In fact, everything has something good in it. If not, it could not really exist. The question is always just how much good, or perhaps what proportion of good to evil. There are some things that can release positive qualities and others that cannot. For example, the chemical element aluminum, one of the most common components in earth and clay, can be extracted with a great deal of difficulty and only from relatively rare bauxite. Bauxite will release the aluminum, while other substances will not."

❧ A Question with No Answer ❧

I explained to the congregation that in my own relationship with Rabbi Steinsaltz, I'd tried to seek a certain kind of balance. There were times when I had so many questions for him, I couldn't wait to see him and to somehow or other weave my personal and theological questions into the conversation. At other times, I'd be quieter and perfectly happy carrying his bags and checking him into his hotel and getting him to wherever he needed to go and not trotting out all of my own stuff.

When Rabbi Steinsaltz visited the United States a year earlier, I decided on my drive to the airport that during this trip, I would keep my mouth shut. I would not talk about my personal problems or my theological issues; I would just carry his bags and get him to his destinations.

On that particular trip, he came to New York for about seven days, and then made a couple of side trips for a day or so to Chicago, Miami, and one other place, giving talks and classes and meeting with community leaders and others.

During that week, I clung to my commitment. I carried his bags, I checked him into his hotel, we went here and there as his schedule dictated, and I did my job. I didn't bring up anything personal.

Finally, at the end of the seven days, on our way back to JFK for the return flight to Israel, I started to chafe under my own restrictions. I was carrying his suitcase, and we were walking toward the El Al terminal when suddenly I blurted out, "Rabbi Steinsaltz, I have a question."

I reminded Rabbi Steinsaltz that I was divorced and that my three children lived a few streets away from me. I also told him that I saw my children all the time, so much that they insisted that I see them more than most of their friends' parents who are married and live in the same home.

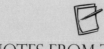

NOTES FROM THE ROAD:
Insanity

This morning, Rabbi Steinsaltz and I were talking about insanity. He suggested that it may be impossible to define the term adequately. He told me about a man who lives in Jerusalem and is known by many people because one can often see him playing his fiddle at hospitals. "People generally don't know that he's a very successful attorney, but his real mission in life, he feels, is to play his fiddle at hospitals. One might think, from looking at him, that he's crazy."

I get it. He may be more sane than most of us.

Rabbi Steinsaltz said to me that there is a paradox concerning the nature of a fool. Sometimes a reason for folly is knowing too much.

"This is one reason why children are often wise. They have natural humility; they can absorb things better and not critically." Rabbi Steinsaltz said that among modern physicists, the creative and innovative periods have been in their youth. "During the rest of their careers, they elaborate on and teach about their original ideas."

And then I said, "What is my responsibility to my family? I travel around so much. Should I be home more?"

Rabbi Steinsaltz looked at me and said, "Well, there is a story in the Talmud of the student who was away from his wife all year to be with his teacher, except for one particular year, he was home on the eve of Yom Hakippurim, because he wasn't feeling well."

We kept on walking to the El Al terminal. I looked at him and said, "I'm asking you what my responsibility is to my family, and you are telling me of someone who is away from his family *the entire year,* except for one particular year when he was home *because he wasn't feeling well?* I don't understand. What does that mean?"

He said to me, "It means that there is no answer to your question. Sometimes, a person has to be home with his family every day. And for someone else, his family is better off if he stays away a little bit more often."

ᘑᕘ More About Good and Evil ᘑᕘ

The next time Rabbi Steinsaltz came to the United States, I saw him only briefly. My sole task, as has often been the case over the years, was to pick him up early in the morning at JFK and get him to his first appointment.

Sometimes I feel guilty, almost jumping on him as soon as he gets into my car, sending my questions his way. I actually suspect that I am not very aggressive about it. But I always feel that I have an agenda far different from just getting Rabbi Steinsaltz to his appointments on time.

For example, I was eager to follow up with the Rabbi on a point of theology. So there I was, 6:30 in the morning, asking him about good and evil.

At a certain point in the conversation, Rabbi Steinsaltz said, "Bad qualities are not necessarily absolute qualities of the soul. They are like modes of expression. For instance, it is said that while depression is evil, a little melancholy is possibly a good thing; in the same way that, while joy is certainly positive, excessive good spirits can be dangerous. It is not the specific qualities; it is the right measure, the correct application. So even love or even compassion can be bad if used in the wrong time or place."

Every pharmacist knows this, I suggested.

"Yes, poisons, when used in certain doses, become medicines."

He then added, "And the other way around. It depends on the use made of them, on the relationship with other things, not on anything intrinsic."

"So we have to make judgments constantly?" I asked.

"Yes. One does have to judge things all the time. We need to investigate matters deeply. Every person and situation has to be examined in the context of the surrounding reality."

"So we assume that God creates everything, even evil?" I asked.

Rabbi Steinsaltz rarely quotes from holy books. He quotes from Dickens, from Lewis Carroll, from Mark Twain, from a broad range of world literature, past and present, but rarely from Scripture. But at that moment he made a rare exception and said, "It says it there in the book of Isaiah, "Who forms light and creates darkness, who makes peace and who creates evil. I am God. I do all these things" (Isaiah 45:7).

When Rabbi Steinsaltz came to the United States the next time, once again my only responsibility was to pick him up and get him to his first appointment.

But once again I took advantage of the situation by discussing a subject of interest. I asked him to explain more about what he meant during his last trip when he said that the Talmud and Kabbalah are really the same.

"Is that indeed what you said?" I asked.

Rabbi Steinsaltz smiled and said, "The commonly held view, that Kabbalah and Talmud are in and about different worlds, is a misconception. It is simply not true. There is an organic unity of the whole. The Kabbalah and the Talmud are different forms of expression of the same thing, but each in its own way."

He then added, "There was never a real separation between the daily obligations that we do and the esoteric or mystical aspects of the tradition. They have always been connected. They are different aspects of the same thing. There was never a separation of any real consequence between Kabbalah and the Talmud. They have always been connected."

I had found a passage in his book *The Essential Talmud* that made the same point, and while we were stopped at a traffic light, I quickly read it to him:

> It should not be assumed . . . that there were two separate areas of "revealed" and "hidden" material. To a certain extent, these were thought of as components of the all-embracing Torah. A well-rounded disciple who absorbed his rabbi's teachings also learned esoteric wisdom. This close connection between prosaic and esoteric matters is one of the outstanding characteristics of Jewish esoteric literature in general. The Jewish mystic is not detached from the Halakhah and practical questions; on the contrary, the halakhic expert is often also a mystic, and the kabbalist studies legal and mystic matters with the same degree of enthusiasm.[9]

Rabbi Steinsaltz then said to me, "There is the story of Rabbi Shimshon of Ostropol. He was a well-known Kabbalist and writer of some famous books on Kabbalah. He decided one day to write a Kabbalistic commentary on the Talmud. He wanted to explain all of the secret meanings in the Talmud.

"He was a great scholar and worked hard at it and finally finished it. He then put the book to what is called 'the test of a dream.' And the answer he received was that his book was far too elaborate and long.

"So he shortened it and again asked that a critique be revealed in his dream. The answer was exactly the same. It is too long a book. Again he cut it down, and again he received the answer that his book was still not precise enough.

"When finally he had made it as concise as he could, he found that what he had basically written was *Perush Rashi,* the accepted commentary on the Talmud."

Saying the Same Thing in Different Ways

I then reminded him of a comment of his that I loved. He said that people often say that the Bible is the *pshat* (literal) and that the Zohar, the great work of Kabbalah, is the *sod* (secret), but it can also be seen the other way: the Bible is *sod:* the secrets are hidden in the text. The Zohar is *pshat:* the secrets are right there on the surface. I wanted to know if I remembered it right.

He said that I did. Then he added, "All the parts of the Torah are, in fact, connected with each other in a way that is organic. They are just like parts of the same thing that are inter-connected. If I try to cut off one of these, it's not just that I am maiming the thing. I am doing something worse. When I try to disconnect one part of it, it is no longer Torah.

"One of the points, a very important one, is that if what I speak is correct halakhically (legally), it is also correct from a Kabbalistic point of view. It is sometimes a matter of what language you want to speak, but the thing is basically identical. I am just changing languages. It's like translating things. All the parts are interconnected. Taking out one part is not just maiming it but is in fact destroying it."

Rabbi Steinsaltz went on, "It's like having the most complex machine, a machine that is made of thousands of parts, like having a rocket that has to get to heaven. It was in the news not many years ago. It was made of thousands, many thousands of parts. And one of them was faulty. So it didn't get into the sky. It burned up. It was nothing but a disaster.

"It is the same way with the Torah: you take one part out of it, and won't get to heaven. It will be the same disaster. So the notion of the completeness is a part of the understanding of what Torah means.

"When people speak about the world of the Kabbalah and the revealed world of, say, the Talmud, the notion that they are two different and distinct worlds is a mistake. They are two sides of exactly the same thing. They are just expressed in different formats."

So I asked Rabbi Steinsaltz if he could give me a concise explanation that I could share with people who are always asking me why Kabbalah was never a part of their Jewish education.

Rabbi Steinsaltz said, "The terms *Ashkenazi* and *Sephardi* are very loose terms, not precise. But we can say that one of the distinctions between the Jewish communities of the West, meaning European or what's called Ashkenazi Jews, and Jews of Asia and Africa, or what's called Sephardi Jews, is that in the world of the non-Ashkenzi Jews, Kabbalah is far more open and far more used.

"In every Sephardi *siddur* [prayer book], you see Kabbalistic formulas that are there for everybody. In an Ashkenazi *siddur,* you hardly ever find them. There are historical reasons. And it is due mostly to the tragedy of Shabbetai Tzvi, which in many ways hit Ashkenazi Jewry far more harshly. And there was a fear of dealing with Kabbalah in an open way. So Ashkenazi Jewry became, I would say, a little bit weary and a little bit afraid of dealing with this whole subject.

"Sephardi Jewry never had this shock, this trauma. And therefore it continued in the same way. If you look, say, at the commentaries of the *Shulchan Aruch,* you'll find a commentary like that of the Magen Avraham that is full of Kabbalah. He lived just before that period, and he was not scared of using Kabbalistic terminology. When you find books written later, they are, so to say, slightly or more than slightly scared of the experience. So they don't use the terminology. They don't use Kabbalistic terminology, but they use other forms."

So I asked, "Why is the study of Kabbalah discouraged by some?"

"It is not because Kabbalah in particular is dangerous but because people should be advised not to deal with subjects that they don't know. A little knowledge is a very dangerous thing in every field.

"Now, sometimes people want to play with the esoteric, which is not Torah. It's something that they think they can play with and not have to be serious about. When people want to play with Kabbalah, they will damage themselves, and the same thing will happen if they want to play with halakhah and if they want to play with Talmud because the thing has to be taken seriously.

"The real danger is not in the field of knowledge. The real danger is of being not educated and being foolish enough to make decisions and to play with things that people don't understand.

"As a young man, I used to work in a laboratory, doing all kinds of chemical experiments. And I can tell you that I know how a little knowledge can become dangerous. You shouldn't dabble with too many of those things because the thing that you are playing with may be, say, potassium cyanide, or it may be some explosive material."

NOTES FROM THE ROAD:
Jewish Mysticism

Rabbi Herbert Weiner, a Reform rabbi who wrote a groundbreaking book on Kabbalah titled *Nine and a Half Mystics,* writes of his encounters with Rabbi Steinsaltz back in the 1960s. He reports that at one point, he asked Rabbi Steinsaltz for a definition of Jewish mysticism. The next day, Rabbi Steinsaltz handed him the following handwritten note:

> The goal of Jewish mysticism is the effort (combined with the practice) to come close to things, a yearning for identification. This yearning includes all things, small and large, but its special goal is an identification with the innermost aspect of everything—the Divine. Mysticism, therefore, is the desire to remove the outer coverings of things which hide their inner quality. Only through finding innerness in our life, as well as the innerness of all things, will this desire for full identification enjoy any kind of gratification. It is possible, therefore, to perceive two processes at work in mysticism. First, an activity which is mainly speculative—that is, the intellectual effort to remove the shells of reality. Second, the activity by which, after the removal of the outer coverings, one binds oneself to the truth. These two processes make up, respectively, the philosophy and practice of mysticism.[10]

❧ **Threads Running Through the Text** ❧

As time went on, I began to receive regular invitations from synagogues asking for lectures or adult education programs using *The Thirteen Petalled Rose* as a text. The book is, after all, the most authentic Kabbalistic text ever published in English. As its reputation spread, more and more people were discovering its special contents and style.

In my studies of Rabbi Aryeh Kaplan's commentary on his translation of the Kabbalistic book titled *Sefer Bahir,* Rabbi Kaplan says that the correct way to study a Kabbalistic text is to discover the "threads" that run through the book.

In other words, sometimes the most important topics in a book are not in the table of contents but rather appear almost constantly throughout each chapter, like threads that run through the whole work. Some ideas seem to appear throughout a book and are so basic that they just become assumed as part of the general backdrop to the subject at hand.

In my study of *The Thirteen Petalled Rose,* reading it again and again, I have discovered that in addition to the countless insights and dazzling ideas in the book, there are indeed threads that run through the work, that in some ways are more basic than the somewhat deceptive table of contents.

I discovered what I thought were three important threads, important for me at least, that run through *The Thirteen Petalled Rose,* three subjects that don't have their own chapters but that seem to appear in almost every chapter someplace or other as an assumption that helps hold up the entire edifice of thought. I remembered the words of Rabbi Kaplan that the only way to study a Kabbalistic text is to recognize the threads, and lo and behold, these three threads began to appear and take form.

Early one morning, seated in my car on the way from the airport to Rabbi Steinsaltz's first appointment, I had between us my current copy of *The Thirteen Petalled Rose* and six sheets of notes. The notes were in fact not really notes on the text but rather quotes of sentences that I had selected from the text and assigned to one of the three categories reflecting the three threads that I had begun to identify. I was eager to share these observations with Rabbi Steinsaltz and ask him if indeed these were the kind of threads that Rabbi Kaplan was referring to.

Encountering Paradoxes

The first thread that seems to consistently run through the text is a paradox. Now I learned a long time ago that when you encounter a paradox, it means you're going in the right direction.

My friend Richard and I once found ourselves, as teenagers, sitting on beach chairs that reclined all the way back in his parent's yard one starry summer night. Richard and I, looking up at the sky, were dazzled by the stars.

We began to have that conversation about whether the sky ends or not. And one of us would say, "The sky goes on forever and ever. It never ends."

The other would say, "How can that be? How can it never end? How is it possible for something to never end? It's got to end."

And the first person would say, "What? Is there a brick wall at the end? That's impossible; there's got to be something on the other side of the wall. The universe never ends."

Our conversation went back and forth until at one point, Richard, who ultimately went on to become a professional actor (you might recognize his face from a popular Brawny paper towel commercial and a Fruit of the Loom commercial where he plays one of the pieces of fruit on the label!) fell off the chair deliberately like a clown and said, "Goodbye," as if to say, "This conversation has blown my mind. I can't contain it any longer."

Over the years, when Richard and I get together and find ourselves talking about certain subjects that bring us to some paradox, he and I at some point will look at each other and one of us will mimic that clownlike gesture from years before and we fall off our chairs and say goodbye, as if to say that at a certain point, the mind can't contain the paradox.

What I did not know back when Richard and I were looking at the stars as teenagers but I do know now is that he and I were having a theological discussion. We were trying to grasp the infinite. We were trying with our finite beings to grasp the infinite; itself a paradox.

At a certain point on the spiritual path, one sees that encountering a paradox is a sign that you are going in the right direction. Rabbi Steinsaltz once said to me, "A paradox is not an absurdity. There is a vast difference."

Beyond Understanding

The first thread of *The Thirteen Petalled Rose* is the thread that I call "what is beyond understanding." I have noticed that in some way or other, Rabbi Steinsaltz includes, in many of the chapters of the book, the notion that the subject under discussion is beyond our grasp.

So, for example, in the third chapter, titled "The Soul of Man," Rabbi Steinsaltz is discussing the soul and at a certain point makes it clear that the nature of the soul cannot be grasped by human comprehension.

In his chapter called "Holiness," Rabbi Steinsaltz makes it clear that the very term *holiness* implies that it is beyond our grasp, beyond our understanding, beyond anything the human mind can conceive of, that *holiness* is, by definition, "distinctly other."

In his chapter called "Torah," Rabbi Steinsaltz makes it clear that it is impossible to define *Torah*. In his chapter "Divine Manifestation," Rabbi Steinsaltz makes it clear that it is impossible, by definition, to conceive of the subject in any way whatsoever and that there is a gap that humans, even at the highest level, cannot bridge.

But while the subjects we are dealing with are beyond our understanding, we pursue those subjects anyway. We learn, paradoxically, that to acknowledge the impossibility of grasping the subject ultimately becomes a great advantage in making progress toward a better and more complete understanding of it.

As Rabbi Steinsaltz writes, "If you think you've arrived, you are lost." Over and over again, Rabbi Steinsaltz urges the reader to acknowledge that the pursuit of the answers to our ultimate questions requires us to acknowledge the impossibility of grasping what we are seeking.

Levels of Consciousness

A second thread in *The Thirteen Petalled Rose* is one that I labeled "levels of consciousness." The book, which came out in 1980, was the only book about Judaism that I had encountered in English that dealt with the subject of consciousness. No other author had dealt with the question. But here, in Rabbi Steinsaltz's introduction to the essentials of Jewish thought, the subject of consciousness is a major thread running throughout the book.

It's no surprise that, as the statistics indicate, a disproportionate number of American Jews are involved in other religions and spiritual pursuits. The Jewish spiritual seeker all too often when exploring Judaism does not encounter a spiritual path but rather, as Rabbi Steinsaltz describes it, "heaps and heaps of unrelated facts."

The Rabbi goes on to say that often education winds up obfuscating rather than clarifying. Jewish spiritual seekers who read books on Jewish thought and practice encounter so many items of history and custom and law that they can barely find a trace of spirituality or practices reflecting inner work, the work of consciousness. But there it is, time after time, in *The Thirteen Petalled Rose*.

Opening Oneself

The third thread I call "opening oneself." Throughout the book, over and over again, Rabbi Steinsaltz indicates that the spiritual path requires one to lend oneself to the subject. The posture we are to take is not one of tightly folded arms or an attitude of "prove it to me."

Rather, as Rabbi Steinsaltz repeatedly urges, it is important for us to lend ourselves in the process of discovery, to taste in order to know from the inside, as an experience and not just as a topic to try to grasp. One cannot know Shabbat, for example, from the outside. No amount of reading or studying about the Sabbath can compare to the simple experience of the Sabbath, but one needs to lend oneself to it.

By Doing, We Will Understand

There is an often quoted line from the Torah regarding this. When the children of Israel accept the Torah, they say, *na'aseh v'nishmah,* often translated as "We will do and we will understand," "We will do and we will hear" (Exodus 24:7).

In other words, this notion of first doing and then understanding is the opposite of what we often do, of the stance we often take. We often say, "Explain it to me, and then I'll do it" or "Prove it to me first, and then I'll do it." But the children of Israel said the opposite. They said first, "We will do it, and then we will understand it."

Pop Culture Kabbalah

Newspaper and magazine reporters occasionally raise questions about spirituality and the popularization of Kabbalah when interviewing Rabbi Steinsaltz.

To one reporter, the Rabbi replied, "There are people in America, in Israel, and in other countries who are selling Kab-

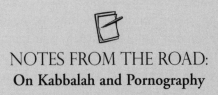

NOTES FROM THE ROAD:
On Kabbalah and Pornography

Tonight, someone asked Rabbi Steinsaltz about the popularization of Kabbalah in great part due to celebrity involvements, most notably that of the singer and actress Madonna.

Rabbi Steinsaltz said that the connection between pop-culture Kabbalah and the real thing "is the relationship between pornography and love. Pornography is intrinsically soulless and doesn't have any obligations attached. It's just using externals. [Pop culture Kabbalists] are doing exactly the same thing."

balah. My low regard for this organization is one thing. But it goes much deeper. It is part of the interest in black magic. They take out of Kabbalah every part that has anything to do with obligation. I would call it freewheeling Kabbalah. These Kabbalah centers sell images of power without any obligation, without any future."

Drunkenness

One weekend, Rabbi Steinsaltz was the Shabbat scholar-in-residence at a particularly upper-class, fancy, and straight-laced Orthodox synagogue. Saturday night, after Shabbat was over,

Rabbi Steinsaltz was scheduled to deliver the final lecture. He came into the packed auditorium a little bit late. There was a buzz in the room that Rabbi Steinsaltz was not going to lecture. Instead, he was going to hold a *fabrengen*.

A *fabrengen* is a Hasidic gathering where one eats and drinks and sings religious songs and shares words of Torah. Rabbi Steinsaltz entered the room with a bunch of cups in one hand and a bottle of whiskey under his arm.

And as he walked through the aisles and passed out the cups to various individuals in the audience, he began to pour the whiskey and proceeded to give a lecture on the benefits of getting a little drunk. He spoke about the importance of sometimes almost losing your balance.

As people began to drink, he spoke eloquently on the subject of the necessity of instability in order for there to be growth, progress, change. He talked about airplanes and how safe the airplane is as it flies thirty thousand feet in the air. It's not stable when it's taking off, and it's not stable when it's landing. It is during those moments of shifting, of transition, from one realm to another, from the land to flying, from flying to the land, that there is a period of instability.

The instability is an essential part of the growth, the shift from one place to another. Change would not be possible if it weren't for that instability. Rabbi Steinsaltz talked about climbing a ladder: as you go up, the moment between rungs is a necessary moment of instability.

Trying to loosen up this very stiff audience, Rabbi Steinsaltz told the group that while he had been to many, many gatherings of Hasidim where there is a lot of drinking, he never saw a Hasid who was drunk or rowdy. The drink was merely a little help to get oneself a little unstable so that the words of Torah could enter and the spiritual songs penetrate.

It was a great evening.

❧ Rabbi Steinsaltz in China ❧

In 1996, Rabbi Steinsaltz was invited to give a lecture at the Academy of Social Sciences in Shanghai. It was part of a more extensive tour of China the Rabbi was making as a guest lecturer at academies and universities in Beijing, Shanghai, and Nanjing.

I was able to obtain a transcript of his talk to the academy. The lecture was titled "*Pirkei Avot* and Chinese Culture: A Comparative Survey."

Rabbi Steinsaltz has said, "The Chinese are convinced that they are the only cultured people in the world. Recently, we published with the Chinese Academy of Social Sciences a translation of the *Pirkei Avot* (Ethics of the Fathers), which is closer to Chinese philosophy than probably any other text. And although they probably have no idea how many we are, they started saying, 'You and us, the Jews and the Chinese, we are the only cultured people in the world.'"

Here is the transcript of the Rabbi's lecture and a few of the questions he was asked by the audience in Shanghai.

> "One initial remark about the title 'Rabbi': in our tradition, it does not designate a ritual position. Unlike a priest—Christian or Buddhist—it is a title given to a Jew who passes certain examinations, to prove that he is a scholar in Jewish subjects.
>
> *Pirkei Avot* is a small part—one of sixty—of a much larger collection, which itself is a part of an even larger series of books, created in the second classic period of our culture (roughly between the years 500 B.C.E. and 500 C.E.). This period began at the time of Confucius and went on for some thousand years, which in China ranges from the time of the Three Kingdoms up to the creation of the Great Empire Dynasties.

Pirkei Avot can be said to be second to the Bible in our classical heritage, because of its very special features. This book deals mainly with morals and ethics, and not so much with fate or religion. In our culture, as in yours, there are some organized books that deal with morality and ethics and outline a worldview. This book, however, is not an organized work about ethical subjects but rather a collection of sayings.

Although edited by one person around the year 200 C.E., it is the fruit of the thought not of one single person but rather of numerous Sages who lived over the course of some 500 years. Yet all of these sayings can, and should be, considered part of a philosophical unit. At the same time, it is obvious that not all of the Sages quoted here speak the same language or say exactly the same thing, and consequently one can find conflicting ideas.

One such instance is found in the fourth chapter of *Pirkei Avot,* paragraph 20: "Studying at a young age can be compared to something written in new ink, on a new sheet of paper. And studying at an old age can be compared to writing on old, reused paper."

The Sage who said this lived around the beginning of the Christian Era. A much later scholar says something similar, but not identical: "A person who learns from young people is like one who eats unripe grapes or drinks wine that has just been pressed. One who learns from old people is like a person who eats ripe grapes and drinks old wine." And a third Sage expressed an entirely different opinion: "Do not look at the container, but look at what is in it. For you may have a new container with good old wine in it and an old container which does not even have new wine."

On the one hand, this is the old problem of who are the masters of wisdom. On the other hand, it is also a very modern problem: Who is it that we should learn from? Is old age an advantage, or is it of no consequence whatsoever? Who should be the ruler of a country? Should he be an old wise man or a young and very modern person? Some say young people are not suitable because they are not ripe and inexperienced; others say that there is no direct correlation between age and wisdom; there can be very young people who are wise and very old people, whose only claim is that they happened to have been born earlier.

There are many more examples of different, even conflicting, ideas in *Pirkei Avot*. Yet despite that—and this is indeed one of the most remarkable aspects of this book—*Pirkei Avot* reflects a unified system of thinking, because it is a reflection of a culture.

I would like now to remark about a few points of similarity and dissimilarity between the Jewish and Chinese cultures.

At a first glance, *Pirkei Avot* looks very much like the collected sayings of Confucius: it has the same style and seems to have the same way of thinking. A more profound examination, however, will show that in fact it is more like the work of Menzius [an outstanding Confucian sage] in terms of its view of morality and of ethical values.

But in fact, in both details of style and the general way of thinking, *Pirkei Avot* bears an inner resemblance to the basic book of Dao. For one thing, *Pirkei Avot* uses a more poetical language, which is much fuller of parables and metaphors than that of Confucius and therefore more similar to that of Lao-tzu. In addition, unlike Confucius,

Pirkei Avot uses ways of thinking that are, in themselves, dialectical and paradoxical.

One string of paradoxes, which deal with the question of what comes before what, is found in chapter 3, paragraph 17: "Rabbi Elazar ben Azariah says, when there is no Torah there is no *derekh eretz;* when there is no *derekh eretz,* there is no Torah." Torah means learning and knowledge, the whole body of learning. *Derekh eretz* means the right conduct.

Derekh eretz is very important in both our cultures, for in both of them there exists a whole code of behavior, which is not necessarily connected with moral or religious conduct but rather deals with how a person should behave in society. This goes from seemingly simple and even trivial matters—such as who should enter or leave a room first, who sits at the head of the table, which hand to use for what functions, and so on—to more complex issues, such as what is the right relationship between young and old, pupil and master, man and woman, and so on. Or the significance of colors: in Chinese culture, yellow is of utmost importance and is always positive. In Western culture, its meaning is either unclear or negative. This difference is not only psychological but also cultural.

All of these details, however superficial they may seem, reflect basic philosophical notions about the universe. Therefore, in both cultures, *derekh eretz* fulfills a very important role not just in determining behavior in life in general but also for deeper guidance.

Let us go back to chapter 3, paragraph 17. "If there is no Torah, there is no *derekh eretz*" means that one should start with high theoretical knowledge and from there seek the right way of conduct in social life. But the other part of this statement contains the opposite idea, namely, that "if there is no *derekh eretz,* there is no Torah," which means that if one does not have good manners, one cannot achieve theoretical knowledge. This statement is only one of a series of statements, which are all phrased in a similarly dialectical manner. Typically, the paragraph contains no synthetic answer, for the synthesis is the work of the learner.

All of this has to do with style. Contentwise, however, there are several very striking similarities between the two cultures. First and foremost, one of the central themes of *Pirkei Avot* is the great importance attached to wisdom. Second is the strong emphasis on tradition. Other points are filial duty toward father and teacher and the importance of ritual.

Another point, which is also a basic moral issue in this book, is the relationship between theory and praxis. I have reason to believe that this problem has been dealt with intensively in this country in the last fifty years. In *Pirkei Avot,* the question is discussed in great detail, and the basic answer is that theory without praxis is unstable.

But in addition to the similarities, there are also profound differences, and I will point to at least one or two.

One major philosophical and cultural difference is in the relationship between morality and religion. In Chinese culture, there is an almost absolute separation between these two spheres, since religion—namely, the relationship between man and God—is basically ritual and has little to do with the world outside of the Temple. Whereas in Jewish culture, the opposite is true: morality is based on religion, and man-and-God and man-and-man relationships are not seen as two separate spheres but rather as two aspects of the same whole.

This difference is not only philosophical but also has great bearing on the development of morality and of the culture as a whole. In Chinese culture, morality is basically a social and interpersonal relationship that has social and political meaning but does not have a relationship with objective, abstract, and absolute values. In other words, this morality is relativistic, seeing good and evil not as absolute values but rather as definitions of what is socially and politically right or wrong.

In sharp contrast to that, Jewish morality contains, from its very beginning, absolute values of good and evil. Chinese culture had one major encounter with a different cultural system that had an absolute value system, though it had no God, and that is Buddhism. (I am speaking now about the theoretical encounter with Buddhism and not about what happened to Buddhism when it became a Lamaistic religion or a Dao-Buddhist popular religion.) In Buddhism, you have this notion that certain things are bad, regardless of social context, and if one does them, it changes one's karma, causes one to have a lower incarnation, and vice versa. And as the respective cultures develop, this point, in itself, creates a sequence of cultural and philosophical differences.

Another, more tenuous point of difference between our two cultures has to do with the attitude toward tradition. *Pirkei Avot* is based on an ancient tradition, to which it continuously refers from its very first paragraph. Likewise, in the writings of Confucius, one gets the similar feeling that everything in these books is really not new but rather is the wisdom of the ancestors.

But underneath this external similarity there is a profound difference. In the Confucian tradition, the scholar always was, or tried to be, identified with the establishment and the contemporary rulers. In Taoism, when a master did not approve of the behavior of his prince, he would just make a very mild remark to the effect that it is not exactly the right way to behave—or if he felt very badly about it, he would resign and go elsewhere; but he would never say that the government should be attacked. Only in the works of Menzius can one find some hinted remarks about the possibility of saying or doing something in that direction. All this is, as I said earlier, one outcome of the relativity of good and evil in Chinese culture.

In *Pirkei Avot* and the other books around it, we find a different view. Although Jewish tradition in general is very much in favor of continuity, and although it also maintains that government should be obeyed, if the government passes a certain red line of immorality, it loses its right to rule, and the people are obligated to revolt against it and overthrow it.

Symbolically speaking, Chinese rulers, whatever titles they had, were always the sons of Heaven, and the scholars were their servants. In Jewish culture, the ruler was never considered a son of Heaven. Chapter 4, paragraph 13, of *Pirkei Avot* says, "The world contains three crowns," that is, three types of greatness: "the greatness of the priest," who deals with ritual; "the greatness of the king," who in certain ways is greater than the priest; and highest of all—"the greatness of the scholar." In another Jewish book (Babylonian Talmud, Tractate Horayot, page 13a), there is an even more precise hierarchy. Highest of all is the king; then come the High Priest and other officials. However, this applies only when all these people are otherwise equal in knowledge. If one is a scholar, even if he comes from the lowest family and is, socially and ritually, of no consequence, he still is considered to be on a higher level than a king.

This difference of approach also had some practical implications. Both the Jewish and the Chinese rulers had an army and a police force, even when their rule was merely theoretical; whereas the scholars sometimes did not even have money. They had knowledge but no money and no power. This was true for both countries. The theory behind this reality, however, was different. Consequently, according to Jewish law, in a case of two people who should be saved from trouble but only one can be saved, if one is a scholar and the other is not, even though the scholar is poor and of low descent and the other a priest or a king, it is the scholar that should be saved first; the priest or king should wait or even die.

This law is connected to the notion that there is an absolute law, which is beyond the power of money, of family origin, even of kingship. And it is the highest power that creates the rules. This does not mean that the scholar is always against the government, but it does mean that the government has no absolute rights; it is subject to a higher law, and if it breaks that law, then one has the right and the duty to fight against it. All of this, however, is ancient Jewish law, which today is purely theoretical in twentieth-century reality.

QUESTION: What Is Torah?

RABBI STEINSALTZ: Linguistically speaking, Torah means both "the body of knowledge" and "teaching." In this sense, it is very much like the meaning of the notion of Dao; it is the way of life, the way in which life should be conducted. However, Torah is not just pure knowledge as such. For example, the term *Torah* does not include mathematics, even though there are intellectual and practical connections between these two areas. To use an image from physics,

Torah is knowledge that has a vector, a direction of movement, whereas other knowledge is nonvectorial. And so Torah is not just an accumulation of connected facts: it is always a knowledge that shows a way of life. Thus the difference between learning Torah and learning other knowledge is like the difference between studying simple dimensional mathematics and vectorial mathematics.

For the sake of precision, I should add that sometimes the word *Torah* has a specific meaning—namely, the Five Books of Moses. But in *Pirkei Avot* and elsewhere, *Torah* always means a general type of knowledge that teaches a way of life. In another book, it says that everything, even heaven and earth, has limitations; only Torah has no limitations (Midrash Genesis Rabbah 10). With all that, however, the study of Torah is not emotional or intuitive; it is dealt with almost like the study of mathematics. It may be defined as a scientific, dialectical, logically organized method of dealing with intuitive material, with a higher knowledge. And it is a learning process that continues forever.

In mathematics, there are axioms: a point, a line, a dimension, measurements, numbers, and so on; and then there is a formal and logical way of combining them. The basic materials of Torah are different; it deals with right and wrong, good and evil, what one should or should not do. And these basic materials are then developed into a logical, intellectual construction.

QUESTION: What is the meaning of wisdom in Judaism?

RABBI STEINSALTZ: In one dimension, wisdom is the right understanding of everything—moral and intellectual problems alike—right not in the moral but in the intellectual sense. That is to say that every subject of knowledge is connected with wisdom. In the above-mentioned series of paradoxes in *Pirkei Avot* (chapter 3, paragraph 17), there is the following paradox: "If there is no knowledge, there is no understanding; if there is no understanding, there is no knowledge." In other words, knowledge is not just a static collection of materials, but it is also the ability to use it correctly. In Jewish tradition, a person who has only knowledge is likened to a basket full of books (Babylonian Talmud, Tractate Megillah 28b). Whereas the official title that we give to the old scholar is *talmid hakham,* which means "disciple of the wise." This is somewhat similar to the Greek concept of *philosophos,* a lover of wisdom.

QUESTION: What is the role of the Jewish scholar?

RABBI STEINSALTZ: In addition to his ability to memorize and understand texts, one of the most central drives for a Jewish scholar is to innovate. To use a possibly low metaphor: Confucian scholars wanted to have an old woman in an old dress, modern culture wants a young woman in modern dress, and Jewish culture prefers a young woman in an old dress. Thus although the Jewish scholar always claims that he is just creating a commentary, he is really constantly driven to create new things as new ideas.

The way in which the Jewish scholar advances is not only analytical but also synthetic, in that he is always trying to create new structures all the time. Consequently, the way in which Judaism relates to nonpractical ideas is very different from that of Chinese culture. Confucian wisdom was always very practical and also strongly connected with science and technology. In this sense, it has had a very strong influence on Western culture. In the Talmud, however—of which *Pirkei Avot* is about the one five thousandth part—there are pages and pages of discussion of subjects of no practical value whatsoever.

NOTES FROM THE ROAD:
Sometimes Small Things Are Big

Rabbi Steinsaltz told me that many years ago, he was asked to speak at a university. When he arrived, he found that no publicity had been done, that it was the first day of the semester, and the location of his lecture was at the far end of the campus in a remote building.

Three people showed up.

Twelve years later, a religious man approached Rabbi Steinsaltz on the street in Chicago and said, "Do you remember the night when you were at a university when three students showed up? Well, I was one of the three students. That evening changed my life."

ᛒᛅ The Advantages of ᛒᛅ
Breaking Rules

A funny incident occurred when I brought Rabbi Steinsaltz to speak at a bookstore in Manhattan shortly after his return from China. It was a Border's bookstore, and Rabbi Steinsaltz gave a wonderful talk to an overflow gathering.

At a certain point, I noticed the employee of Border's who was in charge of the book event signaling the Rabbi that his time was up. Rabbi Steinsaltz clearly saw the timeout signal but kept right on talking.

A number of minutes later, once again I saw the employee signal to Rabbi Steinsaltz. After all, I thought, she wants people to stop listening and to go back to buying books. Nonetheless, Rabbi Steinsaltz seemed again to ignore her signal and kept on talking. The audience was paying rapt attention to what he was saying.

A few minutes passed, and a third time the employee gestured the timeout signal to Rabbi Steinsaltz, at which point Rabbi Steinsaltz stopped what he was saying and remarked to both the audience and the person who was signaling him, "I am a rule breaker. I notice that in my life I often break rules. I know that at home in Israel, I'm sometimes breaking some traffic rules. I know that throughout my life, I've often broken rules that my doctors have given me. As I said, I'm a rule breaker.

"I figure that when I get to the Heavenly Court, the Heavenly Court will see that I've broken a lot of the rules man makes on earth. They'll see me as a rule breaker, they'll see that's the kind of guy I am. I suppose it will be some kind of advantage because after all, God and his Heavenly Court will see that I'm a rule breaker. The Almighty won't be able to say, "Why do you follow all the human rules, and only break my rules?"

"In this way, *HaKadosh Baruch Hu,* the Holy One, Blessed Is He, will see that this is the kind of guy I am. I'm a rule breaker. Perhaps then he'll be more lenient with me."

CHAPTER FOUR

Photo © Flash Rosenberg

"Make the Lives of Your Teachers as Miserable as Possible" (2001)

. . . each person must commit himself to a particular person whom he thenceforth sees as his mentor and guide.

—Rabbi Adin Steinsaltz,
Teshuvah

It is 5:30 A.M., spring 2001. I'm at JFK Airport. Rabbi Steinsaltz's flight has just landed.

The last time Rabbi Steinsaltz was here, he told an audience that philosophers have been pondering the question "How do we *know* that something is true?" for centuries. And he said that the only answer that seems to have any merit is this: we know that something is true because it "clicks."

Jewish tradition teaches that each of us should find a teacher. I have surely found mine. How do I know? I guess it's because it clicks.

Rabbi Steinsaltz's secretary in Jerusalem once told me that it is clear to her that my soul and the Rabbi's grow from the same root. Thank you, Ditsa, for seeing that and saying that.

I know that the root meaning of the word *Kabbalah* is "to receive." The job of the student is to empty himself enough to be able to receive from one's teacher.

In *The Thirteen Petalled Rose,* Rabbi Steinsaltz writes, "If only man as an individual, if only the race of man as a whole, were able to forswear the sin of the Tree of Knowledge—the sin of "knowing" . . . when man knows more than he needs to know, when what he learns are no more than fragments of information, heaps of unrelated facts which, whether they are correct or incorrect, become a barrier to experience itself."[1]

What have I learned from Rabbi Steinsaltz?

I have learned that the material world is a shell and that through wisdom, insight, and experience one can pierce the shell, one can peek behind the veil.

> Only those persons who know the secret of existence in the universe can know the extent to which the duplication between the worlds still exists and can perceive the essential analogy between the physical world and the spiritual worlds. They can make out the hidden paths in the con-

crete reality of the world leading to the upper worlds, and they read into whatever is apprehended as real the symbols and models of a higher world taking us step by step upward to the very pinnacle and source of all the levels.[2]

I have learned that I am not a body, nor am I a body that has a soul. I am a soul that has a body. My soul existed before this body, and it will continue on after I drop this body.

The soul of man functions through its instrument or vessel, which is the body.[3]

I have learned that all human emotions are on the same level and are not intrinsically good or bad but rather are good and bad by how they are used.

Which is not meant to imply that there is no difference at all between a good and bad course of action, between good qualities and bad qualities, between a right and a wrong way of doing things. It is simply that even though these differences clearly and distinctly exist, they are not to be taken as something intrinsic to the attributes, actions, or things involved.[4]

I have learned that all of the tens of thousands of *mitzvot,* the commandments to do or to refrain from doing certain things, are to be seen not as burdens but as spiritual opportunities to connect with and be conscious of the only Reality, which is God.

The Jewish attitude is that life in all its aspects, in its totality, must somehow or other be bound up with holiness. This attitude is expressed in part through conscious action: that is, through the utterance of prescribed prayers and blessings and following prescribed forms of conduct; and, in part, by adhering to a number of prohibitions.[5]

I have learned that the human being is created in God's image.

The structure of man is a paradigm of the structure of the worlds; it is the key to the order of the *mitzvot;* and it is also the configuration that symbolizes the system of relationships among the worlds.[6]

There is Rabbi Steinsaltz now. We're back on the road. . . .

🌿 Request for a Favor 🌿

It was a Thursday afternoon in May 2001 when an urgent call came in to my office from the principal of a yeshiva, a traditional Jewish school, in this case a middle school and high school, located in a suburb of New York City. The head of this yeshiva, a rabbi, introduced himself to me and then asked me if his information was correct: that I would be driving Rabbi Steinsaltz to a certain synagogue the next day where he was to be the scholar-in-residence and honored guest for Shabbos.

"Yes," I said, "I will be the driver."

The principal proceeded to tell me that the students in his school all study Talmud using Rabbi Steinsaltz's edition, that the synagogue to which I was driving Rabbi Steinsaltz was right near his school, and wouldn't it be wonderful if I could stop on the way so that Rabbi Steinsaltz could speak to the children?

"Yes, it *would* be wonderful," I agreed. "But I don't think we will have the time," I said, regretfully. "And who knows what traffic will be like."

The rabbi pleaded, "The school is just five minutes from where Rabbi Steinsaltz is speaking. It wouldn't take long. And it would be so wonderful for the children to meet the man whose words they study. Just imagine that they will grow up knowing that they *met* Rabbi Steinsaltz, one of the greatest rabbis of our time. Perhaps of all time."

Again, I agreed with the principal, but I told him that Rabbi Steinsaltz's schedule was tight, that it would be a Friday afternoon when Jewish schools get out early and when everyone is so busy due to the approach of sundown and the arrival of Shabbos, Shabbat, the Sabbath. I told him that I wouldn't be getting to his area until two o'clock.

"That's perfect," he said. "Dismissal is at two thirty."

"I'm sorry," I insisted. "I just don't think we'll have the time."

"I'm begging you," said the head of the yeshiva. "A visit from Rabbi Steinsaltz to our school would be an amazing event. Even if he just came in for two minutes. Listen—what if I promise that I'll have all the children sitting in the auditorium, waiting for the arrival of Rabbi Steinsaltz? All you will have to do is walk in, we'll all be sitting there, and all Rabbi Steinsaltz needs to do is to say hello to the children. It would be amazing for them."

NOTES FROM THE ROAD:
Fighting with the Almighty

Last night, Rabbi Steinsaltz said to his audience, "I am talking, arguing, fighting with the Almighty. This is my life."

"OK," I agreed. "I know just where your school is. I grew up not far from there. If you can promise me that the children will be ready at two o'clock and that we can just go in and say hello, I will ask Rabbi Steinsaltz's assistant if I can do this."

"So Much That I Know So Little About"

The next day, everything went exactly as planned. Rabbi Steinsaltz and I arrived at the school at precisely 2:00 P.M. and went in. The students and their teachers were assembled in the auditorium. As Rabbi Steinsaltz walked in, they all stood up, as they had been taught to do, out of respect.

There was no time for introductions. Rabbi Steinsaltz went to the stage, stood behind the podium, and spoke into the microphone. One hundred and fifty perfectly silent students and a few dozen of their teachers were now sitting and listening to the renowned, the world-famous, the revered Rabbi Adin Steinsaltz.

In almost a whisper, Rabbi Steinsaltz began to speak.

"Boys and girls," he said. "Hello."

He then went on. "There are so many subjects that I know so little or nothing about."

As he said this, it occurred to me that this never seemed to be true. Regardless of the subject, Rabbi Steinsaltz always seemed to know so much, and I had been present so many times when the Rabbi was with experts in the field of science or art or world affairs or law and he would not only hold his own but actually become the experts' teacher. He seemed to be aware of the most profound questions in every field of human endeavor and could therefore shed light on the deepest concerns of people in whatever field they might be in.

Nevertheless, Rabbi Steinsaltz whispered to the students, "There are so many subjects that I know so little or nothing about."

He paused.

"But I do know a little bit about Torah study. So I would like to offer you some words of advice regarding your Torah studies."

The students strained to hear Rabbi Steinsaltz's whispered words. Rabbi Steinsaltz often speaks in a near whisper. Not always, but often.

He continued, "My advice to you is this: make the lives of your teachers as miserable as you possibly can."

The students sat in shock, as did their instructors. Nobody laughed, nobody coughed, nobody moved.

Rabbi Steinsaltz repeated, "Makes the lives of your teachers as *miserable* as you possibly can. Make their lives *miserable*. Ask them some questions that you don't think they can answer. Try to find contradictions in things that they say and ask them to justify these contradictions. Try to find books that ask particularly difficult questions about the subjects you are studying and ask your teachers these questions. Make the lives of your teachers as miserable as you possibly can.

"Thank you very much."

And then Rabbi Steinsaltz, knowing we were short on time and that Shabbos was coming, began to walk off the stage.

The head of the yeshiva rushed to the podium to thank the Rabbi for coming. "Boy and girls, I want to thank Rabbi Steinsaltz for visiting our school and for taking time from his busy schedule to honor us with his presence." And then, expecting a laugh, he said, "But I want to say, please don't take Rabbi Steinsaltz too literally."

At that moment, Rabbi Steinsaltz, who was approaching the steps to leave the stage, turned around, walked back to the podium, and spoke into the microphone once again, but no longer in a whisper.

"Boy and girls, I have so often been misquoted by journalists over the years, but I don't want to be misquoted here. My advice to you is this: make the lives of your teachers as *miserable* as you possibly can." Rabbi Steinsaltz then walked off the stage and waved to the children.

And we left.

✿❧ Visiting Family ✿❧

Rabbi Steinsaltz has been traveling, almost nonstop, it seems, for as long as I have known him, a quarter of a century. Much of his time is spent visiting Jewish communities and Jewish groups of all kinds, in the former Soviet Union, the United States, Great Britain, France, Australia, Brazil, Canada, and other countries.

He told me that when he is on his way to some remote place in the former Soviet Union and is asked by someone where he is going, he says, "I'm going to visit family."

"For reasons I cannot explain, I like Jews," Rabbi Steinsaltz told an audience.

He said, "My work on the Talmud is not for me to show off but to make that wisdom available to our people. I try to build as many bridges as I can because it's a matter of survival."

An Old Perfume Bottle

The following Sunday morning, I picked Rabbi Steinsaltz up from his hotel in Manhattan to bring him to a lecture he was scheduled to give that afternoon at a Jewish Community Center in New Jersey. As always, the parking lot was filled and the auditorium was standing room only. More and more people were becoming aware of Rabbi Steinsaltz's reputation and his contributions to the Jewish people.

And as always, there was a lot of energy filling the large space as people waited with anticipation for Rabbi Steinsaltz to speak. People think of him in historic proportions. He is the

NOTES FROM THE ROAD:
Rabbi Steinsaltz on School

"I considered all my years of school as a kind of Chinese water torture," Rabbi Steinsaltz told an audience of teachers. "I would say that I hated high school. Not that high school was worse than elementary school. I hated elementary school as much as high school! But still, it was about the age of fifteen, I just left school. I had some far more enjoyable times doing some other things. Of course, I had to finish high school somehow. It was a terrible experience.

"I had a friend who studied in the same class and skipped the same class with me. I would say I was punished several times for skipping school. The teachers didn't like me; I didn't like them either!

"But I had a wonderful experience, one that is almost a child's daydream. I had a teacher that particularly disliked me and told me in so many words that when I left school, both of us would be relieved! We would bump into each other in the street, and he would never say hello.

"And then about six or seven years later, I was invited to speak at my old school and he had the job of introducing me! I enjoyed that very much! Very much! You see, he had to say how good and nice I was when I was in high school. It was surely a hard job of lying!

"That is why I considered all of my school years as a kind of Chinese torture: you have to stay there and suffer and remain more or less silent."

kind of individual you will want to tell your grandchildren you saw in person.

The man who introduced Rabbi Steinsaltz focused on his Talmud work, so Rabbi Steinsaltz began his talk by saying, "When I am working on the Talmud, or when I am building the schools in Jerusalem, or when I go to Russia, it is all for the same reason. In each place and with each project, I am doing one and the same thing. I am trying to preserve the possibility that the remnants of Israel not be lost. And in order that the remnants of Israel not be lost, we must keep the channels open for *all* of Israel."

He went on to say, "The Jewish people have chosen a method of self-destruction, it seems, reminiscent of the ancient Roman custom. How did people commit suicide in ancient Rome? A person would get inside a warm bath and cut his own wrist, and then he would sit there and bleed quietly, peacefully, and would die with a smile on his face. This is what is happening to the Jewish people today. There is constant bleeding. It is not very dramatic, but it is ongoing.

"To put it another way, the Jewish people today can be compared to an old bottle of perfume that has been empty for a long time. You can still get a faint whiff of the beautiful scent that was once in the bottle."

As Rabbi Steinsaltz continued his talk, his concern for the future of the Jewish people remained the theme.

"Some people say that the Four Sons at the Passover Seder are four generations; that the first son, the *Chacham,* what they call the wise son, is the observant grandfather.

"And the second son is the unobservant son.

"And the third son, the grandchild of the observant one, doesn't even know what's going on. All he can say is 'What is this?'

"And the fourth son doesn't even know what to ask because *his* grandfather, the son of the observant grandfather, the original grandfather, doesn't observe anything, so he doesn't even know what to ask."

He then added, "Unfortunately, the majority of our people are not any of those four sons: the majority of our people are the fifth son, who doesn't even come to the Seder."

"But in truth," Rabbi Steinsaltz continued, "in the Passover Seder, today there are six sons.

"The fifth son is the one who doesn't come to the Seder.

"The sixth son is the one who doesn't even know that there is a Seder."

NOTES FROM THE ROAD:
From a Talmud Class

Rabbi Steinsaltz was clarifying an often misunderstood teaching from the Talmud. In tractate Eruvin 13a, we learn, "One who flees from honor, honor will pursue."

Rabbi Steinsaltz pointed out that often people think this means that the way to be honored is to run away from honor.

But the word in the ancient text for "pursue" is *rodef,* a pursuer, as in a murderer or a fetus that will kill its mother. For the person who deserves honor yet runs away from it, honor will become such a "pursuer" until he *accepts* the honor he deserves.

"Spiritual Leprosy"

Later on in the talk, Rabbi Steinsaltz remarked, "The Jewish people today have 'spiritual leprosy.' They lose a finger, they lose a nose, they lose an arm. Whole pieces of our people are falling off of us. This is the state of the Jewish people."

During the question-and-answer period, a gentleman asked Rabbi Steinsaltz if his mission in life is to bring Jews back to Judaism, to get them to believe.

He responded, "I don't say to people, 'You must believe.' In fact, theologically speaking, I would say that to speak about belief is either unnecessary or hopeless. For example, like trying to describe, say, a watermelon. I say, 'Bite into it. Taste and see if it is good.' I cannot describe a taste. I can only say, 'It was good for me. Have a bite. Get involved. See for yourself.'"

A documentary film about Rabbi Steinsaltz and his work, titled *The Talmud and the Scholar*,[7] includes a story about Rabbi Steinsaltz that I have heard many people retell over the years. It is worth repeating.

Rabbi Steinsaltz had been teaching a weekly Talmud class for a number of years that was attended by secular academics. At one point, a filmmaker approached the Rabbi and expressed interest in joining the class. But he said, "Rabbi, I want you to know that I eat bacon every Shabbos."

"*Every* Shabbos?" Rabbi Steinsaltz asked.

"Yes, every Shabbos," the professor replied.

So Rabbi Steinsaltz said, "Why *every* Shabbos?"

And the filmmaker said, "I have a busy week. Most days I barely have time for a cup of coffee. But then the weekend comes, and I fix myself a great breakfast—and I include bacon every time."

Rabbi Steinsaltz responded, "It says in the Torah that we should honor Shabbos. It's surely not my way, but I suppose it has some merit to honor Shabbos with bacon than not to honor Shabbos at all."

ᑭᑫ Trying to Stay on Topic ᑭᑫ

In the fall of 2002, I took Rabbi Steinsaltz to a synagogue in Westchester County, New York. He was invited, as usual, to give a lecture. As always, the place was packed with people. When Rabbi Steinsaltz arrives in a town to give a lecture, the space in which he speaks almost always fills to capacity.

Since there is the general belief within the Jewish world that Rabbi Steinsaltz and his commentaries will stand forever among the great works of Jewish religious writing, his arrival in any town with a Jewish population is a major event.

Although we usually arrive at a synagogue or other location and find that a topic has been announced, I knew from attending dozens of such events over the years that Rabbi Steinsaltz never seems to feel obligated to speak on the announced topic. Sometimes he speaks about why he won't speak on the announced topic. Sometimes he speaks about why there is a topic more important than the announced topic. Sometimes he speaks on one part of a topic and shows that the one part is actually larger than the whole of which it is a part.

I've witnessed introductions when the audience has been told that Rabbi Steinsaltz will be giving a talk on the holy city of Jerusalem and instead he gives a talk on the evil city of Sodom.

I've seen it announced that he will talk about books and he decides instead to speak about television.

Of course, evidence of Rabbi Steinsaltz's genius is that even when it seems like he is speaking on a different topic than the one announced, his talk always sheds profound light on the original topic, without even discussing that subject directly.

Rabbi Steinsaltz once told me that he was invited to Australia to speak about the Holocaust, and he told them he definitely would not speak about the subject. Yet when he arrived in Australia, the publicity said that he would be speaking about the Holocaust. So what he did was to give a talk about why he was *not* giving a talk about the Holocaust.

The topic for the lecture I brought him to on this particular day was "*Ahavas Yisroel*: Pluralism and Polarization." *Ahavas Yisroel* is the mitzvah of love the people of Israel feel for the people of Israel.

Rabbi Steinsaltz began, "It's always a kind of an enjoyment when somebody has the opportunity to stand up before the local rabbi and say just the opposite of what he says.

"You see, I am leaving this town tomorrow, so I can say whatever I want! I mean, the rabbi won't be able to do anything about it. I know it is not Jewish and perhaps not even *Ahavas Yisroel,* but the temptation is too big!"

Objecting to the topic of "Jewish values," Rabbi Steinsaltz said, "I really don't like the notion of Jewish values. What does it mean when I have 'Jewish values'?

"It reminds me of something that I read years ago about the punishment of some people in hell. Sometimes a person sins with a woman. So what is his punishment? In hell, he is given the woman, not as a whole, but in pieces. A hand, a leg, an eye. Just imagine how it looks! This is the kind of punishment one gets in hell.

"When one has to deal with 'Jewish values,' I have always considered it the same basic idea. You took something, being Jewish, and cut it into pieces. It is possible that all the pieces are there, but the result is not very attractive. I have the same view when I hear about Jewish values. Speaking about Jewish values basically takes Judaism and cuts it into pieces."

As usual, Rabbi Steinsaltz gave a wonderful lecture, and then we fled. Those of us who have the privilege of traveling with Rabbi Steinsaltz know that we must get out of the building immediately after the lecture, unless the event is a book signing, which it often is. If we don't leave immediately, Rabbi Steinsaltz will be surrounded by people for hours, each hoping for a moment of his time.

Some people want him to read their manuscripts.

Others want to ask him questions, as I have so many times over the years.

Sometimes people want him to bless them. I have seem single women on a number of occasions ask Rabbi Steinsaltz to give them a blessing that they will find a mate.

I took Rabbi Steinsaltz back to his hotel in Manhattan and picked him up the next day.

🐾 The Paradox of Praying 🐾

The next morning, Rabbi Steinsaltz and I had a long drive up to Connecticut. The Rabbi was delivering a talk that afternoon to the medical staff of a hospital, and although I had to refer to my driving directions countless times, I decided to take advantage of the long ride to talk with Rabbi Steinsaltz about some of my difficulties with prayer.

I found myself beginning the conversation by saying, "How is it possible for little me, a speck in an unimaginably vast universe, to turn to my Creator, who I not only can't imagine but who, I am told, I cannot possibly imagine, and pray to him?"

I wasn't sure how I was going to pay attention to the driving and the unfamiliar driving directions and listen to Rabbi Steinsaltz all at the same time, but I think I did pretty well.

While filling his pipe, Rabbi Steinsaltz said, "Your question is not a modern question. And I would also say it is not a secular question.

"Your question, 'How can one turn to the Divine in prayer and what do the words of prayer mean?' is the same question every worshiper asks in the depths of his heart.

"One might say that the paradox of praying is the very struggle with these questions.

"It is a pity that there are so many teachers and also parents who make their students and children pray regularly in an almost mechanical fashion."

I interrupted and said, "It was so intimidating when I began going to a synagogue regularly. It seemed as if everyone except me knew everything."

I told Rabbi Steinsaltz that thirty years earlier, I went to a retreat held by a few different Jewish groups from Boston, New York, Philadelphia, and Washington, D.C. It was my first time at a Jewish weekend gathering.

In the dining hall, when it came time to say grace after the meal, it seemed like everyone but me knew how to say it, fluently, in Hebrew.

And it's long.

I never thought I could master it. I was so uncomfortable and embarrassed that I would hide out in the men's room while everyone else recited it.

It wasn't until much later that I learned that these people knew how to recite the grace after meals in Hebrew from saying it three times a day in Conservative Jewish summer camps for years and that most of them had little idea what they were saying. They simply had it all memorized.

Rabbi Steinsaltz smiled and said, "I remember once a quite mature young man who had grown up on a kibbutz and had been a student at Bar-Ilan University came to our synagogue to learn how to pray.

"One of the things that shocked him was how the little children in the synagogue knew what to do. He asked over and over how they knew when to stand, when to sit, what page to open to, and so on."

Rabbi Steinsaltz continued, "I personally tried, at one time, to exert pressure that the *siddur* [prayer book] be introduced into the religious schools as a compulsory subject of study so that the children who use it should know what they are saying. One of the inspectors of the religious schools told me that this was unnecessary because 'they all know.' But this is simply not so."

"Of course, once I learned the words," I said, "I realized that this was actually the easy part. The hard part is being able to concentrate on what I am reciting from the prayer book."

Coping with Introductions

One of the most difficult parts of Rabbi Steinsaltz's travels is his having to endure the words of the introductions that people give him before he speaks. People mean well, and far be it from me to criticize people who speak with wild enthusiasm about Rabbi Steinsaltz. But these words of praise are tough to follow.

I reviewed my notes from over the years, looking for some of the ways that Rabbi Steinsaltz begins his lectures. Here are a few:

- When Rabbi Steinsaltz spoke before a group of French Jews, he said, "Ladies and gentlemen, I have been asked to speak in English. That is perhaps symbolic of our Jewish existence. One Jew speaks to a crowd of Jews in a language that doesn't belong to either. English is not my language and it's not most of your language and we are speaking in a third language that is not any of ours. That is possibly the way of our Jewish life."

- At the beginning of a particularly strong speech in which Rabbi Steinsaltz urged his listeners to do more about Jewish education for themselves and their children, he said, "Some of the things I may say may not be terribly pleasant. I can make an excuse. It's an Americanism when people say that their middle name is such-and-such. My first name is Adin, which means "gentle"— that is the meaning of my first name. Now, a person that has this first name has all the rights to be as ungentle as possible. I remain always gentle by definition, so I can say the worst things. And I will say some."

- After something like ten talks in four days, Rabbi Steinsaltz said to the next audience, "Ladies and gentlemen, I have been introduced so many times on this visit, and if I knew that I'd be returning tomorrow to Israel, I would say, 'Well, that's the last straw.' But I have been to Canada and England, where they have that beautiful way of understatement. I am much happier with that than with the overstating in America. In America, I just don't know what to believe. You see, in Canada and England, at least I know that what I get is possibly true." On this particular night, after a long introduction filled with high praise from the hosting rabbi of the congregation where he spoke, Rabbi Steinsaltz began his lecture this way: "About the introduction: I should be accustomed by now to hearing these introductions. They remind me of the state of the Israeli shekel at one time, when everybody was a millionaire! With such introductions, the real problem that I have is that I don't know what the real rate of exchange is. I suppose you know your rabbi, so you'll make the proper discount."

- Rabbi Steinsaltz was asked to speak on the subject of "Jewish values in a modern society." He began his talk by saying, "Now, let me begin with a problem, and that is, I would say, the name of the subject that I'm supposed to speak about.

  I have the misfortune to speak in so many places and to speak about some of the craziest topics imaginable. So by this time I'm rather tough. But still, I would say that a subject like this is one that I'm always getting angry at—Jewish values in a modern society. It's a wonderful title! I know that everybody likes it. I don't."

- One evening, Rabbi Steinsaltz began, "Every time when I have to speak, especially after those beautiful, magnificent introductions, I feel that what is coming is an anticlimax. You hear too much, and you have to be naturally disappointed at the result."

- Rabbi Steinsaltz began a lecture one afternoon, "Well, I have already said what I have to say again about these introductions. I wish they were true. That is the only thing that I can say about it. In America, everything is exaggerated, including praise, especially praise. It is possible that every word has about the value of an Italian lira, what they call a liretta. So I suppose you can take what you just heard with a few handfuls of salt."

"Don't Jail God in the Synagogue"

I love the smell of Rabbi Steinsaltz's pipe. He had his lit and was happily enjoying it, as I was. But the pipe went out moments later when Rabbi Steinsaltz said, "I remember running into an old friend after a number of years of not seeing him. He is now the dean of a yeshiva in Israel.

"I happened to asked him what he does during his prayers and specifically whether he concentrates on the prayer itself.

"'Yes,' he answered, 'I have *kavanah* [correct inner attention].'

"I asked him, 'What kind of *kavanah* do you have?'

"So he explained to me that his intent during prayer was to understand the connection between one sentence and the next, between one word and another, between the various sections, and so on. He thinks about these things and concentrates on them, and he calls this *kavanah* in prayer.

"I told him, possibly in a rude manner, that these are things I do on Shabbat, after eating dinner, and that at times I study these questions and refer to books that deal with and explain prayer in this manner. But to consider the analysis of the text, which is what his *kavanah* amounted to even though he did not use this expression, as a proper form of devotion for prayer is not what I would consider or accept as *kavanah* in the true sense.

"There is a story of a simple Jew, quite ignorant, who stood on Rosh Hashanah and recited, with great fervor, several liturgical poems. Someone asked him why he recited these prayers with such great fervor and what he understood of the prayers.

"The Jew answered, 'What do I care what is written there? I only know that all of the prayers have one meaning: Master of the Universe, help us make a living.'

"To my mind," Rabbi Steinsaltz said to me, "in terms of what is truly connected to the nature of prayer, the Jew in this story was far closer to the depths of prayer than the one who knows the exact date of composition of the prayers and knows all about two- and three-letter roots in ancient and modern liturgical poems."

I said, "Of course, the hardest part is to sincerely feel and know that I am actually speaking with God. I remember you once said that it's hard to be Jewish because we are asked to establish a personal relationship with a God we can't conceive of."

"One suggestion I make," the Rabbi responded, "is to say that if a person wishes to relate to God, he or she cannot jail him in the synagogue, without any connection with the surrounding world."

I quickly said, "I remember that you once told an audience that in America we make our synagogues big and that perhaps this reflects the hope that we can keep God in there. You said that God is not just in the synagogue. He's also in the bedroom and in the kitchen and in the marketplace."

Rabbi Steinsaltz, preparing to relight his pipe, said, "As I have said, when a man prays, he says, 'Blessed art Thou, O Lord.'

"When you say, 'Blessed art Thou, O Lord,' you find yourself standing before God, in direct confrontation with him. The moment a person who isn't a liar says these words, he places himself before God. In every prayer, before all else, we face this issue. When we pray, we address *Hakodosh Baruch Hu,* the Holy One, Blessed Be He.

"Once," Rabbi Steinsaltz continued, "while I was in the middle of my prayers, my daughter, who was quite little at the time, tried to talk to me, and when I failed to respond, she was very angry and said, 'Why don't you speak to me?'

"Later on, I answered her by saying, 'I was busy. I was speaking with God.'

"She replied, with great understanding, that she hadn't noticed that God was answering me. Her comment was very deep and we could discuss it, but in any case, this four- or five-year old girl was prepared to accept the notion that I speak to God when I pray. But what *she* wanted was for it to be a two-way conversation and not just a speech.

"But yes, if I have someone with whom to speak, then I can pray. If I have no one with whom to speak, then what is the point of all the words and all the things I say? What good is it if I have no feeling of Presence, even in the simplest sense?"

Our conversation came to an end at some point, and sooner or later we arrived at the hospital in Connecticut. He said, "Is man, as man, permitted to interfere in God's deeds? God makes a man sick or makes a man ill, or makes him one way or another. What kind of permission do I have to interfere?

"Now, different religions have different answers about it. And in many religions, there is a basic distaste for any kind of interference. This was, among other things, the reason why in so many ages, Jews, not Christians, wanted to become doctors.

"In the Midrash, there is a story about Rabbi Akiva. A person asked him, 'How do you dare interfere in the work of God?'

"And he said, 'What is your profession?'

"The fellow answered, 'I am an agriculturalist.'

"'Well,' Rabbi Akiva says, 'You *always* interfere in God's work. You don't allow the earth to remain as it is. But you do something about it. You treat it, you sow it, you reap it, and so on. Humanity is not only allowed but is *supposed* to interfere in God's will.

"It's almost a commandment to interfere, meaning that the world is an incomplete place. The idea that nature is complete as it is is not a Jewish idea.

"The Jewish notion is that man is imperfect, nature is imperfect. The work of man is to make perfection. And therefore, the role of man is to make changes, to amend what God has done, one way or another way.

"The role of man is to make corrections, to make what's called *Tikun Olam,* the amendment of what is there in the world. This is a very positive statement, not just about the role of the doctor but also the role of the inventor, the role of the person that changes the world.

"I don't see, in any Jewish source, that somebody would say that if God meant man to fly, he would supply him with wings. The basic idea is that God gave man the ability to make changes."

NOTES FROM THE ROAD:
Pipe Smoking

Most of the time when I'm with Rabbi Steinsaltz, he's smoking a pipe. I so enjoy the smell of his tobacco smoke. And there is a hint of that smell in my car for many days after he's left and gone back to Jerusalem or wherever the next leg of his journey takes him.

A number of people over the years have asked him why he smokes. They ask him whether he knows that it's not good for his health.

Rabbi Steinsaltz often points out that halakhic authorities are tending to ban smoking because of the opinions in medical profession that smoking is harmful. He once told me that "halakhah does not deal with smoking as an abstract notion but rather in connection with the accepted notions about this issue in the medical world. In many cases, the halakhic view in such instances changes along with medical knowledge, since it must deal with the facts as we best understand them. Hence the change of stance on this point." And he added that "the research done in the field does not show that smoking a pipe is significantly harmful and therefore it possibly does not fall into this ban at all."

Rabbi Steinsaltz has responded a number of times to the question of his smoking a pipe that he has a personal letter from the doctor who was in charge of the government committee on smoking in Great Britain telling him that pipe smoking is not really dangerous.

On the drive back from Connecticut, Rabbi Steinsaltz and I talked about the Bible, known in Hebrew as *Tanakh.*

Rabbi Steinsaltz said, "I don't think that I learned many things from school, but there were one or two things that I have learned.

"One of them was that I had a teacher of *Tanakh* who really liked the book. This is unusual for a teacher! And he gave advice that I often repeat. His advice was that the first step toward understanding the Bible and appreciating the Bible is just to read it.

"This seems to be commonplace, but I have found, in many cases, that it is the best advice that one can give.

"Before any commentaries and before any kind of involvement, just go on and read it, just open it like any other book.

"There is no rule that says that you have to read it from the beginning to the end. You can do it that way. Or you can skip chapters. Or you can look at different chapters. But try to read it. Just read it.

"Read it and understand everything. Or read it and understand very little. You'll get something from the mere reading of the book, and that is important in every context.

"In the Bible, we have a kind of small universe. A poet whom I rather like, even though he converted to Christianity, was the German Jewish poet Heinrich Heine. Heine described the Bible in one of his books.

"He said that the Bible is like a family medicine box. It contains all the important ingredients. There are some parts for one use; there are other parts for other uses. In fact, in the context in which he speaks about the book of *Kohelet* [Ecclesiastes], he says that this book is also part of the family medicine box because in there you also need a small bottle of poison!

"In the *Tanakh,* the whole twenty-four books, or if they are done in the usual non-Jewish way of separating them, the thirty-nine books of the Bible, they are very backward in style, in form, in content. But altogether they form a strange kind of a unity.

"So you cannot take one part of it and separate it; you have so many questions without answers because in some cases the questions are in one book and the answers are in another book.

"Sometimes the problems are found in one part of the Bible and the solutions are in an entirely different part. When you read the whole of it, it is like having this medicine box that you use and find what you need."

❧ Favorite Part of *Tanakh* ❧

My car was filling up with pipe smoke, as it always does when Rabbi Steinsaltz is my passenger. As I've mentioned, I love the smell, even days after he's gone. He once told me that there is a Hasidic book on pipe smoking as a method of meditation. It is known, for example, that the Baal Shem Tov, the founder of the Hasidic movement, was a pipe smoker who used his smoking as a meditative device to prepare his concentration before prayer. It is even said that the Baal Shem Tov said a blessing over his pipe.

I asked Rabbi Steinsaltz if there was any part of *Tanakh,* the Holy Scriptures, that he was particularly drawn to.

And he said, "I read the Psalms quite frequently. As you know, there are 150 of them. It's a big number.

"Some of them I fell in love with at first sight, and I'm still in love with them."

Rabbi Steinsaltz then joked, "It is something to be in love with anything for thirty-odd years!

"For example, there is a psalm that is my special love. I share this preference with one of the medieval scholars, Rabbi Abraham Ibn Ezra, who also said that this is the most exalted of all psalms—and that is Psalm 139.

"There are others that I took immediately to, but there are some psalms that I have a feeling of distaste for. Psalm 104, "Borchi Nafshi," which is one of the most beautiful descriptions of nature in any kind of literature, I took to immediately. But there are some psalms that seem to be, I would say, weepy— they're weepy and whining and I had a distaste for them."

I told Rabbi Steinsaltz that my favorite parts of the Bible were those written by King Solomon.

He smiled and said, "There are three books in the Bible that are attributed to King Solomon. They are the book of *Shir Hashirim,* Song of Songs; the book of *Mishlai,* Proverbs; and *Kohelet,* Ecclesiastes.

"Do you know that there is a dispute between the scholars in the Midrash? These three books are clearly not products of a person at the same stage of life. The same man, if he wrote them, didn't write them around the same time.

"So one explanation, a very obvious one, goes something like this. When he was young, he wrote the Song of Songs. It is really a love song; it is the fruit of youth.

"When he was around middle age, he wrote Proverbs. This is a book of what I call advice. It comes from a mature man that knows the world, knows what happens in the world and gives advice. That is the book of Proverbs.

"And then when he's an old man, when he has already seen too much and experienced too much, he writes the third book, the book of *Kohelet,* which speaks about despair and death and so on.

"Now, funnily enough, there is another interpretation, just to give you a notion of how it is. When he was very young, he wrote the book of *Kohelet!* When he was middle-aged, he wrote the book of Proverbs. When he was old, he wrote the Song of Songs!

"On the face of it, it seems a strange statement. What is it like to be sixteen or seventeen, especially when one is a very pre-

NOTES FROM THE ROAD:
Finding a Place

I told Rabbi Steinsaltz that sometimes it felt difficult for me to find a place in the world. And he said to me two things. I remember him saying that "no place is also a place." And I remember him saying that the most dangerous place in the road was the intersection but that many of us find ourselves there.

cocious sixteen or seventeen, like King Solomon clearly was? For many young people, the feeling of pain of the world brings the deep feeling of despair, the feeling that the world is useless, senseless.

"Then a person gets to some kind of maturity. And only when he is an old man can he write about love with a detachment that makes it a point of beauty and not just a point of desire, as in *Shir Hashirim,* The Song of Songs."

&∿ The Beruria Incident &∿

In the spring of 2002, Malya, the oldest of my three children, was enrolled in a yeshiva for young Jewish women in the Old City of Jerusalem. The majority of the high school graduates from the Orthodox schools my children have gone to spend a year of religious study and touring in Israel before most of them then go on to college.

Malya's high school in New Jersey was an all-girls yeshiva named Beruria. Beruria is the name of one of the best-known personalities in the Talmud. Her reputation is based on her brilliance and on the fact that she is a woman in the Talmudic world of two thousand years ago dominated by men.

Beruria was the wife of Rabbi Meir. Rabbi Meir was a student and colleague of the great Rabbi Akiva. They lived at the time of the destruction of the Second Temple in Jerusalem, which occurred in 70 C.E.

The Talmud tells a moving story about Beruria and Rabbi Meir. One Shabbat, Rabbi Meir came home from his house of study and prayer and asked his wife where their two sons were. He was looking for them but had not seen them in the house of study.

Beruria was aware that their two sons were dead, but she did not have the heart at that moment to share that with her husband. It was still Shabbat. She would spare him the news for a few hours. The text does not make it clear why the sons were dead. Some say they were part of a Jewish resistance movement against the Roman oppressors and were murdered.

He went back to the house of study and came home later and once again inquired of Beruria, "Where are our sons?"

Beruria responded by saying, "Can I ask you a question, my husband, my teacher?"

He said, "Of course."

Beruria asked, "If someone loans jewels to me and then comes back to retrieve them, must I return the jewels?"

Rabbi Meir said, "Yes, of course you must return what was on loan to you."

And Beruria responded, "Our jewels have been reclaimed by him who lent them to us."

One day, Malya came home from high school at Beruria and was troubled. She said to me, "Abba, did you hear what happened to Beruria at the end of her life?" (Kiddushin 80b).

I told her I did recall that there was an incident that was quite controversial, but I did not remember the details.

Malya told me that the Talmud says that Rabbi Meir left the community to live elsewhere because of some incident regarding Beruria (Avodah Zara 18b). However, the Talmud does not explain what the incident was or why it would prompt Rabbi Meir to leave his community.

But Rashi, the famous biblical and Talmudic commentator who was born around the year 1000, gives us, in his commentary, some details of the incident involving Beruria.

"Beruria made fun of the adage of the Sages that women are lightheaded. Then Rabbi Meir said to her: 'With your life you will have to take back your words.' He sent one of his students to test her, to see if she would allow herself to be seduced. He sat near her a whole day, and she finally surrendered herself to him. When she realized what had happened, she strangled herself. Then Rabbi Meir ran away to Babylonia because of the incident" (Avodah Zara 18b).

Malya said to me, "Abba, I don't understand. Why would they name a school after a married woman who was seduced by another man? Why would they name a school after a woman who committed suicide? And why would Rabbi Meir have put his student up to such a thing?"

She went on to say, "Beruria is such an amazing person. How horrible that this brilliant woman in the Talmud ends up in such a terrible way!"

Well, Malya and I proceeded, over the next several months, to try to find out more about Rashi's horrific story about the "incident regarding Beruria" in the Talmud.

Searching for the Truth About Beruria

The first thing that Malya and I did was to look through our library of books to see whether anybody else shed light on the Beruria incident. We found many books that mentioned the incident but none that contributed to our understanding of it or gave any insight into it.

Malya and I then proceeded to reach out to other people. We brainstormed, trying to think who could help us understand the incident. What's going on here? Why would the brilliant, amazing Beruria and the extraordinary Rabbi Meir have become involved with such matters?

One person Malya asked was one of her teachers at her yeshiva. Malya and I ultimately decided, of all the people we asked, he gave the worst answer.

He said, "Yes, it's a horrible story. I never thought Rashi really said it. I always thought it was stuck in there by somebody else."

Malya and I decided this was the most disappointing answer because, as Malya put it, "You can't just throw out a comment by Rashi and claim that he didn't say it just because you don't happen to like what it says."

We asked two rabbis in our town, each of whom said they would get back to us, but neither of them did. We wrote a letter to a well-known Torah scholar, who wrote back a cryptic letter that didn't do much more than repeat the tale.

In our research, one scholar we found wrote, "It clearly was invented simply to morally annihilate Beruria, the one woman of superior stature in the Talmud, Beruria the feminist—for it was exactly on that point that she was attacked. Because she took an overtly feminist stance of rejecting the rabbinic stereotyping of women as intellectually inferior, she was told she would have to give up her life. Feminism was a capital crime! In male chauvinist fashion, the moral destruction planned for her would reduce her to the female stereotype, a weak sexual creature who could not resist a determined Don Juan."[8]

A Visit to Rabbi Steinsaltz's Office in Jerusalem

At a certain point, Malya and I left our exploration of the question of this story about Beruria; two years later, when Malya was studying in Jerusalem, I traveled to Israel to spend a week with her, and we took the opportunity to pay a visit to Rabbi Steinsaltz.

We arrived at the Rabbi's office after hours. Almost everyone had gone home except for Rabbi Steinsaltz and his assistant, Thomas Nissel. Thomas, who is one of the sweetest men in the world, welcomed us, we schmoozed for a while in his office, and then Rabbi Steinsaltz came out, greeted us warmly, and brought us into his office, where we chatted for the next few hours.

It was my first time as a guest in the Rabbi's office in the Holy City of Jerusalem. For more than two decades, my relationship with Rabbi Steinsaltz had developed while I was driving him around in my car.

I looked around the office; it was a simple space, with some books, a phone, and a computer. A couple of pictures hung on the wall.

Rabbi Steinsaltz greeted us warmly. It was nice for me to see how genuinely pleased he was to see Malya. Rabbi Steinsaltz told us he was expecting a visitor in a few minutes but it would only be a ten-minute meeting. Within a few moments, his visitor arrived. It was the famous Russian refusenik and Israeli politician and writer Natan Scharansky. When I was a college student, Scharansky was a modern-day hero, resisting Soviet anti-Semitism, speaking out on behalf of oppressed Russians Jews, and spending years in a Soviet prison for his belief in religious freedom and his dedication to the Jewish people.

Rabbi Steinsaltz introduced Malya and me to Scharansky, who reached out and shook my hand, saying, "Welcome to Israel."

After ten minutes, Rabbi Steinsaltz was back with us. We spoke about Malya's experience in Israel. We talked a little bit about some of the publishing projects I was involved in, and then I looked at Malya and said, "Malya, why don't we ask Rabbi Steinsaltz our question?"

I was referring, of course, to our pursuit of some understanding of the incident regarding Beruria.

Malya smiled and said, "Good idea," and then paused and said, "Why don't *you* ask him?"

Rabbi Steinsaltz was sitting there patiently as Malya and I were talking about him as if he weren't in the room.

I said to Malya, "I really think *you* should ask him. It was originally your question."

Malya agreed, turned to Rabbi Steinsaltz, and said, "I go to a school named Beruria. All the references to Beruria in the Talmud that I've encountered have caused me to admire her. I also admire her great husband, Rabbi Meir, of course. But one day, I stumbled across a comment by Rashi that said . . ."

She paused upon realizing that she didn't need to tell Rabbi Steinsaltz what the Talmud says. Rabbi Steinsaltz very kindly nodded his head and said, "I know what you are referring to."

Malya then said, "I don't get it."

Rabbi Steinsaltz said, "What don't you get?"

Malya said, "I don't understand what happened. Should I just agree with my Talmud teacher that someone other than Rashi just stuck it in there, that it was really an anti-Beruria comment inserted by someone else? Can you help us understand the incident?"

At that point, Rabbi Steinsaltz did something I've seen him do many times, which I've often thought would be impossible to put into words, but I will try.

When Rabbi Steinsaltz speaks about the Talmud, he speaks about it as though he is on the inside of it.

First of all, he speaks about the individuals in the Talmud in the present tense. So it isn't that almost two thousand years ago that Rabbi Meir *said* something but rather that he *just* said something.

What I mean to say is that when Rabbi Steinsaltz began to speak to Malya and me about this incident, he seemed to speak about it as though he were there. He seemed to speak about it as though he had just come down the street from Rabbi Meir's house, that the incident had happened a moment before and he was familiar with it.

Many times since that day, Malya and I have spoken about the amazing experience of listening to Rabbi Steinsaltz as he speaks so intimately and in such a familiar way about the Talmud. As I said, he seems to *be* there.

"We Don't Have Plastic Saints in Judaism"

I want to put this all into a certain context. There is a controversy in the Orthodox community; my children encounter it on a regular basis in their yeshivas. As a publisher, I also encounter it and the issue is this: How do we describe our great Torah leaders?

Do we describe only their positive traits, resulting in books that portray these Torah teachers as perfect beings? Or do we tell it like it is and see our teachers, even the greatest of the great, as fallible and complex human beings?

In the publishing business, this issue shows its face when certain books are published that are condemned by some loud voices in the Orthodox world because they describe certain highly regarded Torah teachers as human. Certain books have been suppressed and even banned because biographies of individuals painted a human picture.

There are many books published in the Orthodox world that, as Rabbi Steinsaltz puts it, "make people into plastic saints."

In my children's yeshivas, this issue shows its face during class-room discussions that my kids have told me about for years.

Some teachers, as well as some students, are appalled when anyone even suggests that one of the great Torah leaders may have been wrong about something.

When Malya pressed Rabbi Steinsaltz, asking him what had happen in this incident with Beruria, Rabbi Steinsaltz said, "It was, seemingly, a miscalculation."

"What do you mean?" Malya asked.

Rabbi Steinsaltz smiled and said, "The student of Rabbi Meir was possibly in love with both of them. The student comes to the house to see his teacher, his teacher who he loves, he really loves. And he sees his teacher's wife and possibly falls in love with her too."

Again as Rabbi Steinsaltz spoke, Malya and I both felt he was describing something he knew to be a fact, as though he had lived through it himself.

He continued, "Rabbi Meir seemingly miscalculated."

Even though he kept saying "seemingly," it truly felt like he knew precisely that this is how it happened. "It was an experiment gone bad. He didn't think it would go that far."

Malya, studying at a Jerusalem yeshiva where certain teachers wouldn't dare criticize a rabbi, let alone suggest that a sage from the Talmud such as Rabbi Meir could have "miscalculated," said, "How can you say that? How can you say that about a sage from the Talmud? He was a *tzaddik* [righteous man]."

Rabbi Steinsaltz responded, "First, we don't decide who is a *tzaddik*. This is something *Hakodosh Baruch Hu* decides. But even a *tzaddik* can miscalculate. We don't have plastic saints in Judaism. Some people like making them. We don't do it."

A few years later, I asked Malya what details she recalled from the conversation. She wrote me the following letter:

Dear Abba,

I received your message asking me for my recollection of the time we spent discussing Beruria with Rabbi Steinsaltz. I've been thinking about how to describe that meeting for several weeks now, and it's not easy.

For me, that story really encapsulates several pivotal philosophical problems and also demonstrates how awesome Rabbi Steinsaltz is because of the way he addressed them.

First of all, I think an important part of the story is how distressed I was by the issue of Beruria. The doubts it introduced for me were huge. How could people whose lives seemed as torrid as a soap opera plotline be my moral role models?

Moreover, how could I live my life based on a legal corpus crafted by people who seemed to lack not only wisdom but also basic morality? The problem was compounded by the fact that no one around me seemed to appreciate it. I asked lots of people to respond to the story and got all sorts of answers.

Some told me it was a lesson for women not to learn so much. Others said that it was written by chauvinist rabbis to keep women away from the text. The vice principal of my high school said that it might not even have been written by Rashi but was some kind of decoy! I found all these answers offensive and beside the point. No one spoke to the issues that I felt were at the heart of the story. How could one know such a story and be an observant Jew? That was the question I needed answered.

It was with this mind-set that I posed the question to Rabbi Steinsaltz. It was pretty ridiculous asking Rabbi Steinsaltz, "Do you know what Rashi wrote about Beruria?" . . . But anyway, I asked him to explain the story.

And he launched into something very puzzling. He basically began a rather detailed psychological profile of both Beruria and Rabbi Meir. What he said was that both were these very intense, letter-of-the-law, exacting personalities. He cited a couple of anecdotes from other places in the Talmud to support this. He told one story about how Beruria once passed one of her husband's colleagues on the road. He stopped her and asked, "Excuse me, which road is the road to Lidda (a nearby city)?"

Beruria replied, "Haven't you heard the rabbinic dictum not to speak excessively with a woman? You should have said 'Which way to Lidda?'"

Clearly, this was a woman who lived her life in a harsh and exact way. Rabbi Meir was apparently similar.

There is another anecdote in which Rabbi Meir actually prays for a group of heretics to die. Beruria finally stops him, not because of any discomfort with wishing others dead, but because she had found a textual proof from the Torah that he should not do so.

This is why the two of them could create such an intense struggle around a legal debate. This was their total, all-encompassing, and unforgiving reality. It is what made them compatible as a couple and what tore them apart.

The Rabbi then went on to discuss the student's psychological state. He spoke about the idea that a student might fall in love with a beloved teacher and by extension with those his teacher loves. He might have the desire to slip into the life of the teacher, to see how it is to inhabit his place. This is how the student might have come to actually sleep with Beruria, not just seduce her.

Listening to all this, I was very distraught. While what he was saying was interesting, it once again seemed beside the point. The Rabbi was discussing how the story was

NOTES FROM THE ROAD:
Parents

This morning, Rabbi Steinsaltz and I were talking about the potential difficulties that children have when they become more religious than their parents. He said, "My best advice, in so many cases, is not to be pushy. Try not to make life miserable for others, even when you know you are right.

"When parents see their children change, it is a shock. Sometimes the parents think that the change in their children is a criticism of them. My advice is this: one should be as patient with one's parents as one can possibly be. Try to maintain the relationship as much as possible. It is important to show that becoming religious does not mean destroying relationships."

possible psychologically and emotionally. I wanted an explanation of how it was possible *theologically*.

So I interrupted him.

I wanted to stop him, tell him he wasn't addressing what I felt was most important.

"But these are *tzaddikim!* (righteous individuals)," I said. He replied, "Only God judges who is righteous. We have no idea."

And that's when I understood. He was addressing my question. He was painting Beruria and her husband as humans with motives and fatal flaws because that's what they were. Because if we see the personalities of the Torah as otherly beings with desires and feelings completely unlike our own, how can we learn from them?

Of what use are their stories to us? Jewish law has validity precisely because it was created *by* flawed humans *for* flawed humans and therefore can speak to us with all our frailties. Rabbi Steinsaltz, in his inimitable fashion, had forced me into a revelation. This isn't to say that I don't still struggle with these questions. However, he managed to transform the story of Beruria from a disturbing tragedy into the conduit of a crucial new paradigm.

Anyway, I think this conveys my take on the whole incident.

I love you,

Malya

❧ Love and Romance ❧

Not long after Malya and I visited Rabbi Steinsaltz, my younger daughter, Miriam, told me that she wanted to speak with the Rabbi. She had heard me quoting him for years, had heard my stories for a long time, and had some issues she wanted to discuss.

I promised Miriam, who was eighteen at the time, that I would take her with me the next time I drove Rabbi Steinsaltz. And that's just what happened.

Miriam came with me to JFK Airport early in the morning. I knew that Rabbi Steinsaltz would not mind if I brought her, that he would be happy to speak with her. We went to the offices in Manhattan where the Aleph Society does its work of fundraising and coordinating Rabbi Steinsaltz's publications and visits in America. I told Rabbi Steinsaltz that Miriam wanted some private time with him, and he consented.

I left them alone for about twenty minutes.

When I returned to the room, they were engrossed in conversation. Miriam was looking Rabbi Steinsaltz straight in the eye. She said emphatically, "Well, I disagree with you!"

"That's my daughter," I thought proudly. So many people come to Rabbi Steinsaltz for counsel, for advice, to drink up his words. My daughter came for a discussion. And she had no hesitation disagreeing with him.

Miriam taped the conversation and shared it with me a few weeks later.

She began, "My first question is this. You know that my parents are not together."

"Yes, I know," said Rabbi Steinsaltz.

"Well, I have a hard time with it," Miriam said. "If everyone is supposed to have one *bashert* [beloved, soulmate]."

Rabbi Steinsaltz interrupted. "All of these things about everyone having a *bashert*—it's not good for the girls and it's not good for the boys. Is a couple supposed to be together forever? It may be that the person for whom someone is destined will meet that person when he or she is fifty-nine-years old. And before that they were married to other people.

"The Rebono Shel Olam [Master of the World] can make a *shiddach* [match], but it doesn't mean that a *shiddach* that he made is a *shiddach* where both parties will be happy."

"How does that make sense?" Miriam challenged.

Rabbi Steinsaltz responded, "Sometimes you have a *shiddach* where a certain combination of genes will make something worthwhile. They will be unhappy with each other; they won't have a minute of happiness. But they will produce something worthwhile.

"The *shiddach* is the right *shiddach*. It is made from the hand of God. But God possibly didn't consider the happiness of the couple at all."

Miriam asked, "So my parents may have been put together but not for them?"

"Yes, that's what I'm saying," Rabbi Steinsaltz insisted. "It may not be for them. You are the product of this marriage. It may be that *you* are what is worthwhile from it. Your parents had three children. This may be enough."

He continued, "It may be worse. It may be that a man is marrying a woman and the outcome is that she'll make him so miserable that he will not want to be home; home will be hell for him. So he goes and sits and learns. His wife is possibly unknowingly pushing him to a great achievement. It doesn't mean the *shiddach* is for happiness.

"There is a story—I don't know if it is true—about the wife of Socrates. She was supposed to be a model of a miserable wife. She may be the reason that he was in the streets talking with people.

"What was the name of the Rambam's wife? And were they happy together? I don't know at all.

"Your great-grandfather was possibly married. Was he happy in his marriage? It may not matter that much."

Miriam objected. "Why?" she demanded.

"For some people it might matter. For others it doesn't.

"There was a time when a man and his wife didn't call each other by their first name until many years of being married. They didn't think that the relationship should go deeper. There were thousands of people like this. Hundreds of thousands of people like this.

"Sometimes you can call a successful marriage one where people live together, they don't have too many fights, they had

Hollywood is an advertisement for a dream, a very shallow dream—a dream about a simplified Heaven, about life that is supposed to be reality, but is not.

—Rabbi Adin Steinsaltz, *Simple Words,* p. 142

nice children, and their households were well organized. But happiness? Who cares?"

Rabbi Steinsaltz continued, "I know it's a terrible thing to ask, but how old are you?"

"Eighteen," Miriam replied.

"Then it is surely the wrong time to tell it to you. But I'll say it: it is possible that the Almighty is not romantically minded at all."

"He's *not*?" Miriam questioned.

"Perhaps not," Rabbi Steinsaltz replied. "Perhaps he doesn't watch American films.

"If you went to most people in the world to ask for an account of what makes a good marriage, it would be very different from what you think of as a good marriage. A person might not be happy. He might be content."

"Is that enough?" Miriam asked.

"For whom? For most people, it would seem to be enough."

"I wouldn't be happy with that," Miriam said.

"Maybe. But that's because you've seen American films."

"You think that's why?" Miriam asked.

"Mostly."

"Do you think that's good?" Miriam probed.

"I don't want to frighten you. It's not a good thing, even though sometimes when you are frightened, you appreciate more of what you have. But sometimes people want all kinds of things from their marriages. Sometimes people get divorced and remarry other people and they find that they are still not happy. It's possibly because their unhappiness had nothing to do with the other person.

"Do you have friends?" Rabbi Steinsaltz asked Miriam.

"Yes."

"Are you in love with them?"

"I love them," Miriam said.

"Yes, but are you in love with them? You are not. This is what happens to couples. They stop being in love with each other and they begin to love each other. It's a very different feeling. I don't know if you have been in love. When you are overwhelmed, when you have nothing in your head but dreaming about that person, seeing their picture, kissing their picture, you feel that you will always be close. But it usually changes from being in love to loving each other.

"You may, for example, love your parents, but you're not in love with them."

"Do you think that it's better that way?" Miriam asked.

"It is surely a more stable relationship. Being in love is not stable. Being in love romantically can take three months or four months. Later on, you either love that person or you don't love that person."

"Do you think that there is anyone who has a romantic relationship for more than three or four months?" Miriam asked.

"Possibly not. I've never made a study of it. But I would say it is less common. People may have revivals. But usually when you see a young couple, after a short while they like being with each other, but they are not so lively about it.

"If someone were to ask me or my wife if we love chocolate, we would both say yes. We love chocolate. We are obviously not in love with chocolate. It is a long and strange relationship we have had with chocolate for many years. Sometimes chocolate doesn't love us—but that's something else.

"Often people expect things from marriage that marriage cannot provide. In movies, you see that they live happily ever after. In fairy tales, that's the most unreal part of the fairy tale. Not the dragons and the magic. That they lived happily ever after—that's the real fantasy in a fairy tale.

"When people get divorced, sometimes they get divorced because they can't stand each other. I am telling young people that there are more important things than what kind of a nose someone has. Try to find out what kind of a life the person wants. Now, if two people want different kinds of lives, sometimes they have to get divorced even though they like each other. He is going one way, and she is going the other. So they cannot be together. Often people who are divorced get along better than when they were married. They have fights because they can't find a common way.

"Let's say you have a friend and you decide to hike together but you don't want to go to the same place. What happens? You split. Does it mean that you don't like your friend? No. You like your friend, but you're not going to the same place."

"Why do you think that people start out loving each other but don't end up that way?" Miriam asked.

"Being in love is often like being drunk.

"People love each other and then find out that there are other sides to the person that they didn't know before or didn't notice before."

Hollywood is not just a place—it is a world in itself. Hollywood has done something remarkable: it has created a great and very successful religion. Through its successful missionaries—the films produced in Hollywood—it has spread all around the globe, gaining adherents faster than any other religion in the world. If it has not attained the stature of a full-fledged religion, at least it is a very strong cult.

—Rabbi Adin Steinsaltz, *Simple Words,* p. 133

"Do you think that if people paid more attention, it wouldn't happen?"

"It would happen far less, but you never really know what will happen in a relationship."

Seeing that I have mentioned my daughters, I want to add something about my son, Moshe. He was born two months premature. After spending weeks in the incubator, he finally recovered and came home. His bris was not eight days after his birth, as is usually the case, but rather a few months after he arrived.

But it was not until the ordeal was over that I told Rabbi Steinsaltz what had happened.

And he scolded me, saying, "Please don't do that to me. If something is happening of importance in your life, I want to know about it."

Moshe is a now a student at a yeshiva high school. A serious scholar of the world's great spiritual traditions, he is an articulate, lovely young man with a sharp mind. When Moshe celebrated his bar mitzvah four years ago, I sent the Rabbi a note telling him of the occasion. Shortly thereafter, a letter arrived from Rabbi Steinsaltz. "Dear Arthur," he wrote.

> *Mazal tov* on the Bar Mitzvah of your son. I hope that it will be for him an important beginning of a new role and a great number of new duties. I would bless all of your family to use this event as a sign for growth and invigoration,
>
> Please tell your son my usual advice for a Bar Mitzvah boy—that in addition to the regular duties that are imposed on him, to choose a special thing to do voluntarily, like saying a chapter of *Tehillim* [Psalms] every day or learning an additional Mishnah daily.
>
> That should be his recurring thanks, not to his family, but to the Giver of all.
>
> Adin Steinsaltz

CHAPTER FIVE

Photo © Flash Rosenberg.

"If You Think You've Arrived, You're Lost" (2005)

Only when a man can relate his inner center to God
as the first and foremost and only reality,
only then does his self take on meaning.

—Rabbi Adin Steinsaltz,
The Thirteen Petalled Rose, p. 147

It is 5:30 A.M., fall 2005. I am standing in the International Arrivals Building at JFK Airport. Rabbi Steinsaltz's flight has just landed.

I'm more tired than usual this morning. I usually get at least a few hours of sleep when I pick up Rabbi Steinsaltz, despite having to get up at 3:30 A.M.

But last night, I was out very late doing a performance of my one-man show "Searching for God in a Magic Shop," which blends my interest in Jewish theology with my interest in performing magic.

Funny, but in some ways, I see my Jewish magic show as the culmination of all of my work. My genealogical research, my spiritual studies from Jewish sources as well as from other traditions, my countless hours with Rabbi Steinsaltz's books, and my time with the Rabbi himself over the years have all come together in, of all things, a magic show!

The show last night had been at a synagogue just north of Manhattan. The audience consisted of members of three congregations who sponsored the program together.

The audience seemed to love the show, and I went home all wound up and didn't sleep at all.

But I'm so eager to share my thoughts about the show with Rabbi Steinsaltz today.

Wow. I'm in luck. Rabbi Steinsaltz is the first passenger out of customs. We're on the road again. . . .

❧ *"Baruch Hashem"* ❧

As we walked to my car, Rabbi Steinsaltz looked at me and asked, "So how are *you?*"

And I said to him, enthusiastically, "*Baruch Hashem* [Blessed is the Name]."

Rabbi Steinsaltz once told a group of teachers that the most important thing they could give their students was their enthusiasm. I later learned that the original meaning of the word *enthusiasm* was "putting God into it."

I had come to learn that in the Orthodox world, the appropriate response to the question "How are you?" was always "*Baruch Hashem,*" "Blessed is the Name" or "Blessed is God," an expression of gratitude to the Almighty.

So when Rabbi Steinsaltz said to me, "How are you?" I found that I automatically said to him, "*Baruch Hashem.*"

Rabbi Steinsaltz looked at me and stopped walking. I stopped too. He stared at me and said, "What kind of answer is *that?*"

I said to him, "'What kind of answer is that?' I thought that *is* the answer!"

And Rabbi Steinsaltz said to me, "Yes, I know, *Baruch Hashem,* Blessed is the Almighty. I don't disagree with you on that.

"But it doesn't tell me anything. I'm asking you, 'How *are* you?'"

I told Rabbi Steinsaltz that I was fine, my family members were all fine, and I was eager to speak with him about the magic show I had performed the night before.

But our first stop on this trip was, as it had been for several years now, the *ohel,* the grave of the Lubavitcher Rebbe. Rabbi Steinsaltz visits the *ohel* on almost every trip, usually on our way into Manhattan from JFK, since it's only about ten minutes from the airport.

The Rabbi and I both wanted to say our morning prayers and put on tefillin. So first we spent time in the small chapel located in the house adjacent to the cemetery where the Rebbe's grave is located, in Queens, New York.

After our prayers, we sat in an area where one can write out one's own personal prayers, which are then read in front of the

Rebbe's grave by each individual in a whisper, after which the paper is torn and dropped into a dry pool-like area in front of the gravestone. Tens of thousands, perhaps hundreds of thousands, of small pieces of paper with personal prayers on them have been recited and dropped in front of the grave of the Lubavitcher Rebbe. Each of the times that Rabbi Steinsaltz and I have visited the Rebbe's *ohel* over the past few years, we have written our own prayers and have done the same.

We then drove to Rabbi Steinsaltz's first appointment, a meeting with someone in an office in New York City.

Rabbi Steinsaltz noticed that I had a beat-up copy of *The Thirteen Petalled Rose* next to the driver's seat. I said to him, "I'm still reading it."

Before we spoke about my interest in magic and my show, I remembered that I had never told Rabbi Steinsaltz the story of one of the most important moments for me in relationship to that book—which I have been studying for over twenty-five years.

⚘ The Hasid on the Subway ⚘

"Rabbi," I said, "I'd like to tell you a story."

I explained to Rabbi Steinsaltz that after my first child, Malya, was born in 1984, I knew we would have to look for a larger space. We were living in a tiny apartment, not big enough for three of us, let alone more—since we were sure we wanted more children.

At the time, I said, "I don't care where we move, as long as we stay on the F train."

I loved riding that subway line from my home in Brooklyn to my office at Behrman House publishers, where I was a senior editor, working on textbooks for Jewish afternoon and

Sunday schools, on Broadway at Thirty-First Street in Manhattan. On the F train, there were always men studying Talmud, and there were always women reading from the *Tehillim,* the book of Psalms.

Every morning and every evening, on every car, we could have organized a *minyan* [quorum for prayer].

There were Jews all around me in the morning and at night. It felt like a Jewish Disney World. I loved it.

I told Rabbi Steinsaltz that I had remembered learning from my first Talmud teacher, the poet Danny Siegel, that the Talmud says you should not travel even two cubits with a fellow Jew without "talking Torah." A cubit is the distance from the tip of your elbow to the tip of your middle finger, about eighteen inches. It was the ancient yardstick. Thus the Talmud says that one should not travel three feet without talking Torah, making "big talk" as opposed to small talk, with a fellow Jew.

So there I was, every morning and every evening, on a subway car filled with fellow Jews, and yet the etiquette in the New York subway system is that usually nobody talks to anybody. One can be sitting or standing for miles and miles through the winding tunnels of the New York subway system and never hear anyone speak to anyone.

Until one particular day, I had never had the courage to strike up a conversation.

Rabbi Steinsaltz smiled. He seemed to be enjoying the story. And I was enjoying telling it to him.

I continued.

At that time, my subway ride from Brooklyn to New York and back again to Brooklyn was occupied with my close and careful studying of *The Thirteen Petalled Rose.* I had my copy with me all the time, and I spent my traveling time reading it.

Sometimes I was happy to get through a few sentences. Sometimes I was proud to complete a paragraph or a page.

I said to Rabbi Steinsaltz, "Ultimately, after reading and rereading the book, after understanding the ideas and how those ideas build on other ideas to create new structures and new visions, I was able to actually go through an entire chapter in one trip between my home and my office."

I then told Rabbi Steinsaltz that one evening, I was on the F train winding its way back to Brooklyn, and I was sitting next to an old Hasid dressed in traditional clothing.

He had a long white beard, long side curls, a traditional black hat, and a long black suit. He looked to be about eighty years old. And the Hasid was reading the *New York Post,* which many New Yorkers considered a low-brow, sensationalistic tabloid.

And I was reading the mystical Jewish text *The Thirteen Petalled Rose.*

I was feeling good about myself, reading a book of Kabbalah while this Hasid was reading the rag newspaper of New York.

I explained to Rabbi Steinsaltz that I was thinking about the passage from the Talmud about talking Torah with fellow Jews, and for some reason on that day, I got up the courage to look at the Hasid sitting next to me and say to him, "Excuse me. Might I ask you a question?"

The Hasid put his paper down and looked at me and said warmly, "Yes. What can I do for you?"

I showed him the cover of the book I was reading and asked, "Did you ever see this book?"

He took it from my hands, flipped through the first several pages, looked at me, and said, "I usually don't look at books unless they have at least two *haskamas.*"

I knew the term *haskama* from my genealogical research. It was an approbation, a seal of approval, alerting readers that the book was "kosher." In past generations, religious books had *haskamas,* and they often contained biographical information about the author as well as an endorsement.

I was tempted to ask the Hasid where in the *New York Post* he was reading was there a *haskama*? But I resisted the temptation. I remember that Rabbi Steinsaltz once said that when one resists the temptation to say something foolish, it is like a sacrifice on the altar in the Holy Temple.

Then the Hasid surprised me. "But it's not all that important," he said with a Yiddish accent. "What's the book about?"

I told him that the book was about fundamental ideas of Jewish thought.

I turned to the table of contents and showed him that there's a chapter called "Mitzvot" and a chapter called "Holiness" and a chapter called "Repentance" and a chapter called "Torah."

I repeated, "It's a book about basic Jewish ideas."

And then I said to him, "In fact, I have a question. May I ask you a question?"

"Of course," he said.

"Does Judaism teach about reincarnation?"

And as the F train was winding its way into Brooklyn, I turned to a page in *The Thirteen Petalled Rose* and read him a passage.

Rabbi Steinsaltz continued to be amused by the story. And as always, he listened closely.

I then did something that surprised Rabbi Steinsaltz. I recited, perfectly and from memory, the entire passage:

> It has been said that each of the letters of the Torah has some corresponding soul. That is to say every soul is a letter in the entire Torah and has its own part to play. The soul that has fulfilled its task that has done what it has to do in terms of creating or repairing its own part of the world and realizing its own essence can wait after death for

the perfection of the world as a whole, but not all the souls are so privileged. Many stray for one reason or another. Sometimes he misuses forces and spoils his portion and the portion of others. In such cases the soul does not complete its task and may even in itself be damaged by contact with the world. It does not manage to complete that portion of reality which only this particular soul can complete and therefore after the death of the body the soul returns and is reincarnated in the body of another person and again must try to complete what it failed to correct or what it injured in the past.[1]

I stopped there.

"Does Judaism teach about *reincarnation*?" I asked the Hasid.

He said, "Of course."

"I never *heard* of such a thing."

"Well, where did you get your Jewish education?" the Hasid asked.

Rabbi Steinsaltz was smiling, enjoying my story and his pipe as well.

I told the Hasid that I hadn't gotten much of a Jewish education as a child, whereupon he looked at me with an expression that seemed to say, "That's not much of a surprise."

But he then began to ask me questions, and we were suddenly involved in a personal conversation as the F train continued into Brooklyn.

I began to tell this old Hasid that I grew up in a home that did not offer much of the Jewish education but that my parents taught me great respect for Jewish tradition and sent me to a Conservative Hebrew school for a couple of years, perhaps just enough to be alienated from it. It wasn't until I finished graduate school and began to do some genealogy research that I fell in love with Jewish tradition.

I told him that during my genealogy research, there was a point at which I felt that I had more in common with my dead ancestors than I did with my living relatives.

I jokingly added that they were also much easier to get along with.

The Hasid laughed. Rabbi Steinsaltz smiled.

But I told this Hasid that I was trying to reconnect with Jewish tradition, that I was struggling with it, that it was difficult to integrate so many ideas and practices into my life.

I told him of my trials and my stumbling blocks and the general difficulty I was having with all of the laws of Jewish observance and with keeping up with the three prayer sessions a day.

The Hasid looked at me and said, "You are lucky—luckier than me."

"How is that possible?" I said.

"Every Jew is connected to God by a rope. Sometimes the rope has been broken, as in your case and the case of your family, but when a rope breaks and you take the two ends that broke and tie them together, the rope is shorter than it was before it broke.

"You're closer to God than I'll ever get," the Hasid said to me.

I then said to Rabbi Steinsaltz, "It was at that point that I understood some things clearly.

"One is that the Talmud is right. You shouldn't travel two cubits with a fellow Jew without talking Torah.

"The second is that perhaps the Hasid on the subway that late afternoon gave me the metaphor for my whole life. Because between my passion for genealogical research and my search for a teacher and a connection to Jewish tradition, I've really been looking for the ends of the broken rope and trying to tie them back together."

Rabbi Steinsaltz looked at me and was still smiling. I said to him, "Perhaps a third gift I received from that encounter was a personal understanding of a passage that is also in *The Thirteen Petalled Rose,* where you, Rabbi, talk about life being 'a descent for the sake of ascension.'"

And as I had done earlier, I recited the text from memory, this time the very last words of the chapter in *The Thirteen Petalled Rose* called "Repentance":

> The penitent does more than return to his proper place. He performs an act of amendment of cosmic significance. He restores the sparks of holiness which had been captured by the powers of evil. The sparks that he had dragged down and attached to him are now raised up with him and a host of forces of evil return and are transformed into forces of good. This is the significance of the statement in the Talmud "That in the place where a complete repentant stands, even the most saintly cannot enter." Because the penitent has at his disposal, not only the forces of good in his soul and in the world, but also those of evil which he transforms into essences of holiness.[2]

I told Rabbi Steinsaltz that I had read the notion in many books that the *baal teshuvah,* the person like me who is trying to master a process of return to Jewish life, is truly on a high spiritual level.

Rabbi Steinsaltz said, "There is a phrase in the book of Ecclesiastes [12:6]: 'Or ever the silver cord be loosed.' It is said that this cord is like an umbilical cord binding man to God.

"It is a cord that is said to be made up of numerous strands, the six hundred and thirteen *mitzvot.* Whenever we transgress, we cut one of the strands. Strand by strand, we sever ourselves from God.

"Man is given a certain amount of time to try to repair the severed thread, to tie it back together through his good deeds."

Rabbi Steinsaltz took a long puff on his pipe and said, "A broken strand that is tied together is also stronger than one that has never been torn. Just like a broken bone that forms a hard knob as it heals, making it stronger than before.

"This is the *baal teshuvah*. He is more steady and powerful than he was earlier."

A Totally Private Affair

I then said to Rabbi Steinsaltz, "I have been living in the Orthodox community for the past twenty-five years, and the more I live in it, the more I realize that the term *Orthodox* has little real meaning. I know people who are "Reform" Jews who have a deep love for Torah and faith in God, and I know Orthodox Jews who walk through it and follow all the dos and don'ts and never seem to think about it. So there are all kinds of people on the spectrum."

I explained that I don't feel that they are a useful bunch of terms, *Reform, Conservative,* and *Orthodox.*

I said, "When I was growing up, in the 'non-Orthodox world,' I used to think that there are all kinds of different non-Orthodox Jews—there's Reform and Conservative and Reconstructionist and right-wing Conservative and liberal Conservative and all different kinds of other non-Orthodox Jews.

"And then there are the Orthodox.

"Well, once I started living in the Orthodox world, I concluded the exact opposite. There are all kinds of Orthodox Jews—there's modern Orthodox and Satmar and Lubavitch and B'nai Brak and all kinds of other Orthodox Jews.

And then there's the non-Orthodox.

"Well, obviously, both sides are wrong. In fact, everybody's different. We all have our own individual paths."

I said to Rabbi Steinsaltz that an important idea I learned in *The Thirteen Petalled Rose* is that our relationship to God is a totally private affair.

🌿 Magic as Metaphor 🌿

The drive from JFK to the Rebbe's grave and then on to Manhattan didn't take long. We were quite early for Rabbi Steinsaltz's New York City appointment. We sat in the car and talked for about half an hour.

Defining oneself only in relation to secondary things leaves one's being as nothing but a series of empty shells each dependent on the others for meaning. Thus a man is defined as this one's friend, that one's son, the father of another, the one occupied with this or that, the one who thinks this or that, someone engaged with certain problems, and all these are only shadow relationships that leave him a faceless, empty figure trying to clothe itself with some visible individuation. Only when a man can relate his inner center to God as the first and foremost and only reality, only then does his self take on meaning.

—Rabbi Adin Steinsaltz, *The Thirteen Petalled Rose,*
   p. 147

I told Rabbi Steinsaltz that I wanted to speak with him about my interest in magic and to tell him about my show the night before.

"How did you get interested in magic?" Rabbi Steinsaltz asked me. He knew that I had an interest in the subject, but until now we never spoke much about it.

"One day, my father and I drove to a costume store in search of a three-cornered hat for my third-grade class play about George Washington," I told Rabbi Steinsaltz, "and in the shop, I noticed that there was a small counter dedicated to magic tricks. And it was on that evening that my father purchased my first magic trick for me."

"Do you remember the trick?" he asked.

"It was a little box that changed a penny into a dime. And ever since, I've had a serious interest in magic.

"A few years ago, I began performing a ninety-minute show I'd written for myself called "Searching for God in a Magic Shop," combining magic with my interest in Jewish ideas, Jewish history, and Jewish life.

"May I tell you about it? The central idea of my show is that a magician is able to fool his audience because of one fact—the fact that the audience does not *see* everything. If the audience saw everything, the audience would understand how the trick is done.

"Most magical effects are quite simple," I said. "Usually, a small bit of information makes the performance of a seemingly impossible miracle perfectly clear."

I then said, "In modern magical literature, magic is referred to as 'misdirection' because the magician is directing the audience's attention in a certain direction so that the audience does not see the small bit of information that would make everything clear."

I then told Rabbi Steinsaltz that I had been fascinated to learn that in the Talmud, magic tricks and performances by magicians are referred to as "capturing the eye," the idea being that the magician does not want the audience to see everything, and that's how the magic trick works.

I told Rabbi Steinsaltz that I was familiar with the discussion of magic in the Talmud (Sanhedrin 67a-b). Right there in the Talmud, the performance of magic tricks is explored, a few tricks are even described, and the passage has largely become the basis of the answer to the question as to whether performing magic tricks is permitted by Jewish law.

I asked Rabbi Steinsaltz whether in his judgment it is permissible, according to Jewish law, to perform deceptive magic tricks, and he echoed the position expressed by many other rabbis throughout the centuries that magic shows are permitted as long as the magician does not use it to claim that he has special powers. As long as the magic show is for entertainment or education (both of which fit my own show), Jewish law permits it.

And then I told Rabbi Steinsaltz that the whole point of my using magic tricks is to teach. Magic is a metaphor for the profound Jewish notion referred to by the phrase *gam zu l'tova*.

🍃 Everything Is for the Best 🍃

Gam zu l'tova, an Aramaic expression found in the Talmud that means "This too is for the best," represents the perspective that traditional Jewish wisdom urges us all to cultivate: despite appearances, despite all of life's tragedies, nothing happens in the world that God does not allow to happen. Thus in some inexplicable way, everything is ultimately for the best.

The reason we humans do not understand why bad things happen to good people is that we, like the audiences at my magic shows, do not see the whole picture. We see only a part of what is going on around us. If we saw everything, as the magician does at the magic show and as God does in His universe, we would not wonder why things happen the way they do.

I reiterated to Rabbi Steinsaltz my understanding that the reason we say "*gam zu l'tova*" is to cultivate the spiritual idea in our mind and in our being that we don't see everything in life and also to acknowledge that God sees everything, God knows everything, God has a reason for allowing everything to happen the way it happens, and life is so confusing to humans simply because we don't see it all.

So the central idea embedded within my magic show and my main goal in the show is to teach the idea of *gam zu l'tova.*

I said to Rabbi Steinsaltz, "I tell stories related to that idea throughout Jewish history, and I do magic tricks while I'm telling these stories, all in order to share with audiences the notion that our sages ask us to cultivate the awareness that we don't see everything, we receive only a small slice of reality.

"It is like the dog hearing a dog whistle that a human cannot hear. The frequencies that the dog is able to hear are out of range for the human being."

I asked Rabbi Steinsaltz if he would be kind enough to tell me the Talmudic story of Rabbi Akiva and his use of the phrase *gam zu l'tova* as he knows it. I tell the story at every magic show that I do, but I wanted to hear Rabbi Steinsaltz tell it.

Rabbi Steinsaltz said, "Rabbi Akiva was traveling and could not get lodging at the inn. He had with him a candle to read by, a donkey who took him to the forest where he could sleep, and a rooster who would wake him in the morning.

"When he could not get lodging, he said, 'This too is for the best.' That night, a lion came and killed his donkey, a cat ate his rooster, and the wind snuffed out his candle. Rabbi Akiva said, '*Gam zu l'tova,*' this too is for the best.

"He curled up and slept peacefully.

"In the morning, he learned that a band of robbers had come to the inn, looted the place, and taken captives. Had his donkey brayed or had the rooster crowed or had the robbers seen his candle, he would have also been a victim."

Easier Said Than Done

"My faith tells me that God knows what he's doing. But it's difficult to always know it, to really know it," I suggest to Rabbi Steinsaltz.

Rabbi Steinsaltz responded, "It is known to be far more difficult to do than to say. There is the story of Rabbi Meilish, who was a rich merchant as well as a rabbi. He lived in Warsaw and Krakow.

"He was known as a scholar and was a teacher to the most brilliant students. At the same time, he was in the lumber business and sent timber by river to Germany to be sold there at a profit.

"Once there was news that the timber boats were destroyed in a storm. The rabbi lost everything in one day. The people did not know how to tell the rabbi, but one of his prized students did so.

"The student picked a passage in the Talmud and came to the Rabbi with his question: 'It says that one has to thank God with blessings for the evil that befalls one as well as for the good. How can this be done?'

"The rabbi explained various aspects of theology and some of the mystical meanings behind the notion.

"The student said, 'I am not sure I understand. If you, rabbi, learned that all your boats with timber had sunk, would you be happy?'

"The rabbi said, 'Yes, of course.'

"'Well,' said the student, 'all the boats are gone!'

"When he heard this, the rabbi fainted. When he came to, he said, 'Now I must confess I no longer understand this Talmud passage.'"

When Rabbi Steinsaltz finished the story, I said, "It's a difficult idea, but it is obviously central to Jewish teachings on the matter of our relationship to God, isn't it?"

Rabbi Steinsaltz replied, "Yes, everything is good, in the sense that it comes from God. But of course, suffering exists, and suffering is called evil. The good is hidden. Often several levels of excavation are needed to get to it, if at all. At other times, it's on the surface: sometimes your cow breaks its leg and you find a treasure at that spot."

There is an important teaching that goes along with the notion of *gam zu l'tova,* and that is the injunction that we can only say this about our own suffering but we are forbidden to say it to someone else who is suffering.

In other words, if you fall and bang your knee, my response to you must not be "Well, it's for the best." On the contrary, if I see someone suffering, my one obligation is to try to help relieve that suffering. Telling a suffering person that everything is for the best is called, in the Talmud, "the sins of the friends of Job." Job suffered greatly, and his friends said to him, "Don't you have faith in God?"

This is not what the friends should have said. Even though we do believe, as the Baal Shem Tov teaches, that *nothing* happens without God allowing and permitting it to happen, it is not appropriate to speak this theology while a person is struggling with pain or grief.

But if I fall and bang my own knee, I have a choice. I can wallow in my pain, or I can use the experience to stimulate my faith and to prompt me to examine my life more carefully and to grow, in empathy and understanding, from my experience.

Many of us have had terrible experiences, filled with suffering and pain. We would not want it to happen if we could change the course of things. But we also cannot deny that the tragedies we experience often lead to situations, wonderful and glorious situations, that would never have occurred had the tragedy not happened. The entire key to this subject is based on the notion that our souls existed before our bodies and that when we die, our souls continue on their eternal work.

From the point of view of those left behind after a death, for example, death is a sad experience. But from the point of view of the deceased, the soul does not die but rather is eternal and has its job to do.

Ultimately, God knows what he's doing.

NOTES FROM THE ROAD:
Big and Small

One morning, I was telling Rabbi Steinsaltz that I resented newspapers for deciding for us what is important and what is unimportant. I often notice that the headline of a newspaper will be about a story that will be forgotten in a few weeks and in the same paper, on page 22, at the bottom, in a one-inch article, it will say, "New Galaxy Discovered."

We went on to discuss that one of the great tasks in life is to figure out what is big and what is small. And that it's not always easy or even possible.

❧❧ The Story of Reb Zusia ❧❧

I told Rabbi Steinsaltz that I see the same wisdom reflected in the blessing that we are taught to recite on the occasion of hearing bad news and the one we recite when we learn that a person has died. The blessing we say is "*Baruch dayan emes*," "Blessed is the true judge." I then said to Rabbi Steinsaltz that he surely knows the story of Reb Zusia regarding that blessing.

"Yes," he said.

"Please tell me your version," I asked. I then added, "In my opinion, it is the most profound story I have ever heard."

"Well, Reb Zusia of Anipoli," Rabbi Steinsaltz said, "was known to be very poor and living in quite miserable conditions.

"Once two scholars came and asked Reb Zusia's teacher, the Maggid of Mezritch, the meaning of the precept that one has to recite a blessing on the bad as well as the good."

"The Maggid said, 'Go and ask my pupil, Reb Zusia.'

"They went to Reb Zusia's house, saw his impoverished life, saw how he lived, and put their question to him: 'Why are we to bless the bad as well as the good?'

"Reb Zusia answered, 'I really don't know why my teacher sent you to me. I have never known bad in my life at all.'

Rabbi Steinsaltz then said, "You can reach a stage where you transform all darkness into light."

Fooled by Surfaces

I told Rabbi Steinsaltz that one of the attractions I have to magic is that magic reminds me of something we often forget: it is easy to be fooled by surfaces.

That is, it is important to be able to distinguish the relative value of things and try to understand everything in context and from various points of view. I can't just let the *New York Times* or the TV news decide that for me.

Rabbi Steinsaltz said to me, "One of the things that we as people have to pray for is to be able to distinguish between what is important and unimportant, between a major event and a trivial happening. Usually we don't have sense enough to make these distinctions. We don't know what is great and what is small. Sometimes, we somehow mix them up. The important is considered unimportant, and vice versa.

"In fact," Rabbi Steinsaltz continued, "there is, in the Talmud, a story of somebody in a semiconscious state who saw the world and said it was a strange place. All the important people were sitting somewhere in low places, and the unimportant people were sitting above. His grandfather said, 'You saw the true world. We are living in a world in *Olam Hasheker,* in a world which is a lying world, a world which is untrue. You saw the *whole* world.'"

As I shared these ideas with Rabbi Steinsaltz, I saw that he was appreciating what I was suggesting. He recognized that my

Precisely because the Divine is apprehended as an infinite, not a finite, force, everything in the cosmos, whether small or large, is only a small part of the pattern, so that there is no difference in weight or gravity between any one part and another. The movement of a man's finger is as important or unimportant as the most terrible catastrophe, for as against the Infinite both are of the same dimension.

—Rabbi Adin Steinsaltz, *The Thirteen Petalled Rose*, p. 46

The process of the soul's connection with the body—called the "descent of the soul into matter"—is, from a certain perspective, the soul's profound tragedy. But the soul undertakes this terrible risk as a part of the need to descend in order to make the desired ascent to hitherto unknown heights.

—Rabbi Adin Steinsaltz, *The Thirteen Petalled Rose,*
    p. 54

magic tricks were a perfect metaphor for *gam zu l'tova,* this profound theological notion that is so central to Jewish thought.

He said to me, "Arthur, you are creating a new doorway to this material."

I was thrilled. This is precisely what I wanted the magic show to be, and it was wonderful to be able to get a seal of approval, a *haskama,* and words of encouragement and support from my teacher, my Rebbe.

A Family Story from Auschwitz

Rabbi Steinsaltz asked me how I bring genealogy into my magic show.

I told him that one of the things I tell my audiences is my discovery that my great-great-great-grandfather was a Hasidic rebbe in the town of Stropkov in Slovakia. I also mentioned to him that there's a yeshiva in Jerusalem on Chaim Ozer Street that is named after this direct ancestor, Rabbi Chaim Yosef Gottlieb.

One day, when I had the opportunity to travel to Jerusalem, I went to Chaim Ozer Street, a narrow, quiet road, looking for this yeshiva.

When I reached the building, I saw a Hasidic man sitting on a chair right next to the doorway. I walked up to him and saw that he was perhaps eighty years old.

He was dressed in traditional Hasidic clothing, his long *peyis* [side curls] hanging down almost to his shoulders.

I asked, "Is this the Chaim Yosef Gottlieb Yeshiva?"

He said, "Yes, how can I help you?"

I said to him, "Well, I'm a descendent of Rabbi Chaim Yosef."

He looked at me and said, "I *too* am a descendent of Rabbi Chaim Yosef."

We shook hands, we smiled at each other, and he said to me, "My name is Naftali Gottlieb. So tell me, who are you?"

I knew that he meant how am I connected to our shared ancestor, the Stropkover Rebbe?

I said to him, "Well, as you know, the Stropkover had five children, four sons and a daughter. Two of the sons were twins. I descend from the daughter."

In fact, the Stropkover Rebbe's daughter, whose name was Miriam, is the person after whom my daughter Miriam is named.

I repeated to him, "I descend from the daughter, Miriam Gittel."

He told me that he descended from one of the sons and then asked me how I was connected to the daughter.

I told him that the daughter's grandson was my grandfather. My grandfather was Zalman Leib.

The old Hasid looked at me and said excitedly, "*Zalman Leib!*"

I said, "Yes, my grandfather was Zalman Leib."

With great enthusiasm he said, "*Zalman Leib?* Zalman Leib from Bistritz?"

I said, "Yes, my grandfather Zalman Leib came from the town of Bistritz."

He said, "Zalman Leib. You're a grandson of Zalman Leib! Zalman Leib, the brother of Pinchas?"

I said, "*Yes,* that's my grandfather's brother; my grandfather had a brother named Pinchas, who was murdered in Auschwitz."

The old Hasid, my newly found cousin, looked at me and said, "Yes, I know." He rolled up his sleeve and showed me the tattoo on his arm and said, "I too was in Auschwitz. I learned Torah in Auschwitz with Pinchas."

So I was standing on a street in the city of Jerusalem before an elderly cousin of mine who discussed words of Torah in the death camps with my grandfather's brother who was murdered there. I was blown away.

Naftali Gottlieb then looked at me and said, "Can I tell you a story that your grandfather's brother Pinchas told me in Auschwitz?"

And I told Rabbi Steinsaltz that my Hasidic cousin proceeded to tell me the following story and that I tell it to my audiences.

✳ Rabbi Eliezer and Elijah the Prophet ✳

Many times in the Talmud, we learn that some of the great rabbinic sages prayed with the desire to speak to Elijah the Prophet, who subsequently often appeared to them.

One day, Rabbi Eliezer prayed to the Almighty for a vision of Elijah. Elijah the Prophet appeared before Rabbi Eliezer and said to him, "What can I do for you, Rabbi?"

Rabbi Eliezer said, "I'd like to follow you around. I'd like to watch you do your work, your work for the Holy One, Blessed Be He, in the world. I just want to follow you around and watch you do your work."

Elijah the Prophet said to Rabbi Eliezer, "Sorry, you can't follow me around. You'll have too many questions, and I don't have time for your questions."

Rabbi Eliezer said, "I promise I won't ask any questions. Will you allow me the honor of watching you do your work?"

Elijah the Prophet agreed to that condition, and off they went.

That particular night, when the two of them were looking for lodging, they saw a dilapidated shack, approached it, and discovered that it was occupied by a poor young couple who owned little besides one cow, which lived in the shack with them.

They approached the young couple and asked for lodging, and the young couple greeted them warmly, welcomed them in, and gathered some straw to make it as comfortable as possible for the two strangers to spend the night.

They offered the two guests what little they had. And Rabbi Eliezer and Elijah the Prophet spent the night.

The next morning when they awoke, Rabbi Eliezer overheard Elijah praying to the Almighty, asking that the Almighty kill the cow. No sooner did Elijah finish this prayer than the cow suddenly dropped dead.

Rabbi Eliezer was outraged. He said to Elijah, "What did you do? Why did you ask the Almighty to take the life of the cow? They were such lovely people. They have nothing. Why did you take their cow?"

Elijah the Prophet looked at Rabbi Eliezer and said, "See, you have so many questions. You have too many questions. I don't have time for your questions."

Rabbi Eliezer, though confused, quickly responded, "Please forgive me. I want to follow you. I won't ask you any more questions."

Elijah gave him another chance, and off they went.

The next evening, they spied a big mansion as they were looking for lodging. In response to their knock, the owner of the mansion came out, greeted them brusquely, and agreed that they might stay down in his cellar.

He offered them no human warmth, no physical warmth, and no food, so down to the cellar they went.

During the night, Rabbi Eliezer awoke upon hearing a commotion. He noticed that Elijah the Prophet had totally patched up an area of the cellar wall that was unfinished and crumbling.

Like a skilled craftsperson, Rabbi Eliezer watched Elijah repair and finish off the cellar wall.

The next day, off they went, arriving at a synagogue of wealthy congregants. The pews of the synagogue were made of gold and silver, but the people in the synagogue were cold and unfriendly.

When Elijah the Prophet and Rabbi Eliezer entered the synagogue, nobody greeted them, nobody performed the *mitzvah* of welcoming guests. In fact, the two of them noticed people whispering about them behind their backs.

Before they left the synagogue, Elijah looked at the congregation and said, "I pray that you should all become leaders."

And off they went.

They entered a neighborhood that was impoverished. The people were living in squalor, but they were lovely people— sweet, warm, gentle people, unfortunately living in poverty.

Elijah the Prophet looked at this neighborhood and its people and said, "I want to bless you that one of you should be a leader."

It was at this point that Rabbi Eliezer could not hold his questions any longer.

He said to Elijah the Prophet, "I know that you're going to send me away. I know that you required me not to ask questions. But I beg you, please, can you give me some understanding of what you've been doing? I don't understand anything that you're doing. I beg you; can you offer me some kind of explanation?"

Elijah the Prophet looked at Rabbi Eliezer and said, "I will explain my actions, but then you'll have to leave."

Elijah said, "Remember the first night when we encountered that poor couple living in their shack with their cow? And how outraged you were the next morning when you heard me praying to *Hakadosh Baruch Hu* that he should kill the cow?

"What you didn't know was that it was time for the wife to die.

"But I pleaded with Hashem: don't take the wife, take the cow.

"You recall the next night when we were put in that cold cellar of that rich man? And you woke up puzzled when you saw that I was repairing his walls and fixing them up beautifully?"

Elijah said, "I wasn't doing that. I knew that there was a treasure buried within the walls. The man who owned that mansion didn't deserve the mansion, let alone the treasure.

"So I patched and finished up the walls nicely so that no one would discover that treasure for a very long time."

Elijah the Prophet went on.

"Remember the next day, we went to that synagogue that was so wealthy, with gold and silver pews, but all the people were so unfriendly?

"I noticed how confused you were when I said they should all become great leaders.

"That wasn't a blessing; it was a curse. Anyone who has ever been in an organization knows the chaos that results from everyone thinking that he is a leader.

"And then we went to that poor neighborhood, and the people were so sweet and so lovely, and you wondered, in comparison to the earlier so-called blessing, why would I just say, 'I bless you that one of you should be a leader.'

"You see, that indeed *was* a blessing. I blessed them that one of them should become a leader, one good, strong leader who could take them out of the poverty and the squalor they lived in."

Elijah the Prophet then said to Rabbi Eliezer, "You are going to have to leave me now. But please don't forget that what you see in the world is not the whole picture. It's only part of the grand picture in the mind of the Almighty."

This was the story that my grandfather's brother Pinchas told my cousin Naftali Gottlieb when they were both in Auschwitz.

It was time for Rabbi Steinsaltz to get to his appointment. He left my car, and his sweet-smelling tobacco lingered. I stayed

From what has been said, it may be gathered that the trials and tribulations of life are for the good. This does not mean that they are pleasant; there does exist a certain gap between the two. The point is that God tests a person in order to bring him to a higher level of knowledge.

—Rabbi Adin Steinsaltz, *The Candle of God,* p. 213

where I was and waited for him to return. I felt blessed to be able to discuss these things with my Teacher.

More than two decades earlier, during my very first meeting with Rabbi Steinsaltz, I told him that I was "looking for a teacher with a capital *T*."

I knew, deep in my soul, during that first meeting and ever since, that I had found him. Or perhaps he had found me. Nothing in life happens without the Holy One allowing it.

A Special Place in Hell

An hour later, Rabbi Steinsaltz was back in my car. I began talking to him about something personal having to do with a certain kind of rigidity I was experiencing in myself. I wasn't able to let go of something that I had my mind tightly wrapped around.

At a certain point in the conversation, Rabbi Steinsaltz said to me, "Arthur, there is a special place in hell designed for Jews who think that to be Jewish is to follow the *Shulchan Aruch.*"

I almost swerved off the road. I couldn't believe what I heard him say. "What? There's a special place in *hell* designed for Jews who think that to be Jewish is to observe the *Shulchan Aruch*? The *Shulchan Aruch,* the Code of Jewish Law? The most important authority of Jewish practice and Jewish life for centuries?

I said to him, "What? Could you repeat that?"

"Yes," he went on, "there's a special place in hell for Jews who think that what it means to be Jewish is to follow the *Shulchan Aruch.*"

The subject, for some reason, then quickly changed. I don't know what distracted us, but as often has happened over the years, a profound conversation can easily be interrupted in New York City traffic.

NOTES FROM THE ROAD:
Another Woman

Rabbi Steinsaltz said to me that he met a man whose wife became religious and the children became religious but he didn't and doesn't want to. And he asked Rabbi Steinsaltz what he should do.

Rabbi Steinsaltz said, "Well, now, you don't have to get a divorce. Many men want to get a divorce because they want another woman. You already have another woman."

Surely Rabbi Steinsaltz was not advocating the abandonment of Jewish law, nor was he questioning the authority of the Code of Jewish Law. But as he writes in *The Thirteen Petalled Rose,* "If anything is clear, it is that a rigid, unchanging way is wrong."[3]

I have come to understand that Judaism is not a cookbook religion that allows you to simply look something up in a book and know what to do. This is the dreadful error that I believe too many religiously observant Jews make. There is a terrible trend of mimicry in the Orthodox world. It looks and feels too often like a rubber-stamp existence, a cookie-cutter way of life with a bizarre effort to make everyone the same. This, I believe, is part of what Rabbi Steinsaltz meant when he said that there is a special place in hell for people who think that to be Jewish is to just follow the *Shulchan Aruch,* the Code of Jewish Law.

Life is too complex for such an approach. I believe that the sages wanted us to learn, to study, to understand the guidance of the past, and then to integrate that into our being and to choose wisely.

In my own lectures, I've made the point with a reference to my going to the gym. When I went to the gym, I got pretty good at lifting dumbbells. The pity was that I have never found, in my daily life, a dumbbell to pick up. But of course, I don't go to the gym to learn how to pick up dumbbells. Rather, I go to the gym to get into shape so that I can be prepared to pick up the real things I encounter in life.

And so it is with Jewish learning. I don't learn so that I can find out, in every case and every moment, what I should do. Rather, I learn so that I can get into shape and apply what I've learned to the myriad of different circumstances that I encounter. To think that all I need to do is memorize the law and follow it is, in a way, a special place in hell.

The Fifth Book of the *Shulchan Aruch*

After Rabbi Steinsaltz told me about this special place in hell, I told him that once, after teaching a Talmud class using the Steinsaltz edition, one of the people in the class was an Orthodox rabbi who came over to me, thanked me for the class, and told me a great story.

He said, "You know, when I was in the yeshiva, there was one guy who was the most brilliant of all. This one guy was more brilliant than all the other guys. But for some reason, the *rosh yeshiva,* the dean of the school, didn't give him *smikhah,* didn't ordain him.

"And the months rolled on and the years rolled on and the *rosh yeshiva* was giving *smikhah* to various guys and this one guy who was clearly still the most brilliant of all in the yeshiva was overlooked—to the point that he finally left the school.

In Judaism, man is conceived, in all the power of his body and soul, as the central agent, the chief actor on a cosmic stage; he functions, or performs, as a prime mover of worlds, being made in the image of the Creator. Everything he does constitutes an act of creation, both in his own life and in other worlds hidden from his sight. Every single particle of his body and every nuance of his thought and feeling are connected with forces of all kinds in the cosmos, forces without number; so that the more conscious he is of this order of things, the more significantly does he function as a Jewish person.

—Rabbi Adin Steinsaltz, *The Thirteen Petalled Rose,* p. 155

"And when he left the school, a few of us went up to the *rosh yeshiva* and said to him, 'You never gave that guy *smikhah.* How come? He was such a brilliant guy, more brilliant than all of us.'

"The *rosh yeshiva* said, 'He was never able to master the fifth book of the *Shulchan Aruch.'*

"We looked at the *rosh yeshiva* and said, 'The *fifth* book of the *Shulchan Aruch*? There are only *four* books of the *Shulchan Aruch.'*

"The *rosh yeshiva* looked at us and said, 'There aren't four books of the *Shulchan Aruch;* there are five books. Four of the books are written down. They tell us all the laws. The fifth book is not written down. The fifth book is the book on how to take the four books and apply them to life. I didn't believe that that young man was able to do that. So I wasn't able to ordain him.'"

☙ Who Is Really Observant? ❧

We were now on our way to an afternoon lecture that Rabbi Steinsaltz was scheduled to give. I decided to once again bring up my magic show.

I said to Rabbi Steinsaltz, "Near the beginning of the magic show, I say to the audience, "Ladies and gentlemen, this is a magic show, and I am the first illusion. Because if you look at me, you might conclude that I am an Orthodox Jew, but I'm not.

"You look at me, you see my yarmulke and my beard, and you conclude that I must be Orthodox. Well, the yarmulke is relatively easy; all I have to do is put it on my head. The beard is even easier; I do nothing except wash it and just let it grow. And it's been growing and growing for years."

This usually gets a laugh.

Then I say, "I have no use for the word *Orthodox.* I suppose if you followed me around for a week and watch what I do and what I don't do, you'd probably conclude that I'm Orthodox. But I have no use for the term.

"In fact, I think the term is deceptive and even destructive. I don't consider myself Orthodox; I consider myself a Jew."

This usually gets applause.

I say, "There's a law in Jewish tradition, taught by the great teacher Shammai and recorded in the Mishnah. It's in *Pirkei Avot, The Ethics of the Fathers,* and Shammai teaches '*sever panim yafos*'—you should greet everybody with a smile.

"It also says quite clearly in the *Shulchan Aruch,* the *Code of Jewish Law,*" I continue, "that it is not permitted to eat a bacon cheeseburger.

"So I have two laws. One law is that I'm supposed to smile when I greet somebody, and the other law says that I'm not supposed to eat a bacon cheeseburger.

"Now, I know people who always smile when they greet you. And I know that if served, they would eat a bacon cheeseburger.

"I also know people who never in a million years would consider eating a bacon cheeseburger, and yet they rarely seem to smile. So it seems to me that both of them are picking and choosing.

"Which one of the two is the Orthodox one, the observant one?"

❧ Overlooking the Blemishes ❧

We arrived at our destination, a Jewish community center in the New York suburbs where Rabbi Steinsaltz was scheduled to speak to a group of Jewish communal workers.

Among his comments that afternoon, Rabbi Steinsaltz said, "I found, I think, the best definition of love. When someone falls in love, he sees all kinds of good qualities and nothing else. This is called, in plain language, infatuation. It is not love. Love means that I see the blemishes and I can still love. And this is what I would say a Jewish community worker has to do—to see the blemishes, to see them all, and still be so much in love with our people."

Rabbi Steinsaltz went on to say, "People who are Jewish community workers have a tough time because for some unexplained reason, they undertook this job. And what is the job of the Jewish communal worker? Their main job is to make duplicates of themselves. They need to be contagious, to be able to make other people involved, as they are, as professionals or as nonprofessionals, in whatever capacity they can.

"It's not a very specific job. It is not a job of teaching in particular. It is not a job of preaching; it's not a job of donating so much money to Israel—not that I'm against any of these things!

"There is another part of it. Let me say something about the role of a Jewish priest. There were Jewish priests. And let me tell you what a priest is. A priest's work in the Temple is not spiritual work. He has to slaughter animals, to cut animals, to deal with blood, to deal with all kinds of dirty things. Within the Temple, he was doing all these things.

"Now, to be a priest means that you know all these things, you know the things that are not easy to do. You know the things that are dirty; you know the things that are unpleasant. And yet you are still doing them, and you do them with a feeling of love and a feeling of awe.

"A Jewish communal worker has to be like a priest, meaning that you have to see the dark side. There is no sense and no use in trying to pretend that everything is all right.

"There are faults among our people. There are faults that come out of being in exile for so many years. There are faults because we are a small people. There are faults because we had to struggle terribly for survival. We have all kinds of bad traits. All these faults are there, and we should see them. But we still do all these jobs with a feeling of love and a feeling of awe.

"I would define priest, a *kohen,* as a person who looks at things from behind the scenes. He's not in the audience. He's not just a participant. He sees all the secrets. He knows all the wrong things. I know everything. I know all the detail. I know all the dirty secrets, but still I go on."

A People like a Plant
Rabbi Steinsaltz then spoke about the fact that the Jewish people resemble a plant. "As any botanist knows," he said, "the best way to get a plant to grow is to cut it back."

When you cut back a plant, it responds with a burst of growth. Hair works similarly: trimming is the best way to stimulate its growth.

One of the fiercest things Rabbi Steinsaltz ever pointed out to me is that if you look at Jewish history, you will see that after each terrible cutback, there was a burst of growth.

For example, there was the destruction of the Temple, after which came one of the most extraordinary bursts of creativity in Jewish history, the creation of the Talmud.

There was the expulsion of the Jews from Spain, a cataclysm in the history of our people. The Jewish community in Spain had lived comfortably and happily for centuries. Yet in 1492, the Jews were expelled. Shortly thereafter, in the community in Tsfat, in the Holy Land, we saw the fantastic flowering of what we now call Kabbalah.

Some amazing Jewish personalities, including Yitzchak Luria, Moshe Cordovero, Joseph Caro (the author of the *Shulchan Aruch*), and Shlomo Alkebetz (the author of the hymn "*L'cha Dodi*" that we sing on Friday night), all lived at the same time in the mystical Jewish community of Tsfat just a few years after the expulsion.

NOTES FROM THE ROAD:
Everything Is Torah
When he met a reporter this afternoon, Rabbi Steinsaltz said, "I'll talk about anything you like. To me, everything is Torah."

Rabbi Steinsaltz then pointed to the massacres of Jews in the Ukraine in the 1600s that were statistically as great a blow to the Jewish population of the world as the Holocaust was centuries later. But shortly thereafter, we see the greatest revival movement of Jewish history, Hasidism, founded by the Baal Shem Tov and his disciples and their descendents and their disciples.

Then, of course, there was the Holocaust, two generations ago, when one-third of our people were murdered.

We are a rebuilding generation.

The question, of course, is simple, Rabbi Steinsaltz told the audience: In what lasting ways will our generation once again participate in the burst of growth that follows from such a cataclysm?

❧ Contact with Holiness ❧

We drove back to Rabbi Steinsaltz's hotel in silence. Rabbi Steinsaltz was smoking his pipe, and I was driving and just letting him be.

I thought about a passage in *The Thirteen Petalled Rose,* in the chapter called "Holiness," where Rabbi Steinsaltz describes the holiness of being, the holiness of the human soul.

Whenever I read that description, I find that I choke up with emotion. Rabbi Steinsaltz writes:

> The individual who makes inner contact with . . . a holy person, showing him love and devotion, thereby supports the flow of divine plenty in the world.
>
> This is what has been meant in Jewish tradition, from time immemorial, when devotion has been shown to those

persons who are superior in holiness or have an aura of sanctity.

The gift is given such blessed men to create a bond of some sort that will draw them nearer, whether the holy person is connected to God by being a great scholar of the Torah or whether he is just a saintly individual in his life.

To honor, revere, and love the holy person is a mitzvah in itself, besides serving as a means for direct contact with holiness. And just as inner connection with the holiness of place or time consecrates and raises one, so does the holy person—although, to be sure, the additional factor of conscious transfer of blessedness makes this contact the most heart-stirring and consequential of all human relationships.[4]

Over the years, I have seriously wondered, What *is* it about Rabbi Steinsaltz that is so special?

Yes, he's a genius, but there are lots of geniuses.

Yes, he is a genuinely religious man, but there are lots of religious people.

Who is Rabbi Steinsaltz? Why is he so special? And what is it about him that attracts not only me but countless others from so many walks of life and cultures and nations and religions?

I have seen great numbers of people who have encountered Rabbi Steinsaltz over the years who have gone away feeling that the encounter was something out of the ordinary, something special, something rare.

Rabbi Steinsaltz has dedicated students in the world of academics, in the business world, within all of the movements of Jewish life in America, and in countries throughout the world, from private citizens to public figures.

I have come to the conclusion that Rabbi Steinsaltz does indeed have a special quality, and that is his *wholeness.*

There is something *whole* about Rabbi Steinsaltz.

He is a scientist and a man of religion.

He is a faithful believer and a fierce skeptic.

He has a great sense of humor and is absolutely serious about life.

He is interested in the most profound, sublime, abstract ideas and equally interested in the most mundane and matter-of-fact objects before him.

He has eyes of wisdom that twinkle like a child's.

He treats everybody seriously. And whether the person before him is a dignitary of a nation or an average person he will probably never meet again, Rabbi Steinsaltz is present and focused.

There is something *whole* about him. And I believe that merely being in the presence of wholeness is a blessing.

I believe that just by being with him, just by being with a person who seems to be able to contain all the worlds, it is something rare, something uplifting, something exalted.

To be with Rabbi Steinsaltz is in itself a blessing.

✿ The Most Intimate Relationship ✿

When I think back to the very first time I met Rabbi Steinsaltz, one of my questions to him was, "Why isn't everybody talking about God?"

At the time, I was spiritually intoxicated. I had recently found God—or perhaps God had found me.

Rabbi Steinsaltz writes in *The Thirteen Petalled Rose,* "When a man learns that just as he broods over himself so does

NOTES FROM THE ROAD:
Praying with Rabbi Steinsaltz

Sometimes it happens that when I pick up Rabbi Steinsaltz at the airport at 5:00 A.M., I have to wait there for an hour and a half while he passes through customs. But sometimes he's the first person out.

This morning, that happened.

It was 5:30, and we had nothing to do. It's a little strange to be in New York City at 5:30 in the morning with nothing to do. With Rabbi Steinsaltz.

I decided that we would drive to Brooklyn from JFK and go to the *shul* where I *davened* [prayed].

I was eager to do this because until then, I had only once before prayed in the same room with Rabbi Steinsaltz. And when we got to the *shtieble* where I *davened* in Boro Park, not only did Rabbi Steinsaltz *daven* in the same space, in the same room, but he *davened* right next to me.

I confess that since it is usually difficult for me to *daven* with good concentration under normal circumstances, it was impossible for me to *daven* with any concentration knowing that Rabbi Steinsaltz was praying next to me. I was much more eager to watch him pray and to see what I could learn from him—to learn from his praying rather than to do my own prayers. How does one stand before one's Creator?

I'm sure that this morning will affect the rest of my life.

God yearn for him and look for him, he is at the beginning of a higher level of consciousness."[5] My relationship with God, when I first met Rabbi Steinsaltz, seemed to be the deepest relationship in my life. God seemed to be so present for me. It was, at that time, like a new love.

So I said to Rabbi Steinsaltz at our first meeting, "Why isn't everybody talking about God?"

It seemed to me that there was no reality greater than the presence of God. Why wasn't anybody talking about that?

And Rabbi Steinsaltz smiled and said to me, "It's difficult to talk publicly about your most intimate relationship."

We arrived at Rabbi Steinsaltz's hotel. It had been a long day. I was glad that I was able to speak with my Teacher about my work, my ideas, my magic show, and my understanding of some of Judaism's profound notions regarding human suffering and the purpose of the trials of life.

I felt that I had come a long way since my first meeting with Rabbi Steinsaltz over two decades earlier.

At the time, all I had were questions for him. And reverence. And nervousness.

But now I am able to greet and spend time with him with confidence.

I am able to serve him well when he visits New York, not only as his porter but also, as he has called me, as his friend.

I am a fellow student of Torah.

I am a colleague who, like Rabbi Steinsaltz, travels with a burning desire to teach fellow Jews the wisdom of the great sages.

I am always eager, like Rabbi Steinsaltz, to meet other Jews and to tell them of our inheritance.

I am a Jew who, like Rabbi Steinsaltz, is driven to search for the "remnant of Israel."

As I dropped Rabbi Steinsaltz off at his hotel, he started to leave the car and then turned to me and said, "I was once worried about you."

And when I asked him why, he simply said, "You used to put me so high. I see that you've grown up a little."

It is 5:30 A.M. I'm standing in the International Arrivals Building at JFK Airport, waiting for Rabbi Steinsaltz.

In *The Thirteen Petalled Rose,* Rabbi Steinsaltz points out that since we understand God to be infinite and since we ourselves are finite, God will always seem as distant as ever.

And if God is always as distant as ever, how do we know that we are making progress?

And the answer Rabbi Steinsaltz suggests is this: we know that we have made progress not when we look ahead to see how far we have to go but rather when we pause on a summit and look back and see the distance that we have come.

There he is now. . . .

Notes

The following works by Rabbi Adin Steinsaltz are referred to in these notes and throughout this book:

The Candle of God: Discourses on Chasidic Thought (Northvale, N.J.: Aronson, 1999)

The Essential Talmud (New York: Bantam Books, 1976)

In the Beginning: Discourses on Chasidic Thought (Northvale, N.J.: Aronson, 1992)

The Long Shorter Way: Discourses on Chasidic Thought (Northvale, N.J.: Aronson, 1988)

On Being Free (Northvale, N.J.: Aronson, 1995)

Opening the Tanya: Discovering the Moral and Mystical Teachings of a Classic Work of Kabbalah (San Francisco: Jossey-Bass, 2003)

Simple Words: Thinking About What Really Matters in Life (New York: Simon & Schuster, 1999)

The Strife of the Spirit (Northvale, N.J.: Aronson, 1996)

The Sustaining Utterance: Discourses on Chasidic Thought (Northvale, N.J.: Aronson, 1989)

Teshuvah: A Guide for the Newly Observant Jew (Northvale, N.J.: Aronson, 1996)

The Thirteen Petalled Rose (New York: Basic Books, 1980)

We Jews: Who Are We and What Should We Do? (San Francisco: Jossey-Bass, 2005)

Introduction: Becoming the Rabbi's Driver: Stepping Down to a Higher Position (1980—1985)

1. Irving Friedman, "The Private Gate: A Conversation with Rabbi Adin Steinsaltz," *Parabola,* Summer 1978, pp. 22–31.

Chapter One: "A Series of Small Turnings" (1986)

1. Kenneth L. Woodward and Milan L. Kubic, "Israel's Mystical Rabbi," *Newsweek,* May 26, 1980, p. 55.

2. *The Thirteen Petalled Rose,* p. 3.

3. *Ba'al teshuvah* means "master of return," a reference to trying to master the process of returning to traditional Judaism.

4. *Shefa Quarterly* is no longer published, but most of the essays by Rabbi Steinsaltz that appeared in it were reprinted in *The Strife of the Spirit.*

5. Bobov is the town in Poland where this Hasidic dynasty originated. Just as the Lubavitcher Hasidim come from the town of Lubavitch, Lithuania, the Bobover Hasidim come from the town of Bobov.

6. Rabbi Isaiah Horowitz wrote a book called *The Two Tablets of the Law.* Its Hebrew title is *Sh'nei Luchos HaBris.* Following a tradition among Hebrew scholars, the acronym for the book title, Shelah, came to be used as a substitute for the name of its author. Shelah HaKodesh means "the Holy Shelah."

7. The founder of Lubavitcher Hasidism, Rabbi Schneur Zalman, lived from 1745 to 1812.

8. Frances Kraft, "Rivalry and Animosity Not Helping: Rabbi Steinsaltz," *Canadian Jewish News,* May 24, 2001.

9. Bob Dylan, "Do Right to Me Baby," © 1979 Special Rider Music.

Chapter Three: "Kabbalah Is the Official Theology of the Jewish People" (1998)

1. The Vilna Gaon (*gaon* means "genius") was born in 1720 and was a revered rabbi and scholar in Lithuania and a vigorous opponent of the Hasidic movement.

2. The Ari is Rabbi Yitzchak Luria, considered the greatest and most influential Kabbalist who ever lived. As contemporary masters of Kabbalah say, Kabbalah today, and for centuries, has really been the Kabbalah of the Ari. Rabbi Joseph Caro, as noted in the text, is perhaps best known for his *Code of Jewish Law,* the *Shulchan Aruch.*

3. You can read this article at http://www.ajritz.com/jew/brother.htm.

4. *The Thirteen Petalled Rose,* p. 118.

5. *The Thirteen Petalled Rose,* pp. xi–xii.

6. *The Thirteen Petalled Rose,* p. 131.

7. *The Thirteen Petalled Rose,* p. 103.

8. *The Thirteen Petalled Rose,* pp. 103–104.

9. *The Essential Talmud,* pp. 216–217.

10. Herbert Weiner, *Nine and a Half Mystics: The Kabbala Today* (New York: Holt, Reinhart and Winston, 1969), p. 108.

CHAPTER FOUR: "MAKE THE LIVES OF YOUR TEACHERS AS MISERABLE AS POSSIBLE" (2001)

1. *The Thirteen Petalled Rose,* pp. 141–142.

2. *The Thirteen Petalled Rose,* p. 115.

3. *The Thirteen Petalled Rose,* pp. 61–62.

4. *The Thirteen Petalled Rose,* p. 113.

5. *The Thirteen Petalled Rose,* p. 154.

6. *The Thirteen Petalled Rose,* p. 117.

7. This film is available from Ergo Media, Teaneck, N.J. Consult the online catalogue at http://www.jewishvideo.com.

8. Leonard J. Swidler, *Women in Judaism: The Status of Women in Formative Judaism* (Metuchen, N.J.: Scarecrow Press, 1976).

CHAPTER FIVE: "IF YOU THINK YOU'VE ARRIVED, YOU'RE LOST" (2005)

1. *The Thirteen Petalled Rose,* p. 63.

2. *The Thirteen Petalled Rose,* p. 136.

3. *The Thirteen Petalled Rose,* p. 105.

4. *The Thirteen Petalled Rose,* pp. 83–84.

5. *The Thirteen Petalled Rose,* p. 148.

The Author

Arthur Kurzweil, father of three children, has been a spiritual seeker for most of his life. For seventeen years he was editorial director of the Jewish Book Club and editor in chief of Jason Aronson Publishers, where he acquired and published more than 650 books of Jewish interest.

A popular teacher, lecturer, and performer, for almost thirty years he has been a scholar in residence at hundreds of synagogues and Jewish organizations throughout the United States. As coordinator of the Talmud Circle Project under the direction of Rabbi Adin Steinsaltz, he has inspired many people throughout the United States to discover and begin to study the Talmud.

A member of the Society of American Magicians and the International Brotherhood of Magicians, he frequently performs his one-man show, "Searching for God in a Magic Shop," blending his interest in magic and illusions with some of the profound ideas of Jewish theology.

He is the author of the classic work on Jewish genealogical research, *From Generation to Generation: How to Trace Your Jewish Genealogy and Family History* (Jossey-Bass). He is also the author of *My Generations: A Course in Jewish Family History* (Behrman

House) and is the editor of *Best Jewish Writing, 2003* (Jossey-Bass) and coeditor of *The Hadassah Jewish Family Book of Health and Wellness* (Jossey-Bass).

A former president of the Jewish Book Council, he was also a cofounder of the first Jewish Genealogical Society. A contributor to all three *Jewish Catalogs* (Jewish Publication Society) and to *The Jewish Almanac* (Bantam Books), his writing has appeared in *New York* magazine, major newspapers, and most of the leading Jewish periodicals.

Trained as a librarian, he is a member of Beta Phi Mu, the International Library and Information Studies Honor Society. He received the Distinguished Humanitarian Award from the Melton Center for Jewish Studies at Ohio State University for his unique contributions to the field of Jewish education. He also received a Lifetime Achievement Award from the International Association of Jewish Genealogical Societies.

He is currently Jewish Interest Consultant for Jossey-Bass and serves as publisher at *Parabola* magazine.

Index